INTRODUCTION TO LINGUISTICS

INTRODUCTION TO LINGUISTICS

Second Edition

RONALD WARDHAUGH
University of Toronto

McGraw-Hill, Inc.
New York St. Louis San Francisco Auckland Bogotá
Caracas Lisbon London Madrid Mexico City Milan
Montreal New Delhi San Juan Singapore
Sydney Tokyo Toronto

Library of Congress Cataloging in Publication Data

Wardhaugh, Ronald.
  Introduction to linguistics.

    Bibliography: p.
    Includes index.
    1. Linguistics. I. Title.
P121. W22   1977   410   76-14974
ISBN 0-07-068152-X

INTRODUCTION TO LINGUISTICS

131415 QP/K 98765

This book was set in Zenith by York Graphic Services,
Inc.   The editors were Ellen B. Fuchs, Donald W.
Burden, and Susan Gamer; the designer was Anne
Canevari Green; the production supervisor was Den-
nis J. Conroy.

The foreign languages on the cover are, reading from
top to bottom: Chinese, Parsi, Hindi, and Japanese.

CONTENTS

94730

PREFACE

Like the first edition of this book, the second edition is designed to provide beginning students in linguistics with a basic knowledge of the kinds of questions linguists have asked and are asking about language. Some of the various answers that have been proposed are indicated and discussed. The chapter headings show the range of concerns.

The book espouses no particular theoretical viewpoint to the exclusion of all others. However, some preference is given to generative-transformational theory, the most influential of recent linguistic theories. Linguistics continues to be a very exciting discipline, and change occurs rather rapidly; this book also seeks to show why that is the case.

The material comes from a variety of sources, most of which will be readily apparent to those knowledgeable in the discipline. The general approach has been worked out over the years through teaching many students in introductory linguistics courses before they go on to further work in a variety of disciplines. Such students need an overview of linguistics, and this book seeks in its way to provide such an overview.

As a help to beginning students, each chapter concludes with a brief note indicating further sources for material covered in the chapter. A full bibliography appears at the end of the book. A glossary of terms is also included to help students gain a better grasp of the concepts discussed and the terms used in the text. Each chapter concludes with exercises which provide students with further examples of the material included in that chapter. Some of the exercises are open-ended, to encourage students to raise their own questions and formulate their own answers.

An introductory book of this kind draws on the work of many others. Therefore, my thanks go out to all those colleagues, students, secretaries, readers, and friends who have helped make this book possible. What strengths it has I owe to them; its weaknesses are all my own.

Ronald Wardhaugh

INTRODUCTION TO LINGUISTICS

1

THE STUDY OF LANGUAGE

People have long been interested in language, in such matters as its origin, its nature, and its uses, whether in persuasion, poetry, or prayer. Language has always been something of a mystery, not unlike the mysteries of creation, the origin of the sun, and the coming of fire. As such, it has provided people with such a rich source of myth that even today much of the mystery of language prevails.

One important difference which distinguishes linguists from nonlinguists lies in those aspects of language that the two groups consider to be either mysterious or interesting, and another, in how they choose to investigate and discuss the mysteries and problems that are perceived. The central purpose of this book is to show what linguists do when they work with language. They do different things at different times, but everything they do is motivated by principles derived from modern science. Consequently, this book is an introduction to linguistic science. It seeks to provide an overview of how linguists look at language by showing what questions they ask, what evidence they seek bearing on those questions, and what answers they propose.

SOME VIEWPOINTS ABOUT LANGUAGE

One of the greatest mysteries that have confronted people has been the origin of language, a topic on which there has been much speculation. Many of us are familiar with the stories in Genesis concerning the giving of names by a deity and the diffusion of different tongues following the destruction of the Tower of Babel. Another story, this one not biblical, about a Swede, Andreas Kemke, has him conjecturing that in the Garden of Eden Adam spoke in Danish, the serpent in French, and the deity in Swedish (Eve was not mentioned). This conjecture tells us much more about Kemke than it does about the origin of language. A multitude of theories abound on this topic: "bowwow," "singsong," "dingdong," "pooh-pooh," and "gestural" to name some of the more exotic. In each case the concern of the person or persons proposing the theory has been with explaining how human language could have originated in the world, either by referring to other forms of communication, both human and animal, or by invoking a *deus ex machina* solution. Linguists themselves have tended not to become involved in such "theorizing." Indeed, in 1866 the Linguistic Society of Paris banned papers on the possible origins of language from its meetings and publications.

At times, theorists with an inclination toward experimentation have even gone so far as to try to recreate the conditions which they consider necessary for the origin of language. Herodotus, the Greek historian, tells how the ancient Egyptian king Psammetichus raised two children in complete isolation from human speech to see what language they would "naturally" speak. The children's first word is reported to have been *bekos,* the Phrygian word for bread; consequently, Psammetichus decided that children would naturally speak Phrygian and that Phrygian was an "older" language than Egyptian. James IV of Scotland performed much the same "experiment" in the early sixteenth century, but his children reportedly spoke "good Hebrew." Needless to say such conjectures and such experimentation do not qualify as scientific inquiry as such inquiry is understood today.

In the modern world, people still continue to have only the vaguest notions about what language is. These notions are oftentimes just as vague as those of the Spanish Emperor Charles V, for whom English was the proper language for commerce, German for warfare, French for women, Italian for friends, and Spanish for the worship of God. Even today many people regard Italian as "musical," the English spoken by the Welsh as "singsong," German as "guttural," French as "flowing," and American Indian languages as "monotonous and grunt-filled."

Many people think of languages as dictionaries of some kind and consider that learning a new language is equivalent to learning a new set of words which may be related, often on a one-to-one basis, to the set they know in the first language. Another common confusion is that of language with writing. Speech is often perceived to be a less precise, more transitory, and somewhat debased form of the language, which finds its purest or essential expression in its written forms.

We have poorly developed vocabularies for talking about linguistic matters and we do not know which matters are significant. Then again, in our actual use of words we reveal our attitudes about language and the functions of language. We regard some expressions as taboo, so we carefully avoid them by using **euphemisms**; nevertheless, we consider other expressions to be permissible profanities in certain circumstances. We adopt pseudonames, stage names, and nicknames, either as members of a religious order, stage troupe, or social group. We continue to worship in special languages such as classical Arabic, Latin, or Sanskrit, and we allow ourselves to be controlled by such formulas as *I now pronounce you man and wife* or *I divorce thee* thrice repeated. We joke, pun, delight in riddles, and occasionally fall under verbal spells of one kind or another, which, though no longer as potent as those of the witches in *Macbeth* or of Rumpelstiltskin, still exercise some control over our behavior.

We are assailed on every side by language; yet very few of us know what language is. We are told to think positively, constructively, or imaginatively, but there is little agreement on how language is to be used in such thinking. There is considerable anxiety about how language is used in society. We encounter very few other phenomena as important to us as language. Toward many of these phenomena we have adopted a scientific attitude, as for example in the matters of health and well-being. For most of us too astrology has given way to astronomy. However, we must observe that in general the study of language more closely resembles primitive astrology than it does sophisticated astronomy.

A DEFINITION OF LANGUAGE

Linguists are in broad agreement about some of the important characteristics of human language, and one definition of language widely associated with linguistics may be used to illustrate areas of agreement. This particular definition states that *language is a system of arbitrary vocal symbols used for human communication.* The definition is rather imprecise in that it contains considerable redundancy, particularly in employing both the terms *system* and *arbitrary;* some redundancy is perhaps excusable, however, for it allows certain points to be more heavily emphasized than they would otherwise have been.

Language as System

The key term in the above definition is **system.** It is also the most difficult term to discuss. We may observe that a language must be systematic, for otherwise it could not be learned or used consistently. However, we must also ask in what ways a language is systematic. A very basic observation is that each language contains two systems rather than one, a system of sounds and a system of meanings. Only certain sounds are used by speakers of any language, and only certain combinations of these sounds are possible. A speaker of English can say *I saw the bank* but he cannot say the following two sentences, which are starred (*) to show their unacceptability to a native speaker: **I saw the banque,* which makes him sound partly like a Frenchman, or **I saw the nbka,* which makes him feel that he is saying some kind of tongue twister rather than a completely well-formed English sentence. Likewise, he can say *I saw the bank* but not **I bank saw the,* which is nonsense, and, if he says *I bank the saw,* that sentence means something quite different and is rather absurd. The sound system of a language allows a small number of sounds to be used over and over again in various combinations to form units of meaning. The meaning system allows these units of meaning to be arranged in an infinite number of ways to express both simple and complicated ideas.

All languages have dual systems of sounds and meanings, **duality** being a design feature of language, as Chapter 2 will show. Linguists concern themselves not only with characteristics of the two systems but also with how the systems relate to each other within one overall linguistic system for a particular language. The nature of this relationship in all languages is very important and constitutes a most interesting problem. Reference will be made to it throughout this book, particularly in Chapters 4, 7, and 8.

A related problem concerns the coverage of the system; that is, the kind of phenomena that must be accounted for, the principles to be used in deciding which phenomena are relevant, and how relationships are to be expressed. One kind of coverage would require us to do no more than make a catalog of observations of certain kinds of linguistic phenomena according to a preconceived plan. A dictionary is such a catalog of observations about words and their meanings, with different dictionary makers following different plans concerning what is to be included and how included material is to be described. However, we could not possibly make a dictionary of the sentences in a language in the same way that we can make a dictionary of the words in a language: the supply of words is finite but their possible combinations are infinite. A language offers its speakers the opportunity to speak about anything within their knowledge—and many things outside that knowledge, too. It is essentially a creative system in that much of what we say and hear we say and hear for the first time. We must search for satisfactory ways of describing sentences and parts of sentences, and also sounds and combinations of sounds. And we must do so in the knowledge that any system we propose must recognize the unlimited possibilities any language offers its speakers. As we shall see in later chapters, we can devise various sophisticated ways of saying something of interest about the systematic, creative nature of language.

Linguists are also concerned with the units and processes within the system. An utterance is not a continuous phenomenon: it is broken into discrete units of various sizes, and these units are arranged according to various processes. We must seek to understand what these units and processes are. Very likely they are not those that the educated public holds dear, or at least not as they are defined by that public, for example such units as letters and words and such processes as sentences constructed according to some "sense-making" formula. As we shall see in later chapters, we can postulate such units as phonemes and morphemes, and such arrangements and processes as constituent structures and transformations. Our search must be for those discrete units and processes which systematically account for interesting data within a theory that says something of significance to fellow scientists.

Language as Arbitrary

The term **arbitrary** in the definition does not mean that everything about language is unpredictable, for languages do not vary in every possible way. It means that we cannot predict exactly which specific features we will find in a particular language if we are unfamiliar with that language or with a related language. There will be no way of predicting what a word means just from hearing it, of knowing in advance whether or how nouns will be inflected, or of saying whether pronouns will fall into any particular pattern. Likewise, there will be no way of predicting exactly which sounds will occur, of knowing what the ratio of consonants to vowels will be, or of saying whether the nasal passages will be involved in the production of certain vowels. If languages were completely unpredictable in their systems, we could not even talk about nouns, verbs, pronouns, consonants, and vowels at all. However, linguistic systems are not completely unpredictable: all the phenomena mentioned in the previous sentence will be found in any language we choose to examine, taking different realizations, of course, in different languages.

For example, the process of deletion—that is, the permissible omission of a part of a sentence when that part can be predicted from what remains—may be illustrated by the following deletions in a series of English sentences: *I could have gone and Peter could have gone too; I could have gone and Peter could have too;* and *I could have gone and Peter too.* This deletion process will be found in all languages, but the particular variation will depend on the language. All languages will have devices for negation, as in the English example of *The boy ran* negated to *The boy didn't run.* In this example the positive sentence is negated by the insertion of *n't,* the introduction of the verb *do,* and assignment of the "past tense" from the verb *run* to the verb *do.* This particular negation process is rather complicated. However, we would never expect to find a sentence such as *The boy ran* negated by a sentence such as **The boy ran the boy ran* or **The boy ran ran boy the,* or **The boy ran boy the,* that is, through some system of total sentence repetition or total or partial inversion. Language is unpredictable only in the sense that the variations of the processes that are employed are unpredictable. Apparently certain very simple logical processes are never employed, as in the above ungrammatical examples of negation, but certain seemingly illogical and obviously complicated processes are preferred, as in English negation. Of interest to us is what determines the processes that do occur and what exactly is predictable in languages.

The things which are predictable about all languages are called **linguistic universals.** For example, all languages seem to be characterizable as systems of rules of certain kinds. All have nouns and verbs. All have devices which allow speakers to make statements, ask questions, and give commands or make requests. All have consonants and vowels. All have means for referring to "real world" objects and relationships. And all allow their speakers the freedom to create original sentences. The specifics for each language are, however, largely unpredictable and, therefore, arbitrary: what German nouns are like; how questions are formed in Eskimo; what the vowels of Tagalog are; and what speakers of Basque call the various body parts.

Language as Vocal

The term **vocal** in the definition refers to the fact that the primary medium of language is sound, and it is sound for all languages, no matter how well developed are their writing systems. We are *Homo loquens* as much as we are *Homo sapiens*. All the evidence we have, from the continued existence of preliterate societies, through the knowledge we have of language acquisition by children, to the existence of historical records, confirms the fact that writing is based on speaking. Writing systems are attempts to capture sounds and meanings on paper. Even though certain characteristics of writing systems came into being to inform people how to recite correctly, particularly to recite certain religious texts (as, for example, the Vedas, the religious texts of the Sanskrit language), the primary purpose of writing is to lend some kind of permanence to the spoken language and not to prescribe that spoken language in any way. In our attempts to describe a language, we must keep this fact in mind; therefore, we are not free to ignore the sounds a speaker makes in favor of studying the writing system.

We must acknowledge the centrality of speech to any study of language and therefore we must take an interest in phonetics and phonology (Chapters 3 and 4). Very few linguists have ventured to claim that language can manifest itself in either speech or writing and that the two manifestations are somehow "equal." These comments should not be taken as a denial of the importance of writing and writing systems and of the possible effects of mass literacy on language systems and linguistic usage. Writing undeniably influences speaking. An insistence on the vocal basis of language is an insistence on the importance of the historical and developmental primacy of speech over writing and therefore a denial of the common misunderstanding that speech is a spoken, and generally somewhat debased, form of writing.

Language as Symbol

The term **symbol** in the definition refers to the fact that there is no connection, or at least in a few cases only a minimal connection, between the sounds that people use and the objects to which these sounds refer. Language is a symbolic system, a system in which words are associated with objects, ideas, and actions by convention so that "a rose by any other name would smell as sweet." In only a few cases is there some direct representational connection between a word and some phenomenon in the "real" world. Onomatopoeic words like *bang, crash,* and *roar* are examples from English, although the meanings of these words would not be at all obvious to speakers of either Chinese or Eskimo. More marginal are words like *soft* and *harsh* or *slither* and *slimy,* in which any connection between sound and sense may well be disputed by native speakers. More than one writer has claimed that English words beginning with *sl,* and *sn,* as in *slime, slut, snarl,* and *snob,* are used to denote a variety of unpleasant things. In much the same way the vowel sound in *twig* and *bit* is said to be associated with small things and the vowel sounds in *huge* and *moose* with large things. However, once again we are in an area of subjectivity, as counterexamples are not difficult to find; for example, *sleep, snug, hill,* and *spoon.* No more than a slight statistical trend can be established, one on which it would be unwise to base conclusions. In the circumstances, then, little evidence exists to refute the claim that languages are systems of arbitrary symbols. In learning a new language, you cannot escape learning the new vocabulary almost item-by-item, adequate testimony to this arbitrary symbolic characteristic of all languages.

Language as Human

The term **human** in the definition refers to the fact that the kind of system that interests us is possessed only by human beings and is very different from the communication systems that other forms of life possess. Just how different, of course, is a question of some interest, for it can shed light on language to know in what ways human languages are different from systems of nonhuman communication. The differences may be ascribed to the process of evolution that the human species has gone through and result from the genetic characteristics that distinguish it from other species. No system of animal communication makes use of the design feature of duality, that is, of concurrent systems of sound and meaning, and few systems of animal communication employ discrete arbitrary signals. Moreover, none allows its users to do all that language allows human beings to do: reminisce over the past, speculate about the future, tell lies at will, and devise theories and even a **metalanguage** about the system itself. Bees do not discuss last year's supply of food, dolphins are not next-year oriented, jackdaws do not deceive each other with their calls, and dogs do not bark about barking. Further discussion of some of the fundamental differences between human language and animal communication is contained in Chapter 2.

Language is uniquely human in another respect. People can perform acts with language just as they can with objects of different kinds. As we shall see in Chapter 9, sentences like *I pronounce you husband and wife, I'm sorry,* and *I bet you a dollar* can all be acts (**performatives**) because saying something in the right circumstances is also doing something beyond making noises.

Language as Communication

The final term in the definition is **communication:** language is used for communication. Language allows people to say things to each other and express their communicative needs. These needs are strong, whether they are the needs of a Robinson Crusoe for something or someone to address his remarks to, or of Trappist monks who devise sophisticated signal systems to avoid breaking their vows of perpetual silence. Language is the cement of society, allowing people to live, work, and play together, to tell *the* truth but also to tell a lie, or *lies.* Sometimes it is used merely to keep communication channels open so that if any need arises to say something of importance a suitable channel is available. This last function is met through the conventions of greeting and leave-taking, by small talk at parties, and in the chatter of secretaries in a large office. It is most conspicuous in its absence, as witnessed by the image of the tall "silent" stranger in the movies or by such a statement as *She didn't even speak to me when we passed in the street.* Other manifestations of this keeping open of channels are the ubiquitous portable transistor radios of teen-agers and the *Good morning-Nice day* greetings of casual acquaintances. Language also functions to communicate general attitudes toward life and others, creating what the anthropologist Bronislaw Malinowski called "a phatic communion [among speakers] . . . a type of speech in which ties of union are created by a mere exchange of words." We need only notice how absurd it would be to take each of the following expressions literally: *How do you do! Where have you been all my life?,* and *How's everybody?*

The communication of most interest to us is, of course, the communication of meaning. A language allows its speakers to talk about anything within their realm of knowledge. According to one hypothesis associated with the linguist Edward Sapir and his student Benjamin Lee Whorf, languages may make some things easier for their speakers to say than other things. That is, different languages impose different perceptions of the world on their speakers or predispose them to look at the world in certain ways. If such a hypothesis were true, it would imply either that meanings would not be freely translatable across languages or that they would be translatable only with certain difficulties. However, this hypothesis has never had any strong appeal to linguists, who have felt that the linguistic evidence cited in its support has been slight and that not enough is known about how languages convey meaning to justify such a strong claim.

Linguists must be prepared to take an interest in how meaningfulness is achieved in language, even though at times precise questions about meaning cannot easily be formulated or answered even when formulated. The sentences *John opened the door* and *The key opened the door* communicate meaning; however, no general agreement exists as to how that meaning is achieved in each case. A sentence such as *John and the key opened the door,* made by conjoining the subjects of the two sentences, is bizarre; and both **John opened* and **The key opened* are unacceptable. The sentences fail to communicate meaning. We are faced with the problem of explaining such failure; Chapter 9 offers certain tentative explanations.

THE SCOPE OF LINGUISTIC THEORIZING

The above definition of language as a system of arbitrary vocal symbols used for human communication still allows for a wide range of scientific inquiries into language and its functions. It allows for a wide variety of questions to be posed and for very different bodies of evidence to be examined for answers to those questions. At this point, therefore, we should return to a discussion of what it is that we claim to be describing. Should we merely describe what we happen to observe, or should we attempt to make observations of certain kinds and also to filter out some important principles from these observations? We can, for example, report that so many people of such and such a background use sentences like *He be wise* and *He asked did John go,* and make no attempt to relate these sentences to other sentences from the same speakers, such as *He wise,* and to the almost certain nonappearance of a sentence such as *He asked if John went.* A decision as to what constitutes the data which must be described and accounted for will therefore control what we have to say. The decision effectively controls the actual selection of those data. If we feel we must describe certain kinds of relationships, we will look for examples of such relationships and for additional evidence; however, if we are not aware of these same relationships, we will not even notice certain phenomena. Such a situation is not uncommon in the natural or "hard" sciences. No scientist ever approaches a problem without some idea of how the problem should be stated and without some notion of what evidence might or might not be relevant in finding a solution.

Some kind of system is necessary for collecting and organizing data, because science is concerned with the development of systems for handling data and with theory building. One very simple system would involve no more than making a rudimentary catalog of observations according to an elementary scheme of classification, as in the construction of a simple dictionary. Such a system would have what has been called "observational adequacy." It would simply cover the data but would not attempt to get at any very profound relationships that might exist beneath the "surface" of those data.

Some attempt can be made to get beneath the surface to explain relationships. The resulting system would attempt "descriptive adequacy." For example, various kinds of relationships can be shown to hold among apparently unrelated phenomena. Sentences like *John kissed Mary* and *The boy chased the dog* can be related to each other as exhibiting the same "pattern"; words like *Mary* and *dog* can be considered to be "nouns"; *Mary was kissed by John* and *The dog was chased by the boy* can be regarded as "transformations" of the first two sentences; and both **John Mary kissed* and **The boy dog chased* can be regarded as "ungrammatical," and therefore starred, because either they do not apparently occur in real life or they violate certain "rules" which speakers of the language apparently follow. Not all the preceding statements are equally "adequate." The best kind of descriptive adequacy in a grammar would result from that grammar showing not only how the data in the language are arranged but doing so in a way which accords with the linguistic intuitions of the speakers of that language.

But since all languages are somehow alike, a further level of "explanatory adequacy" may be attempted. All language descriptions would draw on the same system of organization, and the same terms and processes would be used in describing them because of the general likeness. For this reason attempts have sometimes been made to describe all language within a particular terminology. For example, attempts have sometimes been made to describe English as though every word must belong to one of eight parts of speech or in terms of phonemes or morphemes which can be discovered by following a prescribed set of procedures, or through possibilities and impossibilities of occurrence, for example the possibility of *Be quiet!* but the apparent impossibility of **Be tall!* Achieving explanatory adequacy is one of the most important goals of modern linguistics.

Each set of terms arises from a theory of some kind, and the theory and terminology together predispose an investigator to look at a language in a certain way. Investigators do not merely fit data into a theoretical framework using the available terminology to do so; rather, that framework helps them to delineate just what are the data and questions with which they must be concerned. Consequently, at various times certain questions about language have been held to be answerable but at other times not. A good theory should lead to the formulation of interesting questions so that gaps in a conceptual framework may be explored and new linguistic evidence used to confirm or deny basic hypotheses.

The "best" theory for a language, that is, the best grammar, will have all the characteristics of any good scientific theory. It will be an abstraction in that it will make reference to idealized units and processes. It will also, of course, acknowledge that these idealizations are realized in various ways in the world in which we live, just as the physicist's gravitational system and the economist's monetary system are abstractions realized respectively in falling bodies and price fluctuations. The grammar will attempt to relate apparently diverse phenomena within a single framework, will provide a terminology for making observations about such phenomena, and will stimulate interesting investigations. A grammar must do all these things if it is to be of scientific value, and its usefulness must be judged by how well it does all three.

The points made in the previous paragraphs are extremely important. Linguistics is a science only insofar as linguists adopt scientific attitudes toward language. Scientific attitudes require objectivity: investigators must not deliberately distort or ignore data but must try to see things clearly and see them whole, all the while admitting that their theoretical inclinations influence their view of the data. However, these theoretical inclinations should be quite uninfluenced by emotions so as to avoid subjectivity. A scientific statement should also be testable, and the techniques and experiments on which it is based should be replicable, since explicitness is an essential requirement of the scientific method. A statement which is not testable is not vulnerable and an invulnerable statement is not a scientific one, for all scientific statements must be subject to disproof. Scientists must also be thorough in their treatment of problems and reject arbitrary solutions. However, different competing theories exist at any one time, each claiming adequacy in covering what purport to be the same data. The result may be vigorous conflict among supporters of the various theories, and developments in a discipline may appear to be revolutionary rather than evolutionary. Such has been the case in linguistics in recent years.

Since there is more than one way to "do" science—that is, since several different methods may properly be labeled "scientific"—we need not be surprised to find that linguists have continually discussed "how to do linguistics." The methodology of linguistics is a serious continuing concern. In later chapters we will see that concern for methodology surfaces on many occasions, particularly as this book to some extent recapitulates in its treatment of topics some of the history of modern linguistics.

SOME BASIC DISTINCTIONS

Before investigating language phenomena in any detail, we should be familiar with a set of distinctions widely recognized in linguistics. These distinctions are between pairs of related terms: *description* and *prescription; synchrony* and *diachrony; form* and *substance;* and *competence* and *performance.*

Description and Prescription

The distinction between description and prescription relates to the fact that we must try not to make prejudicial judgments about data. Linguists are concerned with how languages work, not with how they can be improved (if indeed they can be). A sentence such as *He ain't got none* is to be explained, not criticized or corrected. Such sentences occur, and must be accounted for. They may produce undesirable consequences when uttered in certain circumstances, but this observation is a social rather than a linguistic observation. *He ain't got none* may result in the speaker's being left out of certain social events and being deprived of certain opportunities. To say that *He ain't got none* is a "bad" sentence is to make some kind of prescriptive statement about behavior, not some kind of descriptive statement about a linguistic phenomenon. We would not want to call it an ungrammatical sentence. For example, we should compare it with a collection of words such as *Got he ain't none,* a collection which is definitely ungrammatical for any speaker of English. *He ain't got none* is quite normal, and therefore perfectly grammatical, for people who use this kind of construction, but no speaker of English uses *Got he ain't none.* It is our task to describe the occurrence of the former and, if we can, to account for it in some way within a general theory. In addition, we may consider that we should also account for the nonoccurrence of the other group of words. On no account, though, can we dismiss *He ain't got none* as either "incorrect" or of no interest, merely because such an expression is in low repute in certain social circles.

Much language study in the last century or more has been prescriptive in nature. This prescriptive influence is particularly apparent in some of the language instruction which is given in the schools. The rules taught are often prescriptive, of the form *Do this* or *Don't do that.* On the other hand, the rules of a generative grammar, as we shall see, are entirely descriptive, of the form *X becomes Y (in situation Z).*

Synchrony and Diachrony

The distinction between synchrony and diachrony refers to the fact that languages exist in time and that we can study a language as it exists at any one time or over a period of time. A **synchronic** statement is a statement about a language at one period in time, whereas a **diachronic** statement is a statement about a change or changes that took place over a period of time. Synchronic statements should make no reference to previous stages in the language. For example, *meet* and *meat* are pronounced the same, that is, they are **homophones** in current English. It is irrelevant in a synchronic statement about Modern English that they were once differently pronounced, a fact to which their spelling attests. The historical facts indeed show different sources for the *ee* and the *ea* in the words. However, such a similarity between the synchronic statement for current English and the diachronic evidence, that is, the historical facts, must be regarded as fortuitous and should never influence decisions as to what are the synchronic facts. A synchronic statement may reflect certain historical developments: for example, in one treatment of the sounds of current English the vowels of *reel* and *real* are described as being basically different rather than alike because the second word has a derived form *reality* which contains a two-vowel pronunciation of *ea.* But such a decision is made for synchronic reasons alone.

Valid diachronic, or historical, work must be based on good synchronic, or descriptive, work, because no valid statements about linguistic change can be made unless good descriptions exist of a language for at least two discrete stages of development. In addition, a theory of linguistic change is required in order to relate the two descriptions. Any account of changes in the pronunciation of words such as *mouse, night,* and *name* over the last thousand years in English must be based on a thorough knowledge of English pronunciation today, English pronunciation a millennium ago, and a theory of sound change, a theory which, to be maximally useful, should also find itself in harmony with the theory from which the synchronic statements are derived. These and related problems will be discussed in some of the later chapters. In those chapters we will also see that the distinction between diachrony and synchrony is not an absolute one: a language is a product of history and many of the effects of its history are noticeable in its structure.

Form and Substance

The distinction between form and substance is the distinction between the system we devise and the actual data. The system is a theoretical construct; the data are events in the real world. Of course, we must assume that there is some correspondence between the two, that empirical justification exists for our claims, and therefore that the system "accounts for" or is "behind" certain data. The system is not unlike a bus-company timetable or the rules of a game like chess. On any particular day specific buses are likely to deviate from the schedule because of local conditions, but the schedule is still recognizable as a whole; similarly, each game of chess is different from every other game in some respect or other, yet each is still recognizably the same game, chess. If the system requires us to refer to certain phenomena as nouns, others as phonemes, and still others as imperatives, then we are really claiming that languages have nouns, phonemes, and imperatives, and that these are realized in such substance as *boy* and *John, p, t,* and *k,* and *Get up!,* respectively. In another sense too, substance means that there can be innumerable instances of *boy, John, p, t,* and *k* and *Get up!,* and that each instance may differ slightly from each other instance since no two pronunciations are exactly alike. However, each one is a particular instance of an abstract "boy," "John," "p," "t," "k," and "Get up!" Such abstractions must somehow exist in people's heads when they use language, so one task we have is that of making hypotheses about the complete set of abstractions that exists, in the simplest yet most comprehensive way. Another implication is that language is, in a very important sense, a mental phenomenon.

Competence and Performance

The distinction between competence and performance is closely related to that between form and substance. The formal system we describe accounts for a native speaker's knowledge of his language. This knowledge allows him the potential to understand and produce utterances which he actually may never find the opportunity either to understand or to produce. For example, the reader will have understood the previous sentence, will understand this one, and will understand the next one, but each of these sentences is unique in his or her experience. This ability the reader has to understand novel sentences derives from **competence** in English. This same competence causes us to reject *the ate goldfish John as a possible English sentence, tells us that *Time flies* is ambiguous, and indicates that the speaker got sidetracked in the middle of such a sentence as *I was going along the street and met well no it was raining at the time and as I said to Peter before leaving.* . . . Linguistic **performance** is full of utterances like this last one, as well as slips, as close listening to almost any conversation will reveal. Many linguists consider that the correct approach is not to describe such utterances, but to describe the underlying system, or competence, which leads a speaker-listener to produce and understand them.

That same system should allow us to account for the ambiguity of *Time flies* and the **ungrammaticality** of the collection of words about John and the goldfish. In that way speakers' intuitions about language will be acknowledged. Actual utterances will not, however, be treated all alike because some will be more useful than others in coming to decisions about the underlying facts. Almost universal agreement exists that any grammar which treats a long, well-formed sentence like *I was walking along Old Bridge Street when I met Jim, who was just leaving the hotel after having attended his weekly United Fund committee meeting* on the same basis as the disconnected utterance above is missing more than one important generalization about English in particular and language in general.

LINGUISTICS AND RELATED DISCIPLINES

Linguists are not the only people interested in the study of language. Anthropologists, philosophers, psychologists, and language teachers have long been interested in language, and linguistics has close ties with each of the other disciplines. These ties have been stronger at some times than others as interests change and as the influence of one discipline on another grows or diminishes.

Linguistics and Anthropology

The tie with anthropology is a historical one in that much linguistic endeavor grew out of a necessity for understanding the languages of "primitive" peoples. Exotic languages proved to be very different in many ways from the Indo-European languages beloved of the philologists and grammarians of the nineteenth century. Linguists who wanted to describe the exotic languages of the Americas, Southeast Asia, and the Pacific found that they had to devise completely new techniques of linguistic analysis. The branch of linguistics called structural linguistics derived its characteristic descriptive approach largely from a concern for exotic languages while its approach to historical matters came largely from the discoveries of nineteenth-century philologists. Today the relationship between anthropology and linguistics is less close than in the past; languages no longer appear to vary in all sorts of unpredictable ways as we find out more about different languages. Some of the ideas which intrigued early anthropological linguists, such as the relationship between language and culture (as, for example, in the aforementioned Sapir-Whorf hypothesis), no longer generate the same kind of excitement.

As some of the interest and excitement has diminished, however, a concern for the relationship between language and society has developed. One of the most rapidly growing areas of linguistic study is **sociolinguistics,** the study of language in its social context. We will be concerned with some aspects of sociolinguistics in Chapters 9 and 12, particularly those aspects which seem to require certain revisions of current linguistic theory.

Linguistics and Philosophy

If the relationship of linguistics to anthropology has weakened in recent years, the one between linguistics and philosophy has strengthened during the same time.

Linguists are interested once more in questions of meaning after passing through a period in which they almost totally disregarded the study of meaning. For a long time no suitable procedures seemed to exist for investigating questions of meaning; consequently, meaning in language was largely ignored because it was felt that nothing worthwhile could be said in the absence of suitable procedures. Today, on the other hand, linguists wonder why a sentence such as *John is as sad as the book he read* is bizarre in its meaning, how a sentence like *John doesn't beat his wife because he loves her* achieves its ambiguity, what *When did you stop beating your wife?* presupposes, and how we can "hear music" even when we cannot be exhorted to **Hear music!* Although we can acknowledge that a language is a system for relating sounds to meanings, we encounter great difficulty in understanding how this relationship is effected. We still know very little about what is involved when we say that something "means" something. As we will show in Chapter 9, there is a new interest in some of the same questions of meaning that have long interested certain philosophers.

Linguistics and Psychology

Linguists share an interest with psychologists in the "human" properties of language, in language learning, and in "creativity." Language is uniquely human. Languages also appear to share some universal constraints. We can assume that these constraints exist because of human limitations or predispositions. Children apparently learn languages in the same way no matter how different the cultures in which they are raised. Such universal learning is of interest to both psychologists and linguists. Language is also probably the most creative system possessed by man. Psychologists and linguists, therefore, have an interest in linguistic phenomena, the former to explain behavior in general, the latter to explain behavior in particular. It may even be the case, as Noam Chomsky has suggested, that linguistics is best thought of as being a branch of cognitive psychology.

One important area of interdisciplinary study has emerged in recent years, that of **psycholinguistics.** Psycholinguists are interested in such matters as the acquisition of language by children, speech perception, language processing, and linguistic functioning in various conditions, for example, in deafness and in various language pathologies. As linguists concern themselves more and more with some of the subtleties of language structure, they find evidence from various psycholinguistic studies useful in making decisions about what must be explained and how it must be explained.

Linguistics and Teaching

Finally, although languages are learned, they must also occasionally be taught, or there must be some teaching about linguistic matters. Linguists can be expected to contribute some understanding of language to this teaching; for example, of the native language, of reading, of foreign languages, and so on. We may also sometimes offer advice about the substance of what must be taught, pointing out what appear to us to be the facts that must be mastered. Occasionally, we venture statements about how what apparently must be taught should be taught. When such statements are made with a full understanding of the complex processes of teaching and learning, they should be listened to with attention. However, too often they are not made with such an understanding, for linguists are just as prone as any other professionals to offer gratuitous advice in areas outside their realm of competence. Nor are we always completely objective in our own use of language. But such is to be expected. Language is heady stuff and not even the most self-disciplined linguist can entirely resist being influenced now and again by some of its more mysterious properties nor avoid being trapped occasionally during actual linguistic performance.

BIBLIOGRAPHIC NOTES

It may seem strange to begin these notes by mentioning a book that is not concerned with linguistics at all; however, Kuhn's *Structure of Scientific Revolutions* brilliantly describes what science is and how it changes. Linguistics fits Kuhn's description rather well.

Allen's bibliography *Linguistics and English Linguistics* is very useful in its combination of references on theoretical linguistics and English. Many good introductions to linguistics exist. The "classics" are Sapir's *Language*, Bloomfield's *Language*, de Saussure's *Course in General Linguistics*, Sturtevant's *Introduction to Linguistic Science*, and Jespersen's *Language: Its Nature, Development and Origin*. Two good "older" texts are Hockett's *Course in Modern Linguistics* and Gleason's *Introduction to Descriptive Linguistics* (with an accompanying workbook). Bolinger's *Aspects of Language* (with an accompanying workbook by Alyeshmerni and Taubr), Falk's *Linguistics and Language*, Fowler's *Understanding Language*, Fromkin and Rodman's *Introduction to Language*, Liles' *Introduction to Linguistics*, Lyons' *Introduction to Theoretical Linguistics*, and Langacker's *Language and Its Structure* all reflect some of the most recent developments in linguistic theory. Three interesting general treatments of issues are Farb's *Word Play*, Haugen and Bloomfield's *Language as a Human Problem*, and Minnis' *Linguistics at Large*. The most influential journals are *Foundations of Language, Language, Linguistic Inquiry, International Journal of American Linguistics*, and the *Journal of Linguistics*.

We can gain some knowledge of the historical development of linguistics as a discipline from Robins' *Short History of Linguistics* and Waterman's *Perspectives in Linguistics*. Pedersen's *The Discovery of Language* is an older account emphasizing nineteenth-century work, and Joos' *Readings in Linguistics* contains original papers that show many of the characteristics of the linguistic thought of a considerable part of the first half of the twentieth century. Dinneen's *Introduction to General Linguistics* is more an introduction to the history of linguistics than an introduction to general linguistics, so should be included here.

Brown's *Words and Things* is still probably the best introduction to many of the topics mentioned briefly in the final section of the chapter. However, certain other works may be cited in connection with specific disciplines. The connection of linguistics to anthropology is explored in Greenberg's *Anthropological Linguistics*, Landar's *Language and Culture*, and Burling's *Man's Many Voices*. The connection between language and thought is examined in Carroll's *Language and Thought* and *Language, Thought, and Reality: Selected Writings of Benjamin Lee Whorf*. Other noteworthy books on language and psychology are Deese's *Psy-*

cholinguistics, Greene's *Psycholinguistics,* Osgood and Sebeok's *Psycholinguistics: A Survey of Theory and Research Problems,* and Slobin's *Psycholinguistics.* Malinowski's words are quoted from his essay "The Problem of Meaning in Primitive Languages." A fairly recent exploration of the relationship of linguistics and meaning is made by Katz in *The Philosophy of Language.*

Wardhaugh's *Contexts of Language* discusses language in relation to most of the above-mentioned issues.

EXERCISES

1-1 Check to make sure that you understand each of the terms printed in **boldface** in Chapter 1.

1-2 Chapter 1 makes distinctions between certain terms. Express the distinction between the following terms as clearly as you can: *linguistic description* and *linguistic prescription; synchrony* and *diachrony; form* and *substance; competence* and *performance.*

1-3 Words such as the following have sometimes been cited to show the non-arbitrary nature of language or to argue for phonetic symbolism. How powerful is this evidence? Can you cite any counterevidence?

bang	dingdong	sludge	snoop	swipe
blare	gurgle	snail	snooty	swirl
blast	hiss	snake	snore	swish
bowwow	honk	snarl	snort	swoop
buzz	moo	snatch	snot	swoosh
chatter	murmur	sneak	snub	whack
choochoo	ping	sneer	splash	wham
clang	pitter-patter	snicker	strum	wheeze
clatter	scratch	snide	swat	whisper
crackle	sizzle	sniffle	swig	whistle
crash	slime	snigger	swill	whiz
creak	slop	snob	swing	whoosh

1-4 Why is **ngleikz* both unpronounceable in English and an obvious spelling aberration?

1-5 Which of the following sentences are "good" English sentences? Why are the others "bad"?

  1 Colorless green ideas sleep furiously.
  2 The moon is made of green cheese.
  3 Moon cheese green made the of is.
  4 The moon is completely uninhabited.

1-6 In what sense does a parrot talk? Why does a dog lie down when told to?

1-7 Record and describe two instances of language used for phatic communion.

1-8 Speech and writing are different. Record a short explanation or description exactly as it was spoken. Rewrite that explanation or description to make it into a coherent paragraph. What are some important differences between the two? What can you say about linguistic performance as a result?

2

LANGUAGE IN COMMUNICATION

Chapter 1 emphasized the fact that language is used to communicate meaning and also stated that linguists are concerned with trying to understand the systematic ways in which such communication is achieved. This book will show how they proceed in this attempt and discuss ways of looking at language. The specific focus is on linguistic systems; several general aspects of communication are not covered beyond what is said in this chapter. The remarks about communication in the following pages are included mainly because of the light they throw on matters in which linguists take an interest when they discuss language rather than communication.

This chapter is concerned with certain aspects of two kinds of communication: nonlinguistic human communication and animal communication. Some linguists have shown an interest in nonlinguistic human communication because parts of it are apparently well structured and because it either supports or denies the content of linguistic communication. Animal communication is also of interest because certain systems emerge, but these systems appear to be different in critical ways from the systems we need in describing language. As we shall see, it is difficult to explain how the gap between animal communication and human language can be bridged, or was bridged, in the evolutionary process. Even the recent experiments which have been successful in teaching certain language-like behavior to chimpanzees shed little light on this issue.

NONLINGUISTIC HUMAN COMMUNICATION

Human beings learn to communicate with each other through nonlinguistic means as well as linguistic ones. All of us are familiar with the saying *It wasn't what he said; it was the way that he said it* when, by using the word *way,* we mean something about the particular voice quality that was in evidence, or the set of a shoulder, or the obvious tension in certain muscles. A message may even be contradicted by the accompanying tone and gestures, so that each of *I'm ready, You're beautiful,* and *I don't know where he is* can mean the opposite of any literal interpretation. Often we experience difficulty in pinpointing exactly what in the communication causes the change of meaning, and any statement we make as to the source of the discrepancy between the literal meaning of the words and the total message communicated is likely to be couched in extremely impressionistic terms. It is likely to refer to something like a "glint" in a person's eye, or a "threatening" gesture, or a "provocative" manner.

We are likely to make similar impressionistic statements about communication between members of different cultures and subcultures. Sometimes we remark that Frenchmen "talk with their hands," Japanese "giggle" on inappropriate occasions, and American Indians are "stone-faced." As a result, tendencies exist to stereotype people who come from other linguistic and cultural backgrounds on the basis of impressions about not only their language but also their gestures, customary movements, and use of space. Such stereotyping can be completely false because signs are either misread and given a significance they do not have or not read at all and therefore missed. Members of a subculture in which inferiors avoid eye contact with superiors are likely to have that behavior misconstrued when they come into contact with members of another subculture who do not use their eyes in this way.

Within a particular language or culture, sublinguistic and subcultural patterns may be even harder to describe. Certain behavior may strike us as "effeminate" in a man, "lethargic" in a young person, or "pompous" in a bureaucrat, but again we may have little real understanding of just what makes the various kinds of behavior effeminate, lethargic, or pompous. In each case, though, the person has communicated something about himself, or is assumed by the observer to have done so. The interesting questions to be asked concern how a particular bit of communication has been effected, the ways in which the nonlinguistic signals are patterned if they are patterned, and how the patterns are learned.

We could, of course, make random observations about the kinds of behavior that accompany speech. For example, we can observe that in North American culture normally only females flutter their eyelashes, although no anatomical reason prevents males from doing so. A woman may also on occasion weep in public, but a man's tears must generally be shed privately. Women are not supposed to indulge in the so-called belly laugh, which is reserved for males, and then only in a narrow range of circumstances. Again, only young children can throw tantrums, in public at least, since public tantrum-throwing is considered "immature" behavior in adults. We can also observe that in certain subcultures men stand when women enter a room and that women may kiss each other though men may not. Such behavior is learned, communicates something about the people involved, and varies from culture to culture and within cultures.

The linguists who have looked at such behavior have done so in an attempt to discover in what ways certain characteristics of nonlinguistic behavior might be structured in ways resembling the structures found in language. We know from experience that some people are more responsive than others to the kinds of nonlinguistic signals just mentioned. People exhibiting this kind of ability are often said to be "sensitive," "perceptive," or "skillful at personal relationships." We would like to be able to describe the precise cues to which such people react, so that some explanation can be offered of the total communication process, not just the linguistic part of it. Although language undoubtedly plays the central role in the total process, other parts of the process must be explored if the ultimate goal is a comprehensive description of how human beings communicate with each other. Language itself appears to be used most effectively when there is communicative congruence, that is, when words, gestures, and behavior support one another, being appropriate to the speaker and the listener and to the content and the context of the message.

Paralanguage

Those who have worked on problems of communication claim to have discovered what they call a system of **paralanguage.** In Chapter 1 language itself was described as being systematic. This further claim is that superimposed on the linguistic system is another which adds extra dimensions of meaning to utterances. The paralinguistic system is composed of various scales, and we assume that in normal communication utterances fall near the center point of each scale. For special types of communication speakers move up or down a particular scale or scales. Sometimes such movements occur inappropriately with consequences that are not always predictable.

The first scale of importance is a loudness-to-softness scale. Most utterances do not draw attention to themselves on this scale, but appear to be uttered with just the right intensity of sound. However, an occasional utterance will strike us as being overloud, whereas another will appear oversoft. Likewise, some people seem to speak too loudly and others too softly. Sometimes overloudness is a necessary characteristic of certain types of communication, as when the carnival barker shouts: *Roll up! Roll up! See this beautiful young lady shot 60 feet up in the air from a cannon!* Oversoftness too may on occasion be used to invoke suspense in a story, as in *And then what do you think happened to the little girl when she got lost in the woods and that big bad wolf found her?* Sometimes, however, the degree of loudness or softness may be quite inappropriate: lovers do not normally shout at each other when they sit together holding hands; and a statesman does not normally whisper at a press conference. We would tend to wonder about the durability of the first relationship and to suspect the motives of the whisperer. Overloudness or oversoftness can suggest to the listener that the actual meaning of an utterance is different from its literal meaning. Unfortunately, he may not always be sure of the difference and may be hard pressed to say why he feels one exists.

A second scale is the pitch scale, that is, how high or how low the voice is pitched in speaking. Every speaker has a range of possible pitches available for use in speaking, so that the same message can be communicated in various subranges of pitch, just as a tune can be played in various places on a piano keyboard. We also learn to associate certain ranges of pitch with certain speakers. When speakers use different ranges, we realize that something out of the ordinary is happening. Sometimes these different ranges are considered appropriate in certain circumstances, as when extrahigh pitch is used in speaking to children, as in *Now just what do you kids think you're up to?* Extrahigh pitch is usually interpreted to indicate strain or excitement, whereas extralow pitch is taken as a sign of displeasure, disappointment, or weariness.

A third scale is one of rasping-to-openness. Rasping refers to the presence of an unusual amount of friction in an utterance, as in the *Ugh!* of *Ugh! Another assignment!* Openness, on the other hand, is associated with certain types of speakers, particularly political and religious orators who speak to huge crowds in large and often unenclosed spaces during some kind of ritual. Such speakers typically give their speech what may be called a "hollow" or "resounding" character, to use impressionistic terms. The speeches are also likely to make use of a variety of other devices, for example of certain kinds of metaphors: *Let us put our backs to the wall, turn our faces to the future, stand feet firm on the ground, and resolve never to submit.*

A fourth scale is one of drawling-to-clipping. A drawled *Ye-a-h!* or *W-e-l-l!* can indicate insolence or reservation, whereas a clipped *Nope!* or *Certainly not!* we take to indicate sharpness or irritation. Drawling or clipping can be used to change the literal meaning of an utterance, even to give it a diametrically opposed meaning, as in a drawled *You're a real friend!*

The tempo of an utterance can be varied too, and the variations provide us with a fifth scale. We have all observed the smooth tempos of certain salesmen and some of us the tempo of the student with the obviously rehearsed story, as in *So I went to the Dean and I said to him that I just didn't like the course and he called Professor Smith and they discussed my problem and then I met the chairman and we talked about the college's philosophy and. . . .* We can contrast such a tempo with a spat out: *Now - you - just - listen - to - me - I'm - having - no - more - of - this - silly - nonsense - out - of - you.* These two utterances are near the opposite ends of any tempo scale.

Speakers of English must learn the uses of these various scales, for knowledge of them is not inborn, the ones mentioned above being appropriate for English only. Children learning English in North America learn how to use the scales as they develop competence in the language. They learn what is appropriate and inappropriate, and this learning happens subconsciously, just as does their learning of the grammar of the language. The fact that children have learned the grammar of English is shown by their ability to speak English. The fact that they have learned the paralinguistic system is shown by their ability to react to the signals of that system and to use the signals. Likewise, children learn to use such expressive systems as laughing and crying according to the requirements of the culture. They learn the amount of laughter that is considered appropriate in certain circumstances, so that they know when a good belly laugh is allowed, when a giggle is acceptable, and when even the hint of a smile on the face is completely inappropriate. In some cultures they will learn to associate a type of giggling with embarrassment, just as in an English culture they will learn to associate giggling with childish behavior but not generally with what is regarded as mature adult behavior. The crying system must also be mastered so that a quavering voice, sobbing, emotion-filled declamations, weeping, wailing, and hysterical outbursts can be used appropriately. Even breath control makes an important difference on occasions: Mae West could breathe out a *C'mon up and see me sometime,* but such breathiness in delivery would seem quite inappropriate in a man.

Every time speakers open their mouths, they indicate some degree of involvement with the message they are attempting to communicate. If the message is delivered toward the center of each of the scales described above, the listener may give it some kind of "normal" reading. However, we still cannot easily describe how that meaning is achieved. On the other hand, if the message is not delivered toward the center of one or more of the scales described above, it will take on additional meanings to the listener, and some of these meanings may even be in conflict with each other.

In order for listeners to interpret correctly the messages they hear, they must further relate their content and delivery to such variables as the sex, age, and appearance of the speaker, and to the context of the utterance. Nevertheless, we know almost nothing about the influence of these latter variables on interpretation. Communication among human beings is an extraordinarily complicated affair, even among those who live and work closely together every day. We should not be surprised, therefore, that so many difficulties occur in communication among people from different linguistic and cultural backgrounds and that so much misunderstanding results in the world.

Kinesics

Alongside the paralinguistic system of voice modulation exists another system, a system of gestures. The study of gestures is called **kinesics.** The gestures may be as small as eyebrow movements, facial twitches, and changes in positioning the feet, or they may be larger gestures involving uses of the hands and shrugs of the shoulders. Again, the correct uses of gestures must be learned, and like linguistic usages, they vary widely among cultures and within cultures.

In North American culture we move our heads up and down to agree and sideways to disagree. Certain other cultures reverse the associations or have different devices to accompany agreement and disagreement: the Semang people thrust the head forward to express agreement, and the Ovibundu people shake a hand in front of the face with the forefinger extended to express negation. When we meet people, we greet them by nodding, shaking hands, clasping arms, kissing, or embracing. We do not greet each other by buffeting the other's head with a fist like the Copper Eskimo, or with the backslapping routine of the Spanish American, or with the embracing and mutual back-rubbing of certain Polynesian peoples. Each culture has conventional greeting routines which are quite arbitrary but perfectly natural for the group. Outside the group they may cause amusement or be completely unrecognized for what they are. We should not be surprised to discover that a typical North American gesture, the nose rub which is used to indicate a certain amount of disbelief, can go completely unrecognized elsewhere.

Within a culture, the appropriate use of body parts must be learned. It is interesting to see how some of these uses relate to the differentiation of behavior between the sexes. Men and women walk, sit, and stand in different ways, and only a minor part of the difference has an anatomical basis. We can observe that advertisements in fashion magazines provide useful caricatures of some of these differences. Facial movements also differ between the sexes, particularly movements of the eyes and eyelashes; for example, the amount of closure of the eyes and the occasions for such closure and the freedom to flutter the eyelashes. Shoulder-shrugging and head-tossing styles are different between the sexes, as are the appropriate distances between the feet when standing, the positioning of the pelvis, and the characteristic curvature of the wrist. The preening behavior of the sexes is also different: touching up lipstick, for example, being characteristic of females, and straightening the tie being characteristic of males. These behaviors are learned to the point of becoming habitual and often go unrecognized for what they are.

We can also compare how different parts of the body are used on different occasions, for example the uses of the feet and the legs during different kinds of sitting, standing, and walking. There are appropriate occasions for the feet and legs to be held straight and others on which they may be turned or twisted. Toes may be tapped on certain occasions for various reasons. We can observe how legs are crossed and uncrossed and how they are used in different styles of standing, walking, and running. A sentry standing on guard duty, a bride walking to the altar, and a child running home from school use their legs very differently. Such behavior is learned behavior which communicates something about the person who manifests it. In like manner, other parts of the body can be studied for their use in communication, for example the lips in greetings, pointing, and eating, and on pleasurable and distasteful occasions.

Proxemics

Still a third system involves the uses of space. Those who study **proxemics,** as it is called, focus on how people use the space between speakers and listeners in the process of communication. "Comfortable" distances exist for various activities, and these distances must be learned. There are appropriate distances for talking to friends, for communicating with strangers, for addressing superiors. Sometimes distances are deliberately manipulated, for example by superiors who try to show consideration to inferiors through deliberately "reducing" the usual distance between them. There are "correct" uses of desks and the space around them, and sometimes much time and energy is spent in worrying over appropriate table shapes and seating arrangements at conferences and dinner parties. Conventions concerning space must be observed in designing houses and offices and in planning social events. In all these activities feelings of "territoriality," that is, of rights to certain spaces emerge; however, the exact dimensions of these spaces and the uses to which they may be put must be learned afresh by each human being as part of his process of acculturation.

Any complete understanding of language use requires knowledge of the peripheral systems of human communication: paralanguage, kinesics, and proxemics. Just as the language system itself must be learned—even though some of the basic characteristics of the system may be predetermined by genetic structure—so these other systems of communication must be learned. Apparently the systems are not as complex as the language system; however, they are systems that must be acquired. People must learn to walk and carry themselves in certain ways, to gesture and laugh appropriately, and even to flirt and make love according to the prevailing conventions. They must acquire control of these things while learning the language. Moreover, the two kinds of learning must be integrated. Certain psychiatrists have, therefore, taken an interest in the paralinguistic, kinesic, and proxemic systems so that they might be better able to recognize cues to abnormal behavior during interviews, such behavior being signaled by some deficiency in integration.

ANIMAL COMMUNICATION

Just as students of language need to know that other systems of human communication exist beyond the linguistic one, so they need to know something of the systems of communication employed by other forms of life. We sometimes examine the characteristics of animal communication to try to achieve a better understanding of human language, particularly a better understanding of its unique characteristics. And, from time to time, following such an examination, the occasional linguist has even ventured into an attempt to explain what must have been involved in the genesis of human language at some distant time in the past.

A great deal of myth exists concerning communication between animals and between human beings and animals. One fruitful area of investigation would be intraspecies communication. A considerable literature does exist on this subject, covering creatures as different as bees and dolphins. Bees are generally credited with having a sophisticated system for communicating information about food sources to one another, and dolphins are often credited with having amazing "intelligence" and a sophisticated "language." There are also stories of horses, cats, and dogs so "intelligent" that they can both understand verbal instructions and even read human minds. Another area of potential interest, therefore, is interspecies communication, particularly since recently several ambitious attempts have been made to teach some parts of human language to chimpanzees raised either alongside human children or in specially designed environments.

Of some interest then are questions of the following kinds: Which animals have highly developed communication systems? What are the main characteristics of these systems, and how do these differ from the characteristics of human language? Can animals acquire language through deliberate teaching during the process of rearing? Is animal communication *quantitatively* different from human language, that is, is it really a smaller amount of the same kind of ability? Or is the difference *qualitative,* that is, of a completely different order? If it is the former, how far can the quantitative possibilities be developed in animals? If it is the latter, how did the qualitative difference arise? These questions, of course, are ordered in such a way as to require more and more speculative answers. Given the present state of our knowledge, we must regard some of the answers as expressions of faith rather than as empirically justified conclusions.

Intraspecies Communication

Among the studies of intraspecies communication is that of the jackdaw by Konrad Lorenz. Lorenz noted that jackdaws have a small repertoire of distinguishable calls. One is a male courtship call, and two others relate to flying, one indicating flight away from "home" and the other flight toward "home." In addition to the calls, the birds sometimes emit a rattling sound to signal anger at the sight of a threatening object. Lorenz noted that these calls and the rattle are found in jackdaws in all parts of the world, so they may be regarded as universal character-istics of jackdaws. They are also found in jackdaws reared in isolation. Jackdaws, then, appear to possess only a very limited system of genetically acquired calls enabling the birds to send but a handful of messages in contrast with the infinite number of messages that humans can send with their system.

Just as Lorenz studied life and communication among jackdaws for many years, Karl von Frisch studied the habits of bees in their natural settings. He was particularly interested in the bee dance, the dance performed by a foraging bee on its return to the hive to report information about a pollen source to the other bees. Von Frisch observed that the returning bee used a system which involved the speed of the bee's movements and the direction of the dance in relation to the sun to inform the other bees of the distance and direction of the pollen source from the hive. The jointly shared system allowed the bees to inform one another of sources discovered within four miles of the hive. According to von Frisch, all bees can use the system, for it shows only occasional minor variations among different colonies of bees. Even Austrian and Italian bees have very few differences in their dances. In recent years von Frisch's claims have been disputed, other investigators claiming that the bees communicate either through the smell of the pollen the returning bee carries or through sounds made during the conduct of the dance. Whatever the exact means of communication used, the "dance" does result in messages being passed from one bee to others.

Other investigators have examined the call systems used by gibbons and dolphins. The results show that gibbons employ a small set of calls for various purposes. The calls allow gibbons to communicate certain facts about the location of food, danger, and so on, and also to keep in touch with each other as a group works its way through dense thickets. Dolphins have a still more sophisticated call system. They use it to relate their positions to the positions of other objects, particularly to the positions of other living things. The system is not unlike certain sophisticated pieces of sounding equipment which humans have invented for similar purposes. However, dolphins do not use the system to communicate with each other the way humans do—their communicative behavior is not "intelligent" the way human communicative behavior is. We can easily understand, though, how their "language" talents have been overestimated. Dolphins are clever, trainable animals who have had good publicity, particularly on television and movie screens. Bees are much less fascinating, though undoubtedly much more useful.

Interspecies Communication

From time to time people have attempted to establish some kind of communication with animals beyond the kind of simple stimulus-response systems used with domestic pets. For a while in nineteenth-century Germany it appeared that a horse had been trained by its master to understand everything that was said to it. "Clever Hans" could stamp out replies to questions it was asked. However, experiments showed that while Hans was clever, that cleverness depended on someone that Hans was watching knowing the answers to the questions Hans was asked. Hans actually depended on visual cues for his cleverness, not linguistic ones. But at least Hans was never required to speak!

The earliest experiments which attempted to teach language to chimpanzees, those by the Kelloggs and the Hayeses, with Gua and Viki respectively, did indeed attempt to teach the animals to speak. But to little avail. Even chimpanzees reared like children do not end up speaking. Chimpanzees have neither the articulatory nor the cognitive ability to speak. Gua learned three or four words which she spoke badly. However, both chimpanzees learned to respond to speech to a considerable extent.

In recent years the experiments by the Gardners and the Premacks, with Washoe and Sarah respectively, have not required the chimpanzees to speak. Washoe was taught American Sign Language, the language system of the deaf, and Sarah was taught to manipulate plastic symbols on a magnetic board. Each chimpanzee was successfully taught a large amount of something that has many similarities to human language. Washoe, for example, learned to name objects, string signs together, ask questions, "converse," initiate language activities, and so on. Sarah learned to perform a number of complicated syntactic operations involving naming, questioning and answering, and even joining "sentences" together with appropriate deletions (for example, combining *Sarah insert banana pail* and *Sarah insert apple dish* into *Sarah insert banana pail apple dish*).

Critics of such experiments have said that the behavior acquired by the chimpanzees is "language-like" but not language. The chimpanzees apparently show little or no ability to handle syntax and do not use the systems they have acquired in the variety of ways that humans use their language systems. The critics claim that language is a specific human characteristic, that is, that only humans have and can have language because only they are genetically so equipped. Consequently, all such experiments are doomed to failure. In support of the experiments it can be said that the chimpanzees have learned something. It would be unwise to close the door to such experimentation through adopting a position that failure to acquire language is certain. Just how much language can be learned by other species is still an interesting question.

THE DESIGN FEATURES OF HUMAN LANGUAGE

The linguist and anthropologist Charles Hockett has pointed out that human language has certain design features that no system of animal communication possesses. We can note how many of these features each of the systems of animal communication mentioned above possesses.

An important design feature of human language is its **duality,** the fact that it contains two subsystems, one of sounds and the other of meanings. In this way language achieves a basic economy, because a discrete number of functional units of sound can be grouped and regrouped into units of meaning, and then these units of meaning grouped and regrouped into an infinite number of sentences. The permissible groupings are sometimes called tactical arrangements: phonotactic arrangements when they refer to the possible sequences of sounds, and syntactic arrangements when they refer to the possible sequences of meanings. No system of animal communication possesses duality, or even comes near to possessing it. The calls of a gibbon or of a jackdaw are discrete unitary calls, and the barks of a dog are unanalyzable wholes. The systems taught to Washoe and Sarah did not have this feature as it is usually interpreted. They had it insofar as the meaning units, the signs used in American Sign Language and the plastic symbols used on the magnetic board, were themselves composed out of another "level" of units.

A second design feature is **productivity.** This feature refers to the fact that language provides opportunities for sending messages that have never been sent before and for understanding novel messages. A gibbon call system lacks productivity, for gibbons draw all their calls from a fixed repertoire which is rapidly exhausted and which disallows any possibility of novelty. Likewise, the communication systems of most other forms of life are nonproductive. The bee dance, however, does have a limited productivity in that it can be used to communicate about nectar sources within a few miles of the hive in any direction. We should emphasize though that messages about such sources are the only kind that can be communicated through the bee dance: bees cannot communicate about people, animals, hopes, failures, and so on. Washoe's system was very productive: she "said" all kinds of things. Sarah's was much less productive, since she was required only to respond to the experimenter, not to initiate exchanges.

A third design feature of language is its **arbitrariness.** There is almost no predictability in many of its characteristics, and there is almost never any connection between symbol and object. A bee dance is iconic rather than arbitrary; that is, it rather directly represents its subject matter, because a direct connection exists between the dance itself and the source of nectar in the number and direction of the gyrations. Any search for similar iconicity in language will reveal language to be almost entirely noniconic. For example, the English number system proceeds as follows: *one, two, three, four, . . . ten . . . thousand,* and so on, not *one, one-one, one-one-one, one-one-one-one, . . .* and so on. *Four* is not four times as long as *one.* Of course, most call systems are arbitrary, but in this case the arbitrariness is minimal because the systems themselves are quite limited both in the number of calls available and the uses made of the calls. Both Washoe and Sarah were required to learn many quite arbitrary features in the systems they were exposed to.

A fourth design feature is **interchangeability.** Any human being can be both a producer *and* a receiver of messages. The communication systems of gibbons and bees have this feature, but those of certain other animals do not; for example, some male birds possess calls which females do not have, and certain fish have similar sex-restricted types of communication. The calls and patterns are not interchangeable between the sexes. Washoe enjoyed her exchanges with humans, initiating as well as receiving messages in American Sign Language.

A fifth design feature is **displacement:** language can be used to refer to real or imagined matters in the past, present, or future. It can even be used to talk about language itself. A gibbon's food call results from contact with food and is made in the presence of food. A gibbon never utters a call about something he ate last year, unlike some gastronomically minded human beings. Of course, bees communicate the fact that they have found pollen when they are not in the presence of that pollen, but they must do this immediately on returning to the hive. They do not dance about the pollen they discovered on some previous occasion, nor do they speculate about future discoveries. Only human beings indulge in complicated sessions of questioning and answering, and talk about talking, even to the extent of inventing metalanguages with which to talk about language. Washoe was able to express many of her needs and desires: for example, for food and for entertainment. To that extent the "language" she used showed displacement.

A sixth design feature is **specialization,** which refers to the fact that communicating organisms should not have a total physical involvement in the act of communication. They should not have to stop what they are doing to make a response, nor should the response be totally determined by the stimulus. Human beings can talk while engaged in activities totally unrelated to the subject under discussion: they can talk about strenuous pursuits without making any kind of abnormal effort. A bee in a bee dance, however, is completely involved physically in the communication process. Washoe "spoke" and played at the same time, but Sarah was much more wholly involved in communication when she was communicating, mainly because she was a laboratory animal whereas Washoe was brought up in a much more homelike environment—in a finished trailer and playground.

A seventh design feature is that of **cultural transmission,** which refers to the fact that the details of the linguistic system must be learned anew by each speaker. They are not biologically transmitted from generation to generation. Animal systems, on the other hand, are genetically transmitted. They are completely determined by the genetic structure of the animal with even minor "dialect" differences apparently resulting from small genetic differences rather than from learning. If a particular animal does not develop its characteristic communication system, the cause is almost inevitably either pathologic or a lack of triggering; that is, it is either a genetic or maturational deficiency. Admittedly, the capacity for language in human beings has a genetic basis, but the particular language a human being learns is a cultural fact not a genetic one. On the other hand, all jackdaws, gibbons, and bees have systems which are identical to those of all other jackdaws, gibbons, and bees. All gibbons are mutually intelligible no matter where reared, whereas, of course, a Russian-speaking monolingual and an English-speaking monolingual are not. None of the chimpanzees learned its system from another chimpanzee. It will be of some interest to see whether or not Washoe, for example, will instruct her offspring in American Sign Language. Was the system she acquired just something to be used with human beings and completely inapplicable to chimpanzee social life?

Still other design features of some importance are those of **discreteness** (language makes use of discrete elements, for example, phonemes and morphemes, not continuous waves–it is digital, not analog); **reflexiveness** (we can use language to talk about language–language is its own metalanguage); **semanticity** (language is about something–it is not just "sound and fury," but has a content); and **prevarication** (language can be used to tell falsehoods).

We can conclude from the above brief survey that no system of animal communication has all the features of human language. Particularly lacking are the duality feature so central to human language and the productivity feature, which allows a human speaker the "infinite use of finite means." The symbolic nature of human language and its arbitrariness appear to be a little less important, for obviously some symbolism is involved in animal communication, and some degree of arbitrariness is present. Attempts to teach human language to animals have been only partially successful. An almost unbridgeable gap seems to exist between humans and animals in the kinds of systems that they can use. Attempts to train animals to respond to human language and to use what language items they learn meaningfully have not been successful because in each case the animal has been unable to bridge the duality gap. It has learned no more than to respond to words as whole units and to certain combinations of words also as whole units. There is minimal productivity and little or no duality. Animals appear to have neither the articulatory possibilities which humans possess nor the cognitive abilities which make language and the use of symbols possible.

If we attempt to account for the origin of human language by maintaining that it evolved from one of the kinds of communication systems used by animals today, we must explain exactly how the feature of duality arose. The fact that animals apparently cannot learn human language even with very deliberate instruction might suggest that the difficulty is genetic in origin, so that animals lack the very capacity for language. Not even the "brightest" animal has the "intelligence" to master a human language, whereas all human beings, unless pathologically afflicted, learn to use language—and most of them accomplish this learning in the first three to four years of their lives, to all intents and purposes. No animal is ever as "bright" as a four-year-old child in linguistic matters. The question then becomes one of explaining a genetic change that occurred. However, we must also decide exactly which characteristics of language are genetic, and therefore universal, and which are nongenetic, and therefore learned as individual languages are learned. Once again we can see how important it is in linguistic work to be concerned with theoretical issues having to do with the nature of language.

BIBLIOGRAPHIC NOTES

Relatively little has been written on the topics of paralanguage, kinesics, and proxemics. The most readable introductions to the general topic are Hall's *Silent Language* and *Hidden Dimension*. Fast's *Body Language,* though a more recent publication, is extremely superficial. Two quite technical treatments are Pittenger and Smith's "Basis for Some Contributions of Linguistics to Psychiatry" and Birdwhistell's *Kinesics and Context.*

Animal communication is discussed in a number of interesting studies. Von Frisch discusses communication among bees in *Bees, Their Vision, Chemical Senses, and Language.* Communication among apes is discussed by Lorenz in *King Solomon's Ring,* and communication with apes is discussed by Hayes in *The Ape in Our House,* by Gardner and Gardner in "Teaching Sign Language to a Chimpanzee" and in "Two-Way Communication with an Infant Chimpanzee," and by Premack in "The Education of S*A*R*A*H" and "Language in the Chimpanzee?" Linden's *Apes,*

Men, and Language is a recent assessment of the work done in teaching language to chimpanzees. Sebeok's *Animal Communication* contains a wealth of information on a variety of other systems and problems, whereas the fifth chapter in Brown's *Words and Things* focuses on a few issues.

Chapter 64 of Hockett's *Course in Modern Linguistics* is devoted to animal communication and the design features of language. Lenneberg's *Biological Foundations of Language* points out certain unique characteristics of human biology that affect the capacity for language acquisition. Hockett and Ascher's "Human Revolution" is an attempt to bridge the evolutionary gap between animal and man so far as language is concerned.

EXERCISES

2-1 Check to make sure that you understand each of the terms printed in **boldface** in Chapter 2.

2-2 Use the appropriate parameters of paralanguage to describe an instance of nonverbal communication.

2-3 Make a set of observations concerning two or three persons of the same age and sex involved in identical activities. Note any similarities and differences in their movements, gestures, and postures.

2-4 Compare the office or room arrangements of some people you know. How do the arrangements affect the interactions of the various people who use these spaces?

2-5 In a conversation with someone you know quite well deliberately change the distance between yourself and the other person. Record what happens.

2-6 Examine a ritual such as a sports activity, a wedding, a ceremony of some kind, or a party for the various uses of paralanguage, kinesics, and proxemics.

2-7 Try to devise a suitable coding system for recording uses of gesture or space. Use the system to record a few observations. What difficulties do you find in using your system?

2-8 Watch a particular television program with someone else with the aim of describing a particular performer's paralanguage, kinesics, and proxemics. (It sometimes works best to turn off the sound track.) Compare your observations.

2-9 Describe the repertoire of responses of any animal that you are familiar with. What are the precise cues to which it reacts? Are linguistic cues treated any differently from nonlinguistic cues?

2-10 Read the accounts of the "language" experiments with Washoe and Sarah. Compare their linguistic abilities with those of any three-year-old child you know. What similarities and differences do you observe?

2-11 If a chimpanzee were to be able to converse intelligently with a human being, what consequences, if any, would this have for humanity?

3

PHONETICS

Chapter 1 emphasized the centrality of speech to language and pointed out that writing systems are secondary systems designed to represent language graphically. When we hear an utterance in a strange language or in an unusual variety of our own language, however, we often experience difficulty in writing down what we heard. The utterance may be quite meaningless and sound quite strange, without our being aware of exactly how it was strange. We may be able to hold in memory and mimic a very short utterance, but a long one exhausts any such capabilities. If any part of the utterance sounds particularly strange, we may not be able to write down what was heard because the English alphabet will seem inappropriate. Unless we have had considerable experience with many other languages, we can be sure we will miss hearing many things we should have heard in the new language. Since we understand nothing that is being said, we cannot rely on understanding parts of what we hear to work out the meaning of those parts we did not hear too well. One of the first needs, therefore, of anyone who aspires to do linguistic work with an unknown language is some systematic way of recording utterances graphically.

Most of the discussion of the sounds of languages that we meet outside of that in books on linguistics and **phonetics,** both of the way sounds are produced and of their characteristics, is based on a poor understanding of the facts of pronunciation. One indication of inadequate understanding is the vocabulary which is used. Terms such as *harsh, guttural, melodious, rhythmic,* and *pleasant* are too imprecise and subjective for use in a serious discussion of the sounds of language. When speakers who use such terms are asked to explain them, they are generally unable to associate them with either specific articulatory movements or even specific sounds. Often, a particular term reflects no more than some kind of stereotyped notion about a language, so that German is said to be "guttural" and Italian "melodious" or "musical." Sometimes instructions on how to pronounce certain sounds contain such advice as "make the sound come out of the top of the mouth" or "think the sound out between the eyes." The reason for the existence of the impressionistic phonetic statements is simple: In general, people have little awareness of how sounds are produced by human beings, and consequently, they have almost no vocabulary available to discuss what is happening. To most of us the parts of the throat, mouth, and nose and their uses in speaking are as much a mystery as is the inside of the rest of the skull.

We must also be aware of the fact that the sounds in utterances are not discrete. An utterance is a continuum of sound which we segment into individual sounds because of our experience. We segment utterances in languages we know with ease; we do not find the same ease in listening to utterances in a strange language because we lack any knowledge of how to segment the sound system. Therefore, as linguists, since any and every spoken utterance is actually a continuum of sound, we must know how that continuum is produced and must have some procedure for breaking it down into separate parts that can be examined for their function. Consequently, we must know how human beings produce the separate parts of the continuum of sound in all their variety and we must be able to record the observations in some kind of **phonetic notation.** Such knowledge and ability is a necessary prerequisite to making any statements about the particular sounds of a language and how they function.

ACOUSTIC PHONETICS

Of course, we could go to the other extreme in making statements about the sounds produced by human beings. Since the sounds are physical events and, therefore, have certain physical properties, we can describe them in the language of the physical sciences. Acoustic phoneticians attempt to do just that, to describe the physical properties of the stream of sound that issues forth from the mouth of a speaker. To describe these properties, they record the sound on machines called **spectrographs.** These spectrographs "print out" representations of this stream of sound as sound spectrograms, graphical representations of the sound stream. Since the sound stream is uttered over a period of time, the machine can plot its characteristics on a time axis. The sound stream also varies in intensity, and the various intensities, or amplitudes, can be recorded. Finally, the sound stream varies in its harmonic and frequency composition, so that the variety of frequencies and their interrelationships can be noted. The availability of spectrographs should enable phoneticians and linguists to make all the statements they need to make about the sounds of languages. However, serious difficulties often arise in interpreting the spectrograms and in drawing conclusions from them as to what constitutes either a "sound" or, more difficult still, two or more varieties of what native speakers would regard as the "same" sound.

The first difficulty is that the spectrograph produces a record of continuous rather than discrete observations. As we might expect, there are no readily identifiable boundaries between the "sounds." Moreover, certain difficulties sometimes arise in relating a particular part of the spectrogram to a particular part of the stream of speech which occasioned it. Such relationships are not readily apparent even when sophisticated filtering equipment is used. Even relating certain portions of the spectrogram to specific movements of the speech apparatus is not an easy task. The spectrograph records everything, but listeners do not listen to everything when they listen to their native language. They filter and sometimes even add what is not there, they hear as the same "sounds" which the spectrograph clearly shows as being different, and they hear as different "sounds" which are clearly shown to be the same. Obviously, humans use their brains in listening: they do not hear and interpret what they hear in some sequential manner. If they did, we could possibly feed the sounds into some kind of machine that would type out what went in (the "talking typewriter"). All such attempts have failed because people use their brains in listening and no one has succeeded in replicating a human brain in hardware.

A practical difficulty that we face in using the spectrograph arises from the fact that it is not a piece of equipment that can be easily used outside a laboratory: it is certainly not the kind of equipment that we can readily transport and make to work successfully on a steamy riverbank or in a desert wasteland. Some approach to observations about speech which does not rely on complicated hardware seems called for. The approach would have to make use of procedures which could be replicated and should refer to physical events.

ARTICULATORY PHONETICS

One such approach to the problem of making observations about speech recognizes that speech is produced by some kind of sound making apparatus and that specific sounds may be related to specific movements of the apparatus that produce the sounds. Since these specific movements produce speech, a systematic description of them would constitute the scope of phonetics. In this variety of phonetics, sounds would be related to the articulatory movements in the chest, throat, mouth, and nose which produce them. Furthermore, systems of transcription would be devised to record the movements, making use of parameters derived from the study of the articulatory processes. These parts of the body, of course, have breathing and eating rather than speaking as their principal functions. Consequently, speech is an "overlaid" function and the so-called "speech organs" are not organs in the sense that the liver, kidneys, and heart are organs.

Linguists are likely to base any study of phonetics on articulation and focus on how sounds are made. They will also be concerned with devising a reliable system for recording the necessary observations. The basic assumption will be that the stream of sound and the articulatory movements can be segmented in a systematic way. Actually, an infinite set of possible variations in articulation exists, for no utterance is an exact repetition of another. However, it is not necessary to record every possible variation or even a very large set of variations. Instead they choose a rather small subset of articulatory characteristics and tie the phonetic observations to these characteristics. In reality, although human beings are capable of producing extremely minute distinctions in speaking, without, of course, being consciously aware of this fact, human ears are unable to perceive all these distinctions and human brains unable to deal with them. Therefore, we can safely ignore possible articulatory distinctions which are not at the same time possible perceptual distinctions.

THE ARTICULATORY APPARATUS

Figure 3-1 indicates those parts of the articulatory apparatus that are of greatest interest to us. An examination of the figure suggests that the areas below the

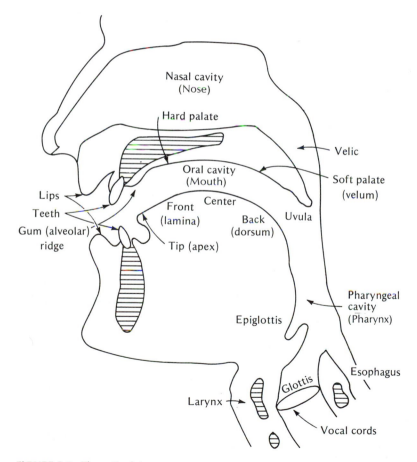

FIGURE 3-1 The articulatory apparatus.

larynx, particularly the lungs, are of no great concern. The lungs are obviously important in speaking, since they provide the airflow to support speech, but they seem to have no function in articulation. A possibility does exist that the lungs are used differently in speaking different languages. Attempts have been made to relate the different syllable structures of languages to different kinds of muscular control in the chest in order to establish relationships between syllables and chest pulses. However, the postulated relationships are very controversial.

The articulatory apparatus in Figure 3-1 contains three important areas or cavities: the pharyngeal cavity (throat); the oral cavity (mouth); and the nasal cavity (nose). The airstream coming from the lungs may be modified in these cavities in a variety of ways. It may also be modified in the larynx or "voicebox" before it reaches any of the cavities. Such modification results from some kind of interference with the movement of the airstream. This modification can be achieved by completely interrupting the airstream or by partial interference in one or more ways. The principal source of such modification is the tongue, and the word *language* itself derives from the Latin word *lingua* meaning "tongue."

Larynx

In any detailed description of the apparatus shown in Figure 3-1 we usually proceed through the whole vocal tract from the "south" to the "north," that is, from the larynx to the lips. The **larynx** is a bony boxlike structure in the front of the throat which contains a valvelike opening consisting of two membranous tissues, the vocal cords. The airstream proceeds to and from the lungs through this opening, called the **glottis.** Normally, only egressive air, that is, air being released from the lungs, is used in producing speech; but sometimes ingressive air, that is, air going to the lungs, may also be used. The membranous tissues can be used to close off the opening in the larynx, just as a valve can be closed. The glottal passage is closed, for example, in lifting heavy objects in order to stabilize air pressure in the chest. In certain pronunciations of *bottle* the middle consonant (only one sound even though spelled with two letters) is pronounced simply by making a brief glottal closure, called a **glottal stop,** rather than, as with the *t* in *top,* by placing the tip of the tongue behind the upper teeth. The symbol for a glottal stop is [ʔ], and it is enclosed within square brackets to show that it is a phonetic symbol. The middle consonant of *bottle,* then, may be pronounced exactly like most pronunciations of the initial part of *ouch,* that is, the part that precedes the vowel, the "gruntlike" sound at the very beginning. More usually in speaking, the tissues, or vocal cords, are either open and vibrating or open and not vibrating. In the first case the vibrations establish a condition called voicing, noticeable in the initial **voiced** sounds of *vat* and *this;* in the second case the condition is called voicelessness, noticeable in the initial **voiceless** sounds of *fat* and *think.* *Bat* and *pat* are also said to begin with voiced and voiceless sounds, respectively. In this case, however, the main difference is in when the condition of voicing begins in the production of the vowel; immediately on release of the *b* in *bat* and with a slight delay on release of the *p* in *pat.* A third kind of opening results in a whisper: the voiced-voiceless distinction is lost and there is a noticeable increase in breathiness.

Pharyngeal Cavity

In the pharyngeal cavity (**pharynx**) the epiglottis serves as a protective cover for the larynx so that food does not "go down the wrong way." It serves no purpose in the production of speech. The pharyngeal cavity may be used as a whole or various parts can be used. The total size can be altered so that its use as a resonating chamber for the sounds produced by vibrations of the vocal cords may vary considerably, either in different languages or in different styles of speaking within a single language. The pharyngeal cavity can also be modified to produce complete stoppages in the airstream or partial stoppages resulting in local friction, as, for example, in Arabic. However, speakers of English do not use the pharyngeal cavity in this way. This is not to say that the pharynx is unimportant. It gives the human voice some of its basic resonantal characteristics. Human infants and apes lack the large adult human pharyngeal cavity because of their high larynxes; they cannot speak partly for this reason.

Oral Cavity

The greatest source of modifications of the airstream is the oral cavity. The modifications result from movements of the uvula, lower lip, and tongue. The uvula is limited in its function in that it can only be made to vibrate to produce a uvular *r* [R], a sound found in very few English dialects but very frequent in French. The lower lip can be moved to meet the upper lip, as at the beginning of *bin* [b], *pin* [p], and *man* [m], or the upper teeth, as at the beginning of *fat* [f] and *vat* [v]. The tongue is much more flexible in its uses than either the uvula or the lower lip. All parts of the tongue can be moved: the back of the tongue can be raised to meet the top of the mouth, as at the beginning of *cat* [k] or *good* [g]; the forward part of the tongue can be raised too, as at the beginning of *tip* [t], *dip* [d], *noon* [n], and *ship* [š]; the tip of the tongue can be thrust between the teeth, as at the beginning of *thin* [θ] and *then* [ð]; and the tongue may even be thrust out to the lips and beyond, so as to protrude from the mouth. This does not usually happen in English except in exaggerated pronunciations of words such as *thin* and *then*. In addition, the tongue can be trilled, curled, and turned back (or **retroflexed**). The tongue is the articulator *par excellence* and, for the purposes of describing most sounds made in the oral cavity, we need to refer only to certain parts of the tongue (the back, center, front, and tip) acting in combination with certain parts of the mouth (the soft palate, the hard palate, and alveolar ridge). The teeth, both upper and lower, and the lips make up the rest of the apparatus we need to refer to in order to describe how sounds are produced in the mouth.

Nasal Cavity

The nasal cavity is easier to describe than the previous two cavities. It is connected to the oral cavity by way of the **velic** at the back of the mouth. The soft part of the roof of the mouth, the **velum,** can be drawn back to close the velic so that all air exiting from the lungs must proceed through the mouth. The velic may also be left open to allow air to exit through the nose. Generally, the velic is either definitely open or definitely closed, although in some styles of speaking or in some dialects partial opening may be observed, the result being speech with a nasal coloring or "twang." Sounds produced with the velic closed are **oral** sounds (all the sounds in the words *pad* [pʰæd], *bat* [bæt], and *loaf* [lof]); those produced with the velic open are **nasal** sounds (the sounds at the beginning and end of *man* [mæn] and at the end of *ring* [rɪŋ]). Some languages have nasal vowels which contrast with oral vowels: French *bon* [bɔ̃] and *vin* [vɛ̃]. No possibility exists for any further modification once air is in the nasal cavity, for there are no parts of that cavity which can be used to produce a stoppage or create friction. There is perhaps one exception. When a speaker has a severe head cold, the nasal passages become unserviceable for speech. Nonnasal sounds, like the beginning sound of *bat* [b] and *doze* [d], are not affected, but nasal sounds, like the beginning sound of *mat* [m] and *nose* [n], are impossible: the nasals are realized like the nonnasals made with the same articulations so that *mat* sounds like *bat* and *nose* like *doze*. A speaker with a very bad head cold is never "nasal," except in popular parlance: the speaker is, in fact, quite the opposite—completely nonnasal.

CONTOIDS

The articulatory apparatus shown in Figure 3-1 is used in a variety of ways. Phoneticians and linguists try to describe certain distinctive activities of the apparatus which seem to recur frequently in the languages they observe. They notice one basic distinction that seems to occur universally: the distinction between consonants and vowels. Many linguists prefer to use the terms **contoid** and **vocoid** rather than **consonant** and **vowel** in discussing phonetic phenomena, reserving the latter terms for discussion of how such phenomena function in the sound system of a particular language. A contoid is a sound characterized by marked interruption in the airstream, ranging from a complete interruption, as at the beginning of *pin* [p], *bin* [b], *tin* [t], *din* [d], *kin* [k], and *Ginn* [g], through an incomplete one accompanied by friction, as at the beginning of *fan* [f], *van* [v], *Sue* [s], *zoo* [z], *shoe* [š], *thin* [θ], and *then* [ð], to various kinds of trills, not usually found in English, and **resonants,** as at the beginning of *red* [r] and **laterals,** as at the beginning of *lip* [l]. A vocoid, on the other hand, is a continuous, therefore uninterrupted, frictionless sound, as in the middle of *bid* [ɪ], *bed* [ɛ], and so on. Such a distinction between contoid and vocoid seems easy and presents no difficulties in words such as *beat, king, pan,* and *fish,* each of which may be said to consist of three sounds, the middle one of which is a vocoid and the other two contoids: [bit], [kʰɪŋ], [pʰæn], and [fɪš]. However, the initial sound of *head, yet, wet, led,* and *red* is not so readily or exclusively classifiable as either contoid or vocoid, as we shall see.

Voice

In classifying contoids, one of the first activities we notice as recurring frequently in languages is activity of the vocal cords, or the lack of such activity. Sounds may be either voiced or voiceless, that is, the vocal cords are either vibrating or not. The initial sounds of each of the following pairs contrast in voicing, the first member of each pair beginning with a voiced contoid and the second beginning with a voiceless contoid. The appropriate phonetic symbol for the sound is provided in each case:

bin [b]	pin [p]
den [d]	ten [t]
goal [g]	coal [k]
vat [v]	fat [f]
zip [z]	sip [s]
thy [ð]	thigh [θ]
joke [ǰ] or [dž]	choke [č] or [tš]

The other voiced contoids in English are the middle sound in *measure* [ž] (compare the middle voiceless sound in *mesher* [š]), the final sound in *rum* [m], *run* [n], and *rung* [ŋ], and the initial sound in *rot* [r], *lit* [l], *yacht* [y], and *watt* [w].

Place of Articulation

A second kind of distinctive activity is related to the location of any interference that occurs in the vocal tract. We must know whether the interference occurs in the pharyngeal cavity or in the oral cavity, what parts of the cavity are involved, and how these parts are involved. Articulation almost always involves the movement of an articulator toward a point of articulation. In very few cases does articulation involve only an articulator being set in motion, as when either the uvula or the tongue tip is trilled by being made to vibrate very quickly. More generally, in contoid articulations, an articulator is made to touch the back of the pharynx or the top of the mouth at some point. The combination of articulator and point of contact is called the place of articulation. For example, the bottom lip may touch the top teeth to produce **labiodental** sounds, as at the beginning of *fat* [f] and *vat* [v]; the two lips may be brought together to produce **bilabial** sounds, as at the beginning of *ban* [b], *pan* [p], and *man* [m]; the tip of the tongue may touch the gum ridge to produce **apicoalveolar** sounds, as at the beginning of *tin* [t] and *din* [d]; the blade of the tongue may touch the hard palate in various ways to produce various **alveopalatal** and **palatal** sounds, as in the middle of *ledger* [ǰ], *lecher* [č], *measure* [ž], and *mesher* [š]; the back of the tongue may touch the soft palate to produce **dorsovelar** sounds, as at the beginning of *cap* [k] and *gap* [g] or at the end of *sing* [ŋ]; and so on, in a great variety of combinations limited only by anatomical impossibility, for example, the impossibility of the bottom lip touching the soft palate. In each case the articulator is located on the lower jaw, whereas the point of articulation is located on the upper jaw. The place of articulation always specifies the articulator first when both terms seem necessary.

Manner of Articulation

The manner of the articulation is also extremely important. *Man* and *ban* share the same articulator and point of articulation in their initial sounds [m] and [b], for both sounds are bilabial and voiced. However, there must be a further difference between the initial sounds because the words have quite different meanings. The difference is a distinction in the manner of articulation of the initial sounds. In *man,* part of the airstream escapes through the nose during the time that the vocal cords are vibrating and the lips are closed. In *ban,* the airstream cannot escape through the nose since the velic is closed. The voicing is actually not apparent until the lips are opened—then it is immediately apparent in comparison to the initial sound [p] of *pin* in which a noticeable delay in voicing occurs. The basic difference in the manner of articulation of the initial sounds of *man* and *ban* arises from the opening of the velic in the first sound [m] of *man* but its closure in the [b] of *ban.* *Man* both begins and ends with nasals: [m] and [n]. The only other nasal contoid in English is that at the end of *sing* or before the *k* in *sink* [ŋ].

Tin, thin, shin are likewise different in the manner of articulation of their initial sounds [t], [θ], and [š]. In *tin* the tip of the tongue completely stops the airstream on the alveolar ridge; in *thin* the airstream is forced through a narrow slit made by the tip of the tongue on the top teeth; and in *shin* the airstream is forced around the edges of the front and tip of the tongue as they are brought into light contact with the alveolar ridge and hard palate. In each case the articulator and point of articulation are quite similar, but the different manners of contact or near-contact produce different kinds of sounds.

The principal manners of articulation are stopping the airstream completely, as in **stops,** for example, the sound at the beginning of *pin* [p], *bin* [b], *toe* [t], *doe* [d], *could* [k], and *good* [g]; interfering noticeably with the airstream as in **fricatives,** for example, the sound at the beginning of *fat* [f], *vat* [v], *Sue* [s], *zoo* [z], *thigh* [θ], and *thy* [ð]; and making a closure as for a stop, but allowing the air to be released through the nose, as in **nasals,** for example, the sound at the beginning of *map* [m] and *nap* [n] and at the end of *sing* [ŋ]. Other manners of articulation involve the production of different curvatures of the tongue as the airstream passes over it: with **laterals** the airstream passes over each side of the tongue but not over the center, for example, the sound at the beginning of *let* [l]; and with **retroflexes** the airstream passes over the tongue tip which is curled back, for example, the sound at the beginning of *red* [r]. Finally, we can have **trills** and **flaps.** Any loose piece of flesh may be trilled, for example, the tongue tip or uvula, or there may be just one quick tap or flap, as when the tongue tip is tapped to the gum ridge in the middle of most North American pronunciations of *butter* to produce a flap [ř].

Airflow Direction

A further distinction involves the direction of the airstream: whether it is going into the lungs and is **ingressive,** or coming from the lungs and is **egressive.** In nearly all languages sounds are made using egressive air only. Ingressives are rare indeed, in English confined perhaps to certain kinds of exclamatory sounds made in moments of pain, surprise, or tension. Naturally, breathing must go on while speaking occurs, and it is remarkable how breathing patterns change during speaking without the physiological disruptions normally associated with marked breathing changes, as, for example, in hyperventilation.

Tenseness

Finally, the tenseness or laxness of the total vocal apparatus, particularly of the tongue and lower jaw, is important in articulation. A noticeable tensing, or tightness, is involved in the production of some sounds, whereas others have no such accompanying tenseness and are lax. The initial sound in *pit* [p], *fat* [f], and *sip* [s] is tense, whereas the initial sound of *bit* [b], *vat* [v], and *zip* [z] is lax. In English the voiceless contoids tend to be **tense** and the voiced contoids tend to be **lax.**

International Phonetic Alphabet Symbols

Using the distinctions referred to above, we can devise a set of symbols for various combinations of phonetic characteristics. The best known system of symbols is that employed in the **International Phonetic Alphabet** (or IPA), of which Figure 3-2 is a simplified version.

A preliminary inspection of Figure 3-2 reveals that terms and symbols other than the ones already used are included in the diagram. These terms are used for certain combinations of the characteristics previously described, such as alveopalatal, and for further modifications. The symbols which indicate modifications are called **diacritic** symbols and are written either above, below, or to the side of the symbol used to denote the basic set of characteristics.

Aspiration is one such modification. The term refers to the fact that a sound is sometimes accompanied by a noticeable outflow of air, or at least a puff of air. The English words *pin, tin,* and *kin* all begin with aspirated stops and can be written [pʰɪn], [tʰɪn], and [kʰɪn]. Affrication refers to another manner in which a stop is released. If the release of the stop is not clear and sharp, we can sometimes observe some friction. The friction may be of the kind that is found at the beginning of *chip* [tˢɪp] and *jet* [dᶻɛt]. It may be of a slightly different kind, not found in English, as when a *t*-like sound is released into an *l*-like sound to produce a *tl* [tˡ]. Such sounds are called **affricates.** Further characteristics such as **palatalization,** a contoid followed immediately by a *y*-like sound, as in [tʸ], **glottalization,** a stop closure made concurrent with glottal closure, as in [t'], and **labialization,** a rounding of the lips made concurrent with the production of a contoid, as in [tʷ], may also be regarded as modifications.

The use of diacritic symbols in Figure 3-2 may be clarified by reference to the following set: [t̪], [t], [t̠], and [tʰ]. The last member of this set, [tʰ], has already been explained, so the main concern is with [t̪] and [t̠]. How does a [t̪] differ from a [t̠], and how do both of these in turn differ from [t]? The unadorned [t] designates a "normal," or "neutral," position of the tongue tip against the alveolar ridge, as in the second sound of *stop*. We can move the tongue tip forward to make the closure on the teeth to make an apicodental [t̪], which is a typical French articulation, as in the initial sound of French *tous,* or initially and finally in French *tête*. If the tongue tip is placed neither on the teeth nor on the alveolar ridge, but is curled a little back, or retroflexed, and made to touch, or come close to, the hard palate, the result is a retroflexed stop [t̠]. The subscripted diacritics [t̪] and [t̠] therefore represent fine variations from some kind of alveolar norm.

		Bilabial	Labiodental	Apicodental	Apicoalveolar	Retroflex	Alveopalatal	Palatal	Dorsovelar	Uvular	Pharyngeal	Glottal
STOPS	vl.	p		t̯	t	t̲	tʸ	k̟	k	q		ʔ
Plain	vd.	b		d̲	d	d̲	dʸ	g̟	g			
Aspirated	vl.	pʰ			tʰ				kʰ			
	vd.											
Affricated	vl.				tˢ		tš					
	vd.				dᶻ		dž					
Laterally	vl.				tˡ							
affricated	vd.				dˡ							
Glottalized	vl.	p′			t′				k′			
	vd.											
Labialized	vl.	pʷ			tʷ				kʷ			
	vd.	bʷ			dʷ				gʷ			
FRICATIVES	vl.		f	θ					x		ḥ	h
Slit	vd.		v	ð					ɣ		ʕ	
Grooved	vl.				s		š					
	vd.				z		ž					
LATERALS	vl.				l̥							
	vd.				l							
NASALS	vl.	m̥			n̥			ɴ̄	ŋ̥			
	vd.	m		n̲	n	n̲	ñ		ŋ			
RETROFLEX	vl.											
	vd.					r						
FLAP	vl.											
	vd.				ř							
TRILLS	vl.				r̥̃							
	vd.				r̃					R		

FIGURE 3-2 Some symbols for contoids, based on the International Phonetic Alphabet.

The symbols in Figure 3-2 represent various articulatory combinations. For example, [b] represents a voiced bilabial stop. The characteristics of the [b] are shown by its position on the grid: place of articulation on the left-to-right axis and other features such as manner and voice on the top-to-bottom axis. The grid provides interpretations for commonly used phonetic symbols and symbols for observed combinations of phonetic characteristics. For example, if a sound appears to have been made by placing the tip of the tongue behind the alveolar ridge and by forcing air over the tongue with audible friction but without voicing, the grid provides the symbol [s] for this combination of characteristics. The grid also enables us to say how two sounds are different from each other; for example, the initial sound of *tin* and *din*. In *tin* the first sound is a voiceless aspirated alveolar stop [tʰ], the aspiration being detectable as a slight puff of air by holding the back of the hand close to the mouth as the word is pronounced. *Din,* however, begins with a voiced alveolar stop [d]. The differences between the initial sounds of the two words, therefore, are those of voicing and aspiration. In *bet* and *met* the difference is one of oral versus nasal articulation: the initial sound of *bet* is [b], a voiced bilabial stop, whereas that of *met* is [m], a voiced bilabial nasal.

In order to be able to record sounds from any language that we may hear, we require a much fuller set of symbols for contoids than the one given in Figure 3-2, which shows mainly sounds used by speakers of English. For some languages we need such symbols as [k͡p] and [g͡b] to represent **coarticulated** stops, that is, two stops made concurrently, just as glottalized stops, such as [t'] and [d'], are concurrently alveolar and glottal stops. Symbols such as [ᵐb], [ⁿd], and [ᵑg] are also sometimes required for prenasalized stops. Prenasalized stops are stops preceded by brief homorganic nasals, that is, nasals made in the same positions as the following stops. Most of the grid shown in Figure 3-2 could be filled out with further symbols and diacritics and several entirely new categories could be added. In each case the same principle would be followed: every symbol or diacritic refers to a member, or members, of a set of articulatory characteristics such as voice, labial, nasal, stop, fricative, and so on, specified with a considerable degree of accuracy.

VOCOIDS

In many ways it is much easier to discuss contoid articulations than vocoid articulations. Vocoids are continuous sounds which are not easily located by reference to movements of the tongue, closures or openings of certain passages, types of interruption and friction, and so on. To use a simple illustration, we can fairly easily say certain things about what happens in the mouth at the beginning and ending of a word such as *bit,* for there is noticeable lip closure at the beginning and a definite closure behind the teeth at the end. However, the sound in the middle of the word is very much more difficult to describe, and the movements in the mouth are much harder to specify. One solution, of course, would be to devise a set of symbols to represent an arbitrary set of sounds. In this way we could pick out the middle sound of *bit* and represent it as [ɪ] without being concerned with how the sound is actually produced or with how it differs from the middle sound of *bet, bat, boot,* and so on. Such a method would hardly be very satisfactory, since it would provide no way of indicating the phonetic similarities that exist in such pairs as *bit-bet* and *bit-beat* but do not exist in such pairs as *bit-boat* and *bit-bout.* We must, therefore, search for those characteristics, or parameters, which are important in the production of vocoids, just as we searched for suitable parameters for contoids.

Tongue and Lip Position

The basic parameters required to discuss vocoids derive from the positions of the tongue and lips. Basically, vocoids are made by holding the tongue in certain positions and sending the airstream over it without any kind of interruption or friction. Further modifications may be made, but all such modifications must be associated with a basic tongue position. A simple understanding of the importance of tongue position can be gained through pronouncing *beat* and *bat,* followed by *beat* and *boot.* In order to pronounce *bat* after *beat* the lower jaw is dropped so that the tongue may be lowered in the mouth. *Beat* contains a **high** vocoid and *bat* a **low** vocoid. To pronounce *boot* after *beat* we pull the tongue back in the mouth. *Beat* contains a **front** vocoid and *boot* a **back** vocoid. A noticeable rounding of the lips occurs as the vocoid in *boot* is pronounced. *Boot* contains a **round** vocoid and *beat* an **unround** vocoid.

This discussion of *beat, bat,* and *boot* introduces the three basic parameters necessary to account for the production of vocoids: the relative height of the tongue, the relative frontness-backness of the tongue, and lip rounding. To sum up the facts for *beat, bat,* and *boot,* we can say that the first word contains a high front unrounded vocoid [i], the second a low front unrounded vocoid [æ], and the last a high back rounded vocoid [u]. We can also find a low back rounded vocoid in *bought* [ɔ].

Figure 3-3 is a schematic drawing of the oral cavity showing these parameters with the front of the mouth to the left of the diagram. It accounts for only four basic vocoid positions: high front, low front, high back, and low back. In addition, the front vowels are specified as unrounded and the back vowels as rounded, in accord with what we regard as the normal relationship of roundedness to frontness and backness. If the roundedness distinction is reversed, an additional four vocoids may be accounted for: high front rounded, low front rounded, high back unrounded, and low back unrounded. A high front rounded vocoid occurs in the French word *lune* [y], which may be distinguished from the English words *lean* and

	Front	Back
High	High front unrounded	High back rounded
Low	Low front unrounded	Low back rounded

FIGURE 3-3 Basic vocoid parameters in the oral cavity.

		Front	Central	Back
High	Upper	i (*beat*)	ɨ	u (*boot*)
	Lower	ɪ (*bit*)	ɨ̵	ʊ (*good*)
Mid	Upper	e (*bait*)	ə	o (*boat*)
	Lower	ɛ (*bet*)	ʌ (*but*)	ɔ (*bought*)
Low		æ (*bat*)	a (*pot*)	ɑ
		Unround		Round

FIGURE 3-4 International Phonetic Alphabet symbols for basic vocoid positions, with illustrative occurrences in English.

loon, which respectively have a high front unrounded vocoid [i] and a high back rounded vocoid [u].

International Phonetic Alphabet Symbols

Although Figure 3-3 provides a basic framework for describing vocoids, it badly lacks details. The round-unround distinction is adequate, but the simple high-low and front-back distinctions are too broad. Further distinctions are necessary, for more heights than two are required. Figure 3-4 uses five. Only three positions on the frontness-to-backness parameter are shown in Figure 3-4, a modified version of the International Phonetic Alphabet, since three appear to be sufficient. Figure 3-4 attempts to illustrate these vocoids with English examples. The illustrations are not very exact because many English vocoids tend to change their characteristics somewhat during the course of production. Anyone with a good knowledge of French will know that the vocoids in the French words *île, doux, beau,* and *les* are "stable" in contrast to the vocoids in the English words *eel, do, bow,* and *lay,* during the production of which some tongue and even lip movement occurs.

Cardinal-Vowel System

An alternative approach to the above principle of dividing up the mouth into certain areas and assigning symbols after the divisions are made derives from the British phonetician Daniel Jones. Jones devised the **cardinal-vowel system.** He used the same parameters given above but arbitrarily located specific vocoids as reference points on these parameters. These vocoids were named the cardinal vowels, and all other vocoids were described in relation to these reference points as being either higher or lower, or further forward or further back, and so on. Jones chose the set of basic reference vocoids himself, and these are illustrated in Figure 3-5. Jones then taught this set orally to his students and they in turn taught

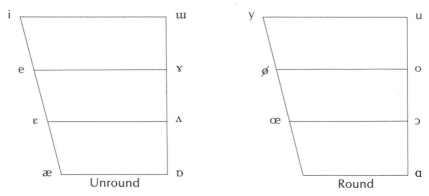

FIGURE 3-5 The cardinal-vowel system of Daniel Jones.

it to their students. The cardinal-vowel system therefore makes use of an arbitrarily chosen set of actual sounds as reference points in phonetic work.'

Voice

Some of the same parameters used for contoids are useful in discussing further modifications of vocoids. Like contoids, vocoids may be either voiced or voiceless; that is, the vocal cords may vibrate or they may be still. Actually, voiced vocoids vastly predominate in languages, but enough of the voiceless kind occur so that a phonetician must be ready to note them. Phonetically, a voiceless vocoid is much like the kind of sound that occurs in English at the beginnings of words such as *hat* and *hot,* except that in English these sounds are accompanied by noticeable glottal friction. If this friction is reduced we can hear pronunciations like[æ̥ æt] and [ɔ̥ ɔt], the [æ̥] and [ɔ̥] representing voiceless vocoids and the [æ] and [ɔ] voiced vocoids. The voiceless quality of the vocoid is shown by the use of the diacritic [̥]. Voiced vocoids are therefore regarded as normal and voiceless varieties as modifications.

Nasality

Vocoids may also be nasal or oral. English vocoids are almost always oral, although in some dialects often a certain amount of nasalization of vocoids occurs, particularly before nasal contoids. An oral vocoid is made with the velic closed. If the velic is open, the result is a nasal vocoid. The French words *bon* and *vin* have nasal vocoids [bɔ̃] and [vɛ̃]; however, *bonne* has an oral vocoid [bɔn]. The use of the diacritic [˜] indicates that the oral vocoid is regarded as the norm in pairs of vocoids which differ only in that one is oral whereas the other is nasal, as with [ɔ] and [ɔ̃] above.

Tenseness

Tenseness was still another parameter we mentioned in the discussion of contoids, when English [p], [f], and [s] were described as tense and [b], [v], and [z] as lax. The same phenomenon of tightness in the tongue and lower jaw may be observed

in the production of certain vocoids. The phenomenon is also of greater importance in describing vocoids than contoids. In the pairs of English words *beat-bit,*
bait-bet, and *food-good,* the first word of each pair contains a tense vocoid and the
second a lax vocoid: [i]-[ɪ], [e]-[ɛ], and [u]-[ʊ].

Further Modifications

Further modification of vocoids may occur if there is any kind of concurrent activity
in the larynx or pharynx which produces special effects such as creaky voice or
unusual openness. More usually, further modification is caused by the tongue
itself, as with *r*-coloring. In most *r*-pronouncing dialects of English the pronunciation of the middle sound in *bird* involves curling back the tongue but no trilling of
the tongue tip or touching it to the palate. The sound is a retroflexed vocoid [ɚ]
with some of the qualities of both vocoids and contoids. This same mixture of
vocoid and contoid quality occurs in the pronunciation of *r* in words such as *red*
and *trench,* and of *l* in words such as *led* and *please.* Consequently, it is not
unusual to see phoneticians use different ways of recording *r* or *l*.

The symbol [ə], **schwa,** which is the basis of the [ɚ] in the preceding paragraph, is usually used to indicate an unstressed central vocoid, as in the first
syllable of *about* or in the second syllable of *comma,* in contrast to the stressed
vocoid [ʌ] in *but.* Unstressed final syllables with central vocoids followed by *r, l,*
or *n* may be transcribed either as schwa plus the contoid ([ər], [əl], or [ən]), as in
weaker [wikər], *riddle* [rɪdəl], and *fasten* [fæsən], or as **syllabic consonants** ([r̩], [l̩],
or [n̩]), resulting in the transcriptions [wikr̩], [rɪdl̩], and [fæsn̩].

Vocoids may vary in length because they are continuous sounds, and during
production, they may also undergo changes in their tensing quality, their degree of
lip rounding, their height, and their frontness-backness. Vocoids which are
noticeably lengthened are generally referred to as long **monophthongs** if there is
no marked change in quality during their production, but as **diphthongs** if there is
a change in quality. English has three obvious diphthongs: the vocoids in *mice*
[aɪ], *house* [aʊ], and boy [bɔɪ]. Lengthening without change in quality is usually
indicated by a macron over the vocoid [ē] or by a colon [e:]. A change in quality is
usually indicated by writing two symbols side by side, the first designating the
starting point of the total vowel movement and the second the end point, as in [ei]
or [au]. **Triphthongs** are also, of course, possible [ieo]. Quite often the two
vocoids in a diphthong are not pronounced with equal intensity or for an equal
duration, and one is perceived to be more important, or central, than the other. If
the second is more important, the diphthong is called a rising diphthong and
written with the first vocoid raised, as in [ⁱɛ]. *Yet* may be said to begin in this way
and may be written [ⁱɛt]. Likewise, *wet* is written [ᵘɛt]. The initial *y* and *w* are
thus described as being basically vocoids in this interpretation. A falling diphthong is apparent in *say* [seⁱ]. In contrast to these rising and falling varieties the
diphthong in *now* [naʊ] is relatively level.

STRESS AND PITCH

Still other phenomena in the sound stream of speech are of interest to us. Certain
vocoids, for example, are uttered with more intensity, or **stress,** than others, as for

example in the different vocoids of *the man* or of *blackboard,* or in the vocoids of a more complicated example *a dusty blackboard.* Stresses must be defined relative to each other, so the distribution of stress is much less easy to describe than the incidences of occurrence of voiceless bilabial stops. The stress on the first vocoid of *the man* can be described as lighter than the stress on the second vocoid, but reference to an absolute scale is impossible, for we can say the total utterance either quietly or loudly. We can try to record what differences in stress we hear by using various accent marks so that *the man* is recorded as [ðə̆ mǽn] and *blackboard* as [blǽkbòrd]. A *dusty blackboard* would be transcribed as [ə̆ dʌ̂stĭ blǽkbòrd]. The heaviest (primary) stress [´] is on *black,* the next heaviest (secondary) stress [^] is on *dust,* the third level (tertiary) stress [`] is on *board,* and *a* and *-y* are unstressed [˘].

Vocoids may also be uttered with different degrees of **pitch.** These differences are also relative differences because the basic pitch of a voice is determined by certain characteristics of the speaker's vocal apparatus such as the length and thickness of the membranes in the larynx. It is often important to note the pitch level of the different vocoids, since in languages like Chinese and Thai pitch differentiates one utterance from another. Thus, an utterance containing a high-pitched vocoid means something quite different from an utterance containing the same vocoid under a mid, low, rising, or falling pitch. Diacritics may also be used to indicate noticeable differences or changes in pitch level. Sometimes pitches work together to produce **intonation contours.** In English, the statement *You're going* and the question *You're going?* have different contours of pitches. These contours differentiate the utterances as statement and question.

PHONETIC NOTATION

Using the approach outlined so far, we can attempt to capture on paper a record of the sounds that speakers make by referring to the articulatory bases of the sounds. Of course, the resulting linear phonetic notation is something of a fiction. The use of discrete symbols is equivalent to a claim that the continuum of sound can indeed be broken up into discrete units and that the right units have been chosen. While we must admit that we have chosen to unite particular combinations of discrete characteristics to form certain units but not to unite others, the claim itself is not without validity, as we shall see in the following chapter.

The linear alphabetic phonetic notation is therefore a partly arbitrary but still convenient fiction. It can be refined and refined, mainly by inventing new symbols for certain complexes of properties which are recurrent or by decorating existing symbols with diacritics. Each individual will also tend to use a slightly different set of symbols and diacritics and even to hear slightly different characteristics depending on his phonetic training and experience. A good observer hears sounds consistently and transcribes them consistently; hence, it is possible to equate the records and impressions of two or more good phoneticians as, for example, in dialect-atlas work, as we shall see in Chapter 12.

FEATURES NOTATION

It is possible to refer to the component properties, or features, of the sounds, if we are willing to sacrifice the convenience of the alphabetic system. Figure 3-6 shows

	bat [b	æ	t]	spin [s	p	ɪ	n]
Contoid	+		+	+	+		+
Vocoid		+				+	
Voice	+	+				+	+
Stop	+		+		+		
Nasal							+
High						+	
Low		+					
Alveolar			+	+			+
Labial	+				+		

FIGURE 3-6 Selected component features of *bat* and *spin*.

one way in which the words *bat* and *spin* can be dealphabetized into selected component features. In Figure 3-6 a plus symbol (+) in the grid denotes the presence of a certain component whereas a blank denotes its absence. Figure 3-6 therefore resolves the two words into component parts which are much smaller than the parts shown in the two notations that use the phonetic alphabet, that is, [bæt] and [spɪn]. Figure 3-6 displays its information more overtly than do the two phonetic transcriptions, which must be interpreted by someone who knows the system, who knows, for example, that [n] denotes a voiced alveolar nasal contoid. This latter information, however, is conveyed quite conspicuously in Figure 3-6 by the pluses opposite the features voice, alveolar, nasal, and contoid. A phonetician must be aware that [ɪ] and [n] share voice as a feature and that [s] and [p] are voiceless, although nothing in an alphabetic transcription indicates such similarities. However, in Figure 3-6 the similarities in voicing are shown by the presence or absence of plus symbols. The representation in Figure 3-6 consequently has certain advantages over an alphabetic system in its overt display of components, particularly in its display of long components, that is, components that appear in two or more successive horizontal segments in the grid. There is an obvious need, however, to look very carefully at the components, listed in the vertical column, and at the use of the plus symbol in order to assess what claims we appear to be making about language. Data may be displayed in all kinds of ways, not all of which have anything of interest to say about language.

In recent years a search has been made for the best set of components to use in the vertical columns of displays such as Figure 3-6. The features are generally known as **distinctive features.** The following set of distinctive features has been found useful for describing the sounds of English. In any particular sound segment the feature is either present [+] or absent [−].

Vocalic sounds are produced by an oral cavity in which the greatest constriction does not exceed that found in the high vowels [i] and [u]. They are also generally voiced.

	p	b	f	v	m	t	d	θ	ð	n	s	z	č	ǰ	š	ž	k	g	ŋ	h	y	w	r	l
Vocalic	−	−	−	−	−	−	−	−	−	−	−	−	−	−	−	−	−	−	−	−	−	−	+	+
Consonantal	+	+	+	+	+	+	+	+	+	+	+	+	+	+	+	+	+	+	+	−	−	−	+	+
High	−	−	−	−	−	−	−	−	−	−	−	−	+	+	+	+	+	+	+	−	−	−	+	+
Back	−	−	−	−	−	−	−	−	−	−	−	−	−	−	−	−	+	+	+	−	−	+	−	−
Low	−	−	−	−	−	−	−	−	−	−	−	−	−	−	−	−	−	−	−	+	−	−	−	−
Anterior	+	+	+	+	+	+	+	+	+	+	+	+	−	−	−	−	−	−	−	−	−	−	−	+
Coronal	−	−	−	−	−	+	+	+	+	+	+	+	+	+	+	+	−	−	−	−	−	−	+	+
Round	−	−	−	−	−	−	−	−	−	−	−	−	−	−	−	−	−	−	−	−	−	+	−	−
Tense	+	−	+	−	−	+	−	+	−	−	+	−	+	−	+	−	+	−	−	+	−	−	−	−
Voiced	−	+	−	+	+	−	+	−	+	+	−	+	−	+	−	+	−	+	+	−	+	+	+	+
Continuent	−	−	+	+	−	−	−	+	+	−	+	+	−	−	+	+	−	−	−	+	+	+	+	+
Nasal	−	−	−	−	+	−	−	−	−	+	−	−	−	−	−	−	−	−	+	−	−	−	−	−
Strident	−	−	+	+	−	−	−	−	−	−	+	+	+	+	+	+	−	−	−	−	−	−	−	−

FIGURE 3-7 Distinctive features of English contoids.

Consonantal sounds are produced by a radical constriction at some point in the vocal tract.

High sounds are produced by raising the body of the tongue above the level that it occupies in neutral position, the position of [ɛ] in *bed*.

Back sounds are produced by retracting the body of the tongue from the neutral position.

Low sounds are produced by lowering the body of the tongue from the neutral position.

Anterior sounds are produced by an obstruction located in front of the alveopalatal region of the mouth.

Coronal sounds are produced by raising the blade of the tongue from the neutral position.

Rounded sounds are produced by rounding the lips.

Tense sounds are produced by increasing the muscular effort in the lower jaw.

Voiced sounds are produced by vibrating the vocal cords.

Continuant sounds are produced by maintaining the airflow in the vocal cavity (but not in the nasal cavity).

	i	ɪ	e	ɛ	æ	ə	a	ɔ	o	ʊ	u
Vocalic	+	+	+	+	+	+	+	+	+	+	+
Consonantal	−	−	−	−	−	−	−	−	−	−	−
High	+	+	−	−	−	−	−	−	−	+	+
Back	−	−	−	−	−	+	+	+	+	+	+
Low	−	−	−	−	+	−	+	+	−	−	−
Round	−	−	−	−	−	−	−	+	+	+	+
Tense	+	−	+	−	−	−	−	+	+	−	+

FIGURE 3-8 Distinctive features of English vocoids.

Classificatory Features	Sounds	Class of Sounds
$\begin{bmatrix} +\text{vocalic} \\ -\text{consonantal} \end{bmatrix}$	i,ɪ,e,ɛ,æ,ə,a,ɔ,o,ʊ,u	vowels
$\begin{bmatrix} -\text{vocalic} \\ +\text{consonantal} \end{bmatrix}$	(p,b,t,d,k,g); (f,v,θ,ð s,z,š,ž); (č,ǰ); (m,n,ŋ)	consonants: (stops); (fricatives), (affricates); (nasals)
$\begin{bmatrix} +\text{vocalic} \\ +\text{consonantal} \end{bmatrix}$	r,l	liquids
$\begin{bmatrix} -\text{vocalic} \\ -\text{consonantal} \end{bmatrix}$	h,y,w	glides (or semivowels)

FIGURE 3-9 Subgroups of English sounds.

Nasal sounds are produced by lowering the velum.

Strident sounds are produced by increasing the turbulence of the airflow.

Figure 3-7 shows the distinctive features of English contoids, and Figure 3-8 shows the distinctive features of English vocoids. We should note that all the vocoids are voiced, continuants, nonnasal (that is, oral), and nonstrident.

An examination of Figures 3-7 and 3-8 shows that the vocalic and consonantal pluses and minuses actually delimit four classes of sounds, for all combinations of vocalic and consonantal features are possible, as indicated in Figure 3-9.

The subgroupings that are indicated in Figure 3-9 are classes of sounds which share a "natural" characteristic. They are, therefore, **natural classes** of sounds. Still other natural classes appear from an inspection of Figures 3-7 and 3-8: for example, a class of back round vowels [+vocalic, −consonantal, +back, +round] comprising [ɔ, o, ʊ, u]; a class of coronal stridents [+coronal, +strident] comprising [s, z, č, ǰ, š, ž]; and a class of labial consonants [+anterior, −coronal] comprising [p, b, f, v, m]. Such natural classes are extremely important in describing the **phonological processes** which operate in languages and in accounting for the changes which occur over time. The distinctive-features approach to phonology more than compensates in this way for its unwieldy nonalphabetic character so far as actual phonetic notation is concerned.

BIBLIOGRAPHIC NOTES

A basic focus of this chapter is on certain practical skills a linguist must have in order to work successfully with informants in linguistic fieldwork. Two books, Samarin's *Field Linguistics* and Gudschinsky's *How to Learn an Unwritten Language,* provide useful introductions to fieldwork.

A variety of introductions to phonetics are available. Acoustic phonetics is best covered in Ladefoged's *Elements of Acoustic Phonetics,* but Chapter 22 of Gleason's *Introduction to Descriptive Linguistics* also contains useful basic information on this topic. Articulatory phonetics is the concern of Abercrombie's *Elements of General Phonetics,* Gimson's *Introduction to the Pronunciation of English,* Heffner's *General Phonetics,* Jones' *Outline of English Phonetics,* Kenyon's *American Pronunciation,* Malmberg's *Phonetics,* and Thomas' *Introduction to the Phonetics of American English.* Pike's *Phonetics,* Denes and Pinson's *Speech Chain: The Physics and Biology of Spoken Language,* and Hockett's *Manual of Phonology* are more technical treatments. The last two cover a particularly wide range of topics. Ladefoged's *Course in Phonetics* is the best available general treatment. The International Phonetic Association's *Principles* pamphlet is, of course, the most authoritative introduction to the International Phonetic Alphabet.

Distinctive features are covered in Halle's "On the Bases of Phonology," Jakobson and Halle's *Fundamentals of Language,* Jakobson, Fant, and Halle's *Preliminaries to Speech Analysis,* and Schane's *Generative Phonology.*

EXERCISES

3-1 Check to make sure that you understand each of the terms printed in **boldface** in Chapter 3.

3-2 Chapter 3 makes distinctions between certain terms. Express the distinction between the following terms as clearly as you can: *acoustic phonetics* and *articulatory phonetics; oral* and *nasal; voiced* and *voiceless; contoid* and *vocoid; stop* and *fricative; articulator* and *point of articulation; tense* and *lax; round* and *unround; front* and *back; high* and *low; stress* and *pitch; phonetic feature* and *distinctive feature.*

3-3 Try to reproduce from memory the diagram of the articulatory apparatus that is given on page 33. Label the various parts.

3-4 Give the correct technical term for each of the following locations or activities:

1 both lips
2 appendage above back of tongue
3 opening between vocal cords
4 teeth
5 hard roof of mouth
6 ridge behind upper teeth
7 tip of tongue to upper teeth
8 articulated in opening between vocal cords
9 lower lip to upper teeth
10 back of tongue to soft rear roof of mouth
11 tip of tongue to ridge behind upper teeth
12 velic opening maintained

3-5 Each of the following sets contains an inappropriate member. Choose the inappropriate symbol and explain why you have chosen it.

1 [m n r ŋ]
2 [p b d g]
3 [d t n g]
4 [ɪ ʊ s o]
5 [b z d g]
6 [g ŋ k t]
7 [ɪ æ ʊ ɛ]
8 [o r l w]
9 [f v d m]
10 [e o ɪ u]
11 [ʒ m n b]
12 [f v p x]

3-6 Give the phonetic symbol for each of the following sounds together with an illustration of the use of the sound in an English word wherever possible:

1 voiceless bilabial stop
2 voiced apicoalveolar nasal
3 voiced apicoalveolar affricate
4 voiced retroflex
5 voiced bilabial nasal
6 voiceless labiodental fricative
7 voiceless dorsovelar stop
8 high front tense unrounded vowel
9 mid front lax unrounded vowel
10 voiced apicoalveolar stop

11 voiceless interdental fricative
12 voiced dorsovelar nasal
13 voiceless frontopalatal sibilant
14 voiced lateral
15 high back tense rounded vowel
16 glottal stop
17 voiced apicoalveolar flap
18 voiced interdental fricative
19 mid central lax vowel
20 low back rounded vowel

3-7 The following is a list of English words recorded in one system of phonetic transcription. Write out the words in their normal English spellings. If more than one spelling exists, write out all the possibilities.

1 [tʰek]	7 [kʰæst]	13 [résəz]	19 [rʌsl̩]
2 [wɪl]	8 [tʰʌŋ]	14 [ɛθl̩]	20 [skul]
3 [fit]	9 [fɪŋgr̩]	15 [si]	21 [fɪkst]
4 [wɚld]	10 [plaʊz]	16 [bekr̩]	22 [kʰɔɪn]
5 [tˢip]	11 [bətwín]	17 [raɪts]	23 [éprən]
6 [šɪp]	12 [ɪ̣ɛt]	18 [rɛsl̩]	24 [tʰɔt]

3-8 Provide an articulatory description of each of the sounds symbolized below together with a word in which the sound occurs in English, if that is possible.

1 [tʰ]	7 [s]	13 [n]	19 [ɔ̃]
2 [g]	8 [æ]	14 [ʔ]	20 [b]
3 [o]	9 [u]	15 [ʊ]	21 [f]
4 [ɪ]	10 [ə]	16 [x]	22 [ñ]
5 [m]	11 [ɛ]	17 [ŋ]	23 [w]
6 [ð]	12 [ž]	18 [p]	24 [ɔ]

3-9 Transcribe each of the following words as completely as you can in phonetic notation in the way that you say each:

1 aloud	10 cup	19 loud	28 thank
2 and	11 ether	20 link	29 then
3 bottle	12 example	21 measure	30 under
4 boot	13 fasten	22 mule	31 while
5 boy	14 goal	23 neither	32 would
6 cape	15 Harry	24 peace	33 wise
7 chief	16 him	25 prince	34 which
8 choose	17 island	26 shed	35 yes
9 Cuba	18 Jack	27 take	36 Z

3-10 Describe the similarities and differences between the sounds represented by the underlined letters:

1 house, houses	5 goose, gosling	9 phone, phonic
2 prescribe, prescription	6 divide, division	10 meter, metric
3 medical, medicine	7 face, facial	11 deduce, deduction
4 life, lives	8 choice, choose	12 provide, provision

4

PHONOLOGY

In Chapter 3 we saw how articulatory information can be used to describe the stream of sound produced by human beings in communication with each other. We also saw what possibilities exist for segmenting the sound stream in various ways and recording the resulting segments. It is still another task to understand how these segments, or individual sounds, function to make communication meaningful. As was indicated in Chapter 1, communication is possible only if the parties involved share a system. Two human beings can make sounds at each other, and sometimes do when they do not know each other's language, but unless some agreement exists between them as to the particular sounds to be used and how these sounds are to function, no communication can take place. There will only be *noise,* in both the everyday and technical meanings of that term. A crucial problem, then, for us, is to determine how sounds, which can be described as in Chapter 3, are organized into systems that allow meaningful communication to occur.

The basic function of a system of communication is to allow different messages to be sent and received. Messages may, of course, be repeated, but repetitions offer little or no help in understanding how individual parts of the sound stream function. However, messages which are different in meaning but have only very small differences in sound are useful to anyone who wishes to understand how sounds function to convey meaning. The small differences that exist are obviously significant in that the consequences of the differences are different messages. What seems to be required is some kind of procedure for isolating these significantly different sounds.

CONTRASTIVE UNITS

One approach that we might adopt involves a search for a set of utterances which are different in meaning and minimally different from each other phonetically. Brief utterances appear to be the best kind, because the brevity puts a limit on the possible variations we must consider in the individual utterances and in the comparisons. We may also hypothesize that long utterances make use of the same basic set of significantly different sounds as the short utterances used to establish the set. There is no reason to assume otherwise: the length of an utterance should not affect the system out of which it is constructed.

Initial Consonant Contrasts

We can use the following set of English words in order to formulate a procedure for discovering, or postulating, a set of differences in sound that might prove to be of interest: *big, pig, rig, brig,* and *prig.* A basic observation is that these words have different meanings. There is no repetition of meaning within the set, nor is there any instance of the repetition of a word. This last point could be important if any such set of words were recorded in a phonetic notation because two slightly different phonetic notations of the same word could conceivably be recorded. In fact, no two pronunciations of the same word are ever exactly alike and sometimes the tolerable phonetic differences may be quite considerable, but such free variation may be ignored.

The words in the list above are all different. The crucial issue concerns the ways in which the words differ in sound. *Big, pig,* and *rig* are minimally different from each other. We can also argue that the difference between the first two, *big* and *pig,* is more minimal phonetically than the difference between *big* and *rig,* being a difference of voicing only, whereas there are differences in both manner and position of articulation in the second pair. The differences of interest at this time are those that result in meaning differences, not detailed phonetic differences. The words *brig* and *prig* also appear to be minimally different in exactly the same way that *big* and *pig* are minimally different, because the same kind of contrast exists at the beginnings of words. The pairs are called **minimal pairs.** However, neither of the pairs *big* and *brig* nor *pig* and *prig* is a minimal pair, because the second word in each pair contains an extra possible contrastive unit that native speakers of English identify with the initial contrastive unit in *rig.*

This procedure of finding minimal pairs can be continued using other words. To *big, pig,* and *rig* we can add *fig, mig, dig, gig, jig, wig,* and *zig.* All these words appear to be minimally different from each other, and no extra contrastive unit is present, as there was in *brig* and *prig.* On the basis of such a list, we may hypothesize the existence of a set of contrastively different beginnings for English words. The next problem that arises is that of determining the exact composition of the set. A solution of this problem requires the use of further sets of similarly brief utterances: for example, utterances ending in —at and having a single initial consonant. Words like *bat, pat, rat, fat, cat,* and so on are required. We can also align some of these beginning consonants with the beginning consonants of the previous list on the grounds that they are the "same," as in the following list:

big	bat
pig	pat
rig	rat
fig	fat
mig	mat
dig	—
gig	—
jig	—
wig	—
zig	—
—	tat
—	sat
—	cat
—	vat
—	Nat
—	hat
—	chat
—	that

The gaps in the two columns of the above list appear to be accidental in that most native speakers of English would accept as an accident of history that words like *jig* and *chat* exist but words like **jat* and **chig* do not. The last two examples would make good English "nonsense" words.

This same procedure can be continued using further lists of contrasts in initial utterance position. We can also assign a set of symbols to the contrasts that occur, so that the initial of *pat* can be designated as /p/, the initial of *chat* as /č/, and so on. These symbols, called phonemic symbols, are enclosed in diagonal bars to distinguish them from phonetic symbols in square brackets. The symbols designate contrastive units called **phonemes,** and the full set of contrasts we require for a language is called the phonemic system of that language. Figure 4-1 presents the list of phonemic symbols generally used to show the possible initial consonant contrasts in English utterances, along with examples of words that can be used to establish or, in this case, verify the list. The lists in Figure 4-1 establish certain contrasts better than others: for example, the contrast between /p/ and /t/ is well established in *pin-tin, pat-tat, pip-tip, and pack-tack,* whereas the contrast between /θ/ and /ð/ is not really established at all in the lists since only *thin* and

Phonemes	Contrastive sets					
/p/	pin	pat		pip	pet	pack
/t/	tin	tat	Ted	tip		tack
/č/	chin	chat		chip	Chet	
/k/	kin	cat				
/b/	bin	bat	bed		bet	back
/d/	din		dead	dip	debt	
/ǰ/	gin		Jed		jet	Jack
/g/	Ginn				get	
/f/	fin	fat	fed			
/θ/	thin					
/s/	sin	sat	said	sip	set	sack
/š/	shin		shed	ship		shack
/v/		vat			vet	
/ð/		that				
/z/			Zed	zip		Zach
/m/		mat	Med.		met	Mac
/n/		gnat	Ned	nip	net	knack
/r/		rat	red	rip		rack
/l/	Lynne		led	lip	let	lack
/y/					yet	yak
/h/		hat	head	hip		hack
/w/	win		wed	whip*	wet	whack*

* In those dialects in which the h is not pronounced so that *wear* and *where* sound alike.

FIGURE 4-1 Initial consonant phonemes in English.

that are cited and these words are not a minimal pair. However, /θ/ and /ð/ can be shown to contrast by using minimal pairs like *thigh-thy* and *ether-either*.

In this chapter, the term *consonant* is used instead of the term *contoid* because we are now concerned with the systematic units that allow for communication in one language. We have reserved the terms *consonant* and *vowel* for use in discussing the phonological system that underlies the phonetic substance we observe. Chapter 3 employed the terms *contoid* and *vocoid* for making observations about the substance. When we talk about the system, we talk about **emic** differences; when we talk about the actual substance, we talk about **etic** differences.

Medial and Final Consonant Contrasts

We cannot content ourselves with finding only the initial consonants in utterances because utterances end as well as begin with consonants, and there are also consonants interspersed among the vowels. Native speakers of English will maintain that the final sound in *pat* is the same as the initial sound in *tap* even though a phonetician notes that the two sounds are phonetically different, the final

Phonemes	Contrastive sets				
/p/	rap	pap	seep		reap
/t/	rat	pat	seat	light	
/č/	ratch	patch			reach
/k/	rack	pack	seek	like	reek
/b/	Rab				
/d/		pad	seed	lied	reed
/ǰ/			seige		
/g/	rag				
/f/				life	reef
/θ/	wrath	path			wreathe (n.)
/s/		pass	cease	lice	Reese
/š/	rash				
/v/				live	reive
/ð/			seethe	lithe	wreathe (v.)
/z/	razz		seize	lies	
/m/	ram	Pam	seam	lime	ream
/n/	ran	pan	scene	line	
/ŋ/	rang	pang			
/r/			seer	lyre	rear
/l/		pal	seal	Lyle	reel

FIGURE 4-2 Final consonant phonemes in English.

sound in *pat* being unaspirated [t] whereas the initial sound in *tap* is aspirated [tʰ]. Native speakers are able to equate nearly all the contrastive units, or phonemes, listed as occurring initially in Figure 4-1 with similar contrastive units occurring finally in English utterances such as *ship, rat, patch, back,* and so on. These final units are contrastive units because the contrasts in final position result in meaning differences, in that *map, mat, match, Mac,* and so on, mean different things. Figure 4-2 lists possible final consonant phonemes in English.

From Figure 4-2 we may note that not all the contrasts which occur initially also occur finally. There are special problems in finding /y/, /h/, and /w/ in final position; consequently, these contrasts are not shown in Figure 4-2. Discussion of final /y/, /h/, and /w/ is reserved till later. The contrastive use of /r/ in final position will also occasion some later comments in the remarks on neutralization. One phoneme appears in the list in Figure 4-2 that does not appear in the list in Figure 4-1: the /ŋ/ phoneme. This phoneme is necessary to distinguish *sing* from *sin;* however, /ŋ/ does not occur initially in English.

ENGLISH CONSONANTS

If we were to list all the possible consonant contrasts for English, we would need only one more in addition to those already given in Figures 4-1 and 4-2: /ž/ to distinguish *measure* (with /ž/) from *mesher* (with /š/). Figure 4-3 provides the full list of contrasting English consonants along with the phonetic features used to

Phoneme	Distinguishing phonetic features
/p/	voiceless bilabial stop
/t/	voiceless alveolar stop
/č/	voiceless (palatal) affricate
/k/	voiceless velar stop
/b/	voiced bilabial stop
/d/	voiced alveolar stop
/ǰ/	voiced (palatal) affricate
/g/	voiced velar stop
/f/	voiceless labiodental fricative
/θ/	voiceless dental fricative
/s/	voiceless alveolar sibilant
/š/	voiceless palatal sibilant
/v/	voiced labiodental fricative
/ð/	voiced dental fricative
/z/	voiced alveolar sibilant
/ž/	voiced palatal sibilant
/m/	bilabial nasal
/n/	alveolar nasal
/ŋ/	velar nasal
/r/	retroflex
/l/	lateral
/y/	front glide or semivowel
/h/	glottal
/w/	back glide or semivowel

FIGURE 4-3 The distinguishing phonetic features
of English consonant phonemes.

distinguish them from each other. We should note that phonetic features which
do not distinguish the consonants from each other, as for example the voicing
feature of nasals, are excluded from Figure 4-3. The nasal feature of /m/, /n/, and
/ŋ/ distinguishes these contrasts from all others so that the concurrent voicing is
redundant in making distinctions. English nasals are always voiced so the phonetic
feature of voicing is predictable from the feature of nasal itself. The nasals are
distinguished from each other by differences in place of articulation. On the other
hand, stops and fricatives must be specified as either voiceless or voiced, because
/f/ contrasts with /v/, /θ/ with /ð/, and so on.

Figure 4-4 contains much the same information as Figure 4-3; however, in
Figure 4-4 this information is displayed in a manner reminiscent of the previous
chapter on phonetics, for example Figure 3-2. Figure 4-4 shows an interesting
symmetry in its patterning: four voiced stops and four voiceless ones, four voiced
fricatives and four voiceless ones, and so on. This patterning is maintained only if
/č/ and /ǰ/ are treated as members of the stop series. Phonetically, /č/ and /ǰ/ are
affricates, that is, sequences of stop plus fricative, so that /č/ is [tš] and /ǰ/ is [dž].
However, since /č/ and /ǰ/ function as single units in English, we include them in
the chart among the stops.

		labial	dental, alveolar, palatal			velar	
Position							
Stop	vl.	p	t	č		k	
	vd.	b	d	ǰ		g	
Fricative	vl.	f	θ	s	š		
	vd.	v	ð	z	ž		
Nasal		m		n		ŋ	
Retroflex				r			
Lateral				l			
Semivowel				y		w	
Glottal							h

FIGURE 4-4 The phonetic distribution of English consonant phonemes.

Allophones

As we have already indicated, a good phonetician will observe that an initial /t/ and a final /t/ sound rather different from each other, and both are different again from the /t/ in the middle of the usual North American pronunciations of *butter* and *later*. The differences, though, are predictable and do not affect meaning: the initial /t/ is always aspirated [tʰ], the final one is quite often unreleased [t̚], that is, the tongue tip is left on the gum ridge after the utterance is completed, and the medial one is always flapped [ř]. Roughly similar distributions of aspiration and release occur for the initial and final variants of /p/ and /k/. Patterning is apparent not only in the phonemic system as a whole but also in the distributions of the variants of the individual phonemes in that /p/, /t/, and /k/ all have aspirated variants initially and unaspirated variants in other positions. Similar variations can be found in the phonetic realizations of other phonemes. For example, /l/ has two variants: a "dark," or velarized, variant [ɫ] which occurs after vowels, as in *full* [fʊɫ], or before back vowels, as in *look* [ɫʊk], and a "light" variant [l] elsewhere, as in *lip* [lɪp]. The phonemes /k/ and /g/ have front variants, [k̟] and [g̟], before front vowels (*keep* [k̟ʰip] and *geese* [g̟is]) and back variants, [k̠] and [g̠], before back vowels (*cool* [k̠ʰul] and *goose* [g̠us]). We can also write the above variations as follows:

/t/ [ř] between a stressed and an unstressed vowel
  [tʰ] initially
  [t̚] free variant in final position
  [t] elsewhere

/l/ [ɫ] after vowels and before back vowels
  [l] elsewhere

/g/ [g̟] before front vowels
     [g̱] before back vowels
     [g] elsewhere

The previous paragraph used the term *phoneme* to refer to one of the reference points in the phonological system, that is, to a formal unit. Each formal unit must be realized in phonetic substance, though it may be realized differently in different environments. The different variants of a phoneme brought about by the environment in which it appears are called the **allophones** of the phoneme. Allophones are described in phonetic terms, but phonemes are defined through the principle of contrast. When, as in Figure 4-3, we associate certain phonetic features with phonemes, we must remember that these features are those of the allophones of the phonemes rather than of the phonemes themselves.

Consonant Clusters

Returning once more to a consideration of *prig* and *brig,* we can observe that the set of phonemes given in Figure 4-3 can be used to show how such words begin: *prig* begins with a /p/ followed by an /r/, or /pr/, and *brig* with a sequence of /br/. *Tricks* begins with /tr/ and ends with /ks/, and *glimpsed* begins with /gl/ and ends with /mpst/. Not all possible combinations of phonemes occur, for there are restrictions in the combinatorial possibilities of the consonants and in the maximal lengths of possible consonant sequences. These restrictions differ between initial and final positions: the combinations that can occur in each position are called the permissible **consonant clusters** in each position, or the **phonotactic** possibilities. An examination of sets of English words shows that the maximum initial consonant cluster in English is three consonants, the first of which must be an /s/. *Scream* /skr-/, *sclerosis* /skl-/, *skewer* /sky-/, and *squelch* /skw-/ illustrate these possibilities. If an /n/, or a /z/, or an /r/, or an /l/ occurs initially in a word, no other consonant can occur after that consonant, except in those dialects which have /ny-/ at the beginning of *new* or /ly-/ at the beginning of *lute*. If the initial consonant is one like /f/, /p/, or /k/, only one of /r/, /l/, /y/, or /w/ may follow, although not all the possibilities actually occur. In final position the possibilities are different, but the same principles operate: only certain sequences, or clusters, are possible, so that an initial /skr-/ and a final /-mpst/ are phonotactic possibilities in English, whereas an initial */slm-/ and a final */-gs/ are not.

ENGLISH VOWELS

An analysis of the vowel system of English through the use of minimal pairs is considerably more complicated than an analysis of the consonantal system. We can find sets of English utterances containing only a single vowel which contrast only in the vowels: *beat, bit, bait, bet,* and so on. A set of symbols could be devised to represent the members of the total set of contrasts, but representing each such contrast with a different symbol might result in an underanalysis of the data. For example, the "short" vowels in *bit* and *bet* seem to many speakers of English to belong to a different set of vowels from the set of "long" vowels, as in *bite* and *bout* in the amount of tongue movement that is noticeable in the production of the vowel. If some other English vowel contrasts are added to the list, for example the contrasts in *Boyd* and *flood,* we can observe that the vowel in *Boyd* seems to pattern with those of *bite* and *bout,* whereas the vowel in *flood* seems to pattern with those in *bit* and *bet.* Then again the type of the "long" vowel in *beat* is different not only from the "short" vowel in *bit* but also from the type of "long" vowel in *bite, bout,* and *Boyd:* there is much more tongue movement in the vowels of the last three than in the vowel of *beat.*

An inspection of the phonetic substance which realizes each of the above-mentioned contrasts throws some light on the problem of analysis. The vowels in *beat* and *bit* have some subtle phonetic differences: both vowels are high front vowels, but the vowel in *beat* is a little higher than the one in *bit;* the vowel in *beat* is also tense, whereas the vowel in *bit* is lax; and the vowel in *beat* is slightly longer and accompanied by forward and upward tongue movement, particularly noticeable when it occurs before silence, as in *bee.* Similar differences can be observed between the vowels of *bait* and *bet* and between the vowels of *boot* and *good* except that the vowel movement in *boot* is toward a more back position with consequent lip rounding rather than toward a more front position. The vowel of *boat* has characteristics similar to those of the vowel of *boot.* One possible conclusion is that these subtle differences between neighboring pairs of vowels are the very differences which establish the contrasts so that the vowels in the above words, and certain others falling in the same category, should be represented as follows:

/i/ beat   /u/ boot
/ɪ/ bit   /ʊ/ good
/e/ bait   /ə/ but   /o/ boat
/ɛ/ bet
/æ/ bat   /a/ god   /ɔ/ bought

Fries-Pike System

The linguists Charles C. Fries and Kenneth L. Pike followed the reasoning given in the last paragraph to arrive at unit phonemic representations for the vowels of English illustrated above. They were still faced with providing an analysis for the vowels of *Boyd, bout,* and *bite.* The vowels in these words are "long" but the various features are different from those of the vowels of *beat* and *bait.* There is much more movement of the tongue in all three cases and definite lip rounding in *bout.* The solution to the problem seemed to reside in treating the vowels as diphthongs, that is, two-vowel sequences so that *Boyd* contains /ɔɪ/, *bout* contains /aʊ/, and *bite* contains /aɪ/. Fries and Pike, therefore, proposed the phonemic system for English vowels which is shown in Figure 4-5.

Trager-Smith System

Of course, alternative interpretations of the same data are possible, and two other linguists, George L. Trager and Henry Lee Smith, proposed one such alternative. They proposed that the phonetic features which distinguish *beat* from *bit* and *fool*

		Front	Center	Back
Monophthongs				
	High	i (*beat*) ɪ (*bit*)		u (*boot*) ʊ (*good*)
	Mid	e (*bait*) ɛ (*bet*)	ə (*but*)	o (*boat*)
	Low	æ (*bat*)	a (*god*)	ɔ (*bought*)
Diphthongs			aɪ aʊ (*bite*) (*bout*)	ɔɪ (*Boyd*)

FIGURE 4-5 English vowel phonemes for one dialect, according to Fries and Pike.

from *full*—that is, the features of tenseness and tongue movement—are the same features that characterize the consonants /y/ and /w/ when these occur initially in words. In this explanation /y/ is essentially represented by a movement of the tongue either toward or away from a high front position, whereas /w/ is essentially represented by a movement of the tongue either toward or away from a high back position. We may even argue that the word *yes* begins in very much the same way as the word *say* ends, and that the beginning and end of *woe* are almost identical. According to the interpretation offered by Trager and Smith, the distinction between *beat* and *bit* results from the presence of the glide /y/ in *beat* as against its absence in *bit,* the basic vowels being identical phonemically. *Beat* is phonemically /biyt/ and *bit* is /bit/, while *fool* is /fuwl/ and *full* is /ful/. The same symbols /y/ and /w/ can also be used for the second elements in the vowels in *Boyd, bout,* and *bite:* /boyd/, /bawt/, and /bayt/. Figure 4-6 sets out the Trager-Smith system for English vowels.

Figure 4-7 sets out the Fries-Pike and Trager-Smith systems side by side so that we can compare them for their phonemicization of English words.

Returning to Figure 4-6, we can observe the same kind of symmetry that appeared in a display of the consonantal system of English. However, two noticeable "holes" are apparent in the otherwise symmetrical pattern, in the high central and mid back positions. Trager and Smith decided to see whether they could fill these holes by making a thorough examination of all dialects of English. They observed that some speakers differentiate between the second vowels in

	y-glide	Front	Center	Back	w-glide
High	iy (*beat*)	i (*bit*)		u (*good*)	uw (*boot*)
Mid	ey (*bait*)	e (*bet*)	ə (*but*)		ow (*boat*)
Low		æ (*bat*)	a (*god*)	ɔ (*bought*)	oy (*Boyd*)
		ay (*bite*)	aw (*bout*)		

FIGURE 4-6 English vowel phonemes for one dialect, according to Trager and Smith.

	Fries-Pike	Trager-Smith
beat	/bit/	/biyt/
bit	/bɪt/	/bit/
bait	/bet/	/beyt/
bet	/bɛt/	/bet/
bat	/bæt/	/bæt/
but	/bət/	/bət/
god	/gad/	/gad/
boot	/but/	/buwt/
good	/gʊd/	/gud/
boat	/bot/	/bowt/
bought	/bɔt/	/bɔt/
bite	/baɪt/	/bayt/
bout	/baʊt/	/bawt/
Boyd	/bɔɪd/	/boyd/

FIGURE 4-7   English vowel phonemes: Fries-Pike and Trager-Smith systems.

words such as *Rose's* and *Rosa's* in pairs of sentences like *They're Rose's* and *They're Rosa's.* They concluded that such speakers must have /ɨ/, the high central vowel, in *Rose's* and /ə/, the mid central vowel, in *Rosa's.* They found too that a simple /o/, an unglided mid back vowel, exists in some dialects, for example in certain pronunciations of *gonna* in *I'm gonna do it,* and in others in *road* /rod/ as opposed to *rowed* /rowd/. It was this evidence that led them to claim the existence of /o/.

This last discovery of the existence of certain vowels in certain dialects tempted Trager and Smith to extend the system given in Figure 4-6 to cover *all the dialects of English.* At the same time, they thought they could remedy another apparent gap in the distribution of consonants, the nonoccurrence of /h/ finally. They claimed that the vowels of any English dialect can be described by the use of nine simple vowels, either singly or in combination with one of the three glides /w/, /y/, or /h/, the /h/ in this case being a glide toward or away from a mid central position. A dialect with a short *o* in *gonna* would have a phonemic /o/ and *gonna* would be represented as /gonə/; however, a dialect with a glide would have /ow/ and *gonna* would be represented as /gownə/. A dialect in which *marry, merry,* and *Mary* were distinguished would have /mæriy/, /meriy/, and /meyriy/ or (/mehriy/) as the phonemicizations of these words. Each dialect of English would be described in terms of a selection made from the overall inventory of the thirty-six possibilities given in Figure 4-8.

The postulation of an overall inventory of phonemes for a language is, of course, extremely controversial. The phonemic inventory of a language is usually established from data obtained from speakers of a single dialect of the language, the phonemes being contrasts within that dialect. The overall inventory of phonemes employs contrast within a wide variety of dialects in order to establish the phonemes. Consequently, the term *phoneme* is used very differently in the two approaches, and in the view of many linguists improperly so within the

	Simple vowel	Vowel with /y/-glide	Vowel with /w/-glide	Vowel with /h/-glide
Front	i	iy	iw	ih
	e	ey	ew	eh
	æ	æy	æw	æh
Center	ɨ	ɨy	ɨw	ɨh
	ə	əy	əw	əh
	a	ay	aw	ah
Back	u	uy	uw	uh
	o	oy	ow	oh
	ɔ	ɔy	ɔw	ɔh

FIGURE 4-8 Trager-Smith overall vowel inventory for English: all English dialects.

overall-inventory approach. Of course, the particular system for English proposed by Trager and Smith could be shown to be inadequate by the discovery of facts that cannot be handled within it, as for example, the discovery of a tenth simple vowel. Such an inadequacy has been pointed out.

AN ALTERNATIVE PROCEDURE

The procedure for establishing phonemic contrasts which has just been described requires that we have available a very large inventory of utterances in the language, because it requires the use of minimal pairs to establish the phonemic contrasts. The procedure almost demands that the analyst be a native speaker of the language so that even rather obscure contrasts can be searched out, such as those in English between *measure* and *mesher* and *either* and *ether*. A thorough knowledge of the language is necessary because, theoretically, every phoneme must be shown to contrast with every other phoneme in at least one environment, or if a certain contrast does not exist, as for example, between certain pairs of vowels in front of /r/ in English, an explanation must be offered. This procedure requires control of a large amount of data; however, linguists attempting to work out the phonemic system of a strange language do not always have such control. Often the data are extremely limited, little opportunity exists to collect more, and other tasks demand attention, such as making a grammatical analysis. Some other procedure for establishing the phonemic inventory of a language must, therefore, be available to the linguist in the field.

Phonetic Similarity

Another so-called **discovery procedure** does exist. This procedure requires the availability of a good phonetic transcription of a corpus of utterances in the language to be analyzed. We then inspect the transcription for sounds which are phonetically similar to each other in order to see how these phonetically similar sounds distribute in relation to other sounds. Phonetically similar sounds are sounds that share a phonetic feature, such as nasality ([n] and [ŋ]), or labial quality ([p] and [b]), or front vowel quality ([i] and [e]), or stop quality ([t] and [ʔ]). In practice, linguists sometimes experience difficulty in defining the concepts of "phonetic similarity" and "sharing a feature" to cover all known cases, so proceed on intuition in such work. However, we should note that the best intuitions in such matters are usually possessed by those who have acquired considerable experience through working with a variety of unrelated languages.

Complementary Distribution

Having discovered sets of phonetically similar sounds, for example [p] and [f], or [k], [x], and [g], or [e] and [ɛ], we must then ask whether the variations in each set can be accounted for in terms of the phonetic environments of the members of the set. If utterances can begin with either [p] or [f] and the same vowels can occur following both [p] and [f], then nothing in the environments would seem to produce the variation between [p] and [f]. The variation is apparently important, reflects a significant difference to the speaker, and establishes /p/ and /f/ as contrasting phonemes. Such is the case in English, in which *pin* contrasts with *fin*. If, in examining the distribution of [k], [x], and [g] in a language other than English, we find that [k] always occurs initially and finally in utterances, [x] always occurs before consonants, and [g] always occurs between vowels, we might well hypothesize that in this language really only one functional unit, or phoneme, exists. We could write this phoneme as /k/ and say that it has three variants, or allophones, [k], [x], and [g], the first initially and finally, the second before consonants, and the third intervocalically. Alternatively, we can state the distribution as follows:

/k/

    [x] before consonants

    [g] intervocalically (that is, between vowels)

    [k] elsewhere

In this statement *elsewhere* is used instead of *initially and finally* because the latter seem to be the least restricted environments and the [k] allophone appears to be somehow the "basic" allophone of the phoneme: hence the use of *k* in the **phonemic notation** /k/. A still more concise statement would read as follows:

/k/

    [x] /-C

    [g] /V-V

    [k]

In this statement / refers to the environment specified by the dash, and C and V to consonant and vowel respectively. The final [k], the "elsewhere" statement, automatically covers all other cases not specified in the first two ordered statements.

If, again in a language other than English, [ɛ] occurs always before consonants and [e] occurs always before vowels or a pause, only one contrastive unit is established, and this phoneme might be written as /e/. The distribution of the variants of /e/, that is, of its allophones, can be stated as follows:

/e/	or	/e/
[ɛ] before consonants		[ɛ] /-C
[e] elsewhere		[e]

The choice of the symbol between the diagonal bars could be quite arbitrary because it represents a contrastive unit, not a sound. Nevertheless, the symbol has a mnemonic value which should not be ignored if it is chosen to suggest the most characteristic allophone associated with the phoneme. It is also important to order the allophones in the statement so as to achieve the greatest economy by avoiding redundancy and by using a simple "elsewhere" statement for the distribution of the final allophone in any list or an alternative convention.

The important principle just illustrated is the principle of **complementary distribution.** Phonetically similar sounds in complementary distribution are allophones of a single phoneme. An alternative way of stating the principle is to say that a phoneme may be realized by slightly different sounds in different environments. This fact should not surprise us: we would expect the environment in which something appears to have an effect because environment affects most things. We should regard a phoneme as a kind of ideal reference point in an ideal contrastive system of phonemes which speakers of a language share. When speakers say something, they realize a selection of these phonemes in phonetic substance. The phonetic substance for any particular phoneme is not a constant but varies within certain limits according to the environment in which it occurs.

It is interesting to observe how the principle of complementary distribution works with certain English phonemes. We find an aspirated voiceless bilabial stop [pʰ] initially in *pot,* a voiced bilabial stop [b] initially in *big,* finally in *rob,* and medially in *robber,* an unreleased voiceless bilabial stop [p˹] in *mop,* and a voiceless bilabial stop [p] in *spin.* All these sounds—[pʰ], [b], [p˹], and [p]—are phonetically similar, for they all possess the features of bilabial and stop quality. The basic linguistic problem is to see how they distribute in relation to each other. First of all, [b] and [pʰ] contrast in initial position, for both can appear in the same environments, as in *bin* [bɪn] and *pin* [pʰɪn]. In final position both [b] and [p˹] can be found to contrast, as in *robe* [rob] and *rope* [rop˹]. But [pʰ], [p˹], and [p] never contrast with each other. We can therefore say that in English there is a phonemic contrast between /b/ and /p/. The first of these phonemes seems to have only one allophone [b]; however, the second has three allophones [pʰ], [p˹], and [p] in complementary distribution. When speakers of English pronounce a word which begins with /p/, they must choose an aspirated allophone [pʰ]. If the word has a /p/ in the middle, they must choose an unaspirated allophone [p] for that occurrence, and a final /p/ will probably be unreleased [pᶰ]. A more economical way of stating this complementary distribution of the three allophones is as follows:

/p/	or	/p/
[pʰ] initially		[pʰ] /#- (where # indicates a word boundary)
[pᶰ] finally		[pᶰ] /-#
[p] elsewhere		[p]

In reality, any one of the three allophones of /p/ may occur in final position without a resulting difference in meaning. Such variation in certain environments among allophones is called **free variation.** We must note that the same variation may not exist in other environments.

Symmetrical Patterning

A third principle is often used in addition to those of phonetic similarity and complementary distribution. This third principle, that of symmetry, or **symmetrical patterning,** has already been mentioned earlier in the chapter, in connection with Figures 4-4, 4-6, and 4-8. Languages seem to have symmetrical phonological systems, so that if we establish four "voiced stop" phonemes, four "voiceless stop" phonemes, and four "voiced fricative" phonemes for a particular language, we would expect to find that any set of "voiceless fricative" phonemes in the same language would number four rather than three or five. Likewise, if three of the voiceless stops had aspirated allophones in initial positions but unaspirated allophones in other positions, we would expect the allophones of the fourth phoneme to share the same distributional characteristics. Although this principle of symmetrical patterning appears to be used on occasion to force data to fit a pattern, as perhaps with the overall vowel inventory devised for English by Trager and Smith, it often produces results which are in accord with a native speaker's intuitions about the structure of the language.

NEUTRALIZATION

The use of this second method of establishing phonemic contrasts sometimes results in just as many difficulties as the use of the first method. For example, the vowels in *beat, bit,* and *beer* are at the same time phonetically different and phonetically similar; that is, they all sound a little different from one another, but are all, nevertheless, high front unrounded vowels. *Beat* and *bit* form a minimal pair in which the vowels contrast. On the other hand, the vowel in *beer* is in complementary distribution with the vowels in both *beat* and *bit.* We could say that the vowels in *beat* and *beer* are variants of the same vowel phoneme, but we could equally well say that the vowels of *bit* and *beer* are variants of one phoneme. Since the vowel in *beer* is in complementary distribution with each of the other two vowels, a decision in one direction rather than the other is quite arbitrary, and there should be no place in a scientific endeavor for arbitrariness of this kind. No easy solution suggests itself to the predicament of assigning the vowel in *beer*. Should we simply note that /iy/ and /i/ (or /i/ and /ɪ/ depending on one's choice of notation) contrast before /t/, as in *beat* and *bit,* but do not contrast before /r/, as in *beer?*

This lack of contrast between two phonemes in one particular environment is sometimes referred to as **neutralization** of the contrast in that environment. The phenomenon is not infrequent, but linguists are sometimes at a loss in dealing satisfactorily with it. How can the facts be stated while maintaining the principle of contrast? In order to avoid assigning the vowel in *beer* to one phoneme rather than to the other in a completely arbitrary manner, a separate symbol, or **archiphoneme,** is sometimes used in the neutralized environment. The result is the use of an /ɪ/ in *beer* in contrast to an /iy/ in *beat* and an /i/ in *bit* in a basic Trager-Smith type notation. This solution sets up further units for the phonological system but fails to provide clear guidelines as to how many additional units might be necessary, since for example, all pairs of stops can be said to be neutralized after initial *s*'s in English, there being no contrasting pairs of words such as *spin*⚹*sbin* and *stop*⚹*sdop,* and so on. Another important neutralizing environment in English is before *r*. Vowels before *r* can lose their distinctiveness, so that *Mary, merry,* and *marry* (and sometimes even *Murray*) can become **homophones.** A conflict obviously exists between the need to devise a system which accounts for *all* the facts of a language according to a set of well-defined principles and the principle of not multiplying entities beyond necessity.

BIUNIQUENESS

Using either set of principles outlined above, we should be able to assign every part of a phonetic notation to a phoneme except features of stress and pitch, which have so far not been mentioned. We should be able to assign every "sound" recorded in the notation to one of a small inventory of contrastive reference points, or phonemes, by means of the statements which relate phonemes and their allophones. These sounds are therefore allophones of the phonemes. Every sound which is distinctly different from every other sound should be assignable to a phoneme and always to the *same* phoneme according to a procedure that is rigorously specified. The procedure should allow for the rewriting of a phonetic notation as a phonemic notation with absolute certainty. Likewise, given a phonemic notation and a statement of the allophones of the phonemes, we should be able to say exactly what the phonemic notation "sounds" like to a speaker of the language and be able to rewrite the phonemic notation as a phonetic notation with absolute certainty. This principle of being able to go in either direction, from phonetic notation to phonemic notation or from phonemic notation to phonetic notation, in a completely explicit way which accounts for every detail is called the principle of **biuniqueness.**

We must emphasize at this point that phonemic transcriptions are not pronounceable. They are symbolizations employing units selected from formal systems; they are not symbolizations of actually occurring phonetic substance, the symbolizations for which are phonetic transcriptions. However, phonemic transcriptions usually have a distinct mnemonic value, because the same symbols are used as in phonetic transcriptions. There would be little point in choosing any other than a /p/ to symbolize a phoneme which has [pʰ], [p], and [p˥] as its allophones, although /2/, /☐/, or /x/ could actually be used to represent this abstract formal unit.

SUPRASEGMENTAL UNITS

Phenomena other than those discussed above may be important in an analysis of the sound system of a language. Stress and pitch differences, for example, might result in differences of meaning. In one dialect of Chinese /má/ with a high, level pitch means "mother," but /mà/ with a low and mainly level pitch means "horse." We must therefore say that in this dialect of Chinese, pitch is phonemic because we have a minimal pair, just as *bit* and *pit* are a minimal pair in English. In Thai there are four phonemic pitch levels: high (/náa/ *uncle* or *aunt*); mid (/naa/ *rice paddy*); falling (/nâa/ *face*); and rising (/nǎa/ *thick*). In English, pitch differences function syntactically, that is, they function in relation to whole utterances, rather than in relation to the individual meaning-bearing parts of utterances.

In English, the stress in words such as *perfect, permit,* and *pervert* shifts according to how these words are used in context:

a pérfect day	to perféct the idea
a new pérmit	to permít him to go
a sex pérvert	to pervért justice

Consequently, we may argue that stress is phonemic in English and postulate several stress phonemes because the different syllables of certain expressions have different degrees of stress. For example, in a *dusty briefcase, brief* carries the most heavy stress/´/, *dust* the second most heavy stress/ˆ/, *case* the third most heavy stress/`/, and *a* and −*y* the lightest stress /˘/, (or, alternatively, are unstressed), so that the four degrees of stress distribute as follows:

ă dûstў bríefcàse	/´/ primary stress
	/ˆ/ secondary stress
	/`/ tertiary stress
	/˘/ unstressed

Furthermore, many minimal pairs can be found to justify these contrasts:

ă hót-ròd	a car
ă hôt ród	a hot *piece of metal*
or	
ă hót rôd	a *hot* piece of metal
ă bríefcàse	a container for papers
ă bríef câse	a case *that was brief*
or	
ă brîef cáse	a brief *case* (not a brief something else)

English stress patterns have sometimes been related to pauses between words. For example, we can say that such words as *nitrate, night rate,* and *Nye trait* require the postulation of a phoneme of juncture to show the difference:

nitrate

night /+/ rate   /+/ plus juncture

Nye /+/ trait

This juncture phoneme apparently indicates a significant pause. Its allophones are difficult to define, however, since it is a significant "nothing." However, it has been claimed that in the presence of /+/ other phonemes have final allophones preceding /+/ and initial allophones following /+/.

In the same way we can say that utterances such as:

He left.

He left?

"He left," I said.

must be differently represented phonemically because of the way the pitch of the voice falls on *left* in the first case, rises on *left* in the second, and stays level on *left* in the third. Three phonemes have been postulated to account for the differences:

/#/ falling terminal contour

/ / / / rising terminal contour

/ / / level terminal contour

The utterances themselves show pitch variations during the course of their production as well as in the production of the final phoneme or phonemes. Consequently, we may postulate four different phonemic pitch levels for English. These pitch levels are generally marked with numbers: /4/ is used for the highest pitch level and /1/ for the lowest, with /3/ and /2/ for the intermediate levels.

The result of such searches for additional phonemes for English is the postulation of a phonemic system that requires the use of both **segmental phonemes** and **suprasegmental phonemes,** the latter term being employed for the phonemes which must always be "overlaid" on the segmentals since they cannot occur without them:

Segmental phonemes:

24 consonants /p, b, t, d, č, ǰ, k, g, f, v, θ, ð, s, z, š, ž, m, n, ŋ, r, l, w, y, h/

14 vowels   /iy, i, ey, e, æ, a, ə, ɔ, ow, u, uw, oy, ay, aw/

Suprasegmental phonemes:

4 stresses   /ˊ ˆ ˋ ˇ/

1 juncture   /+/

4 pitches   /1 2 3 4/

3 terminal contours /# // //

Such a system should allow us to transcribe any English utterance in all its significant contrastive characteristics. For example, a full transcription of *"He left," I said*
would look as follows:

"He left," I said.

$/_2$hîy $+ _3$léft$_1/_1$ây $+$ séd$_1\#/$

The segmental phonemes require no comment, but it may be useful to summarize
what the transcription indicates about the suprasegmental phonemes. There are
two junctures indicated by $/+/$, a level terminal contour between *left* and *I*, a
$/231/$ pitch sequence over *He left* and a $/11/$ sequence over *I said* and a final falling
terminal contour on *said*.

There are undoubtedly many weaknesses in such an approach to suprasegmental phonology. Linguists have disagreed about the facts, and no system that
has been devised has successfully revealed the "facts" of intonation in English.
One weakness is treating suprasegmentals as discrete phonemes just as segmentals
are treated. Pitches, pauses, and stresses act more like contours "spread over"
utterances than like discrete entities added one on to the other. Then, too, as the
meaning of an utterance varies, so does the contour given to it; and so long as
questions of meaning are ignored in any analysis, difficulties are likely to be created
rather than overcome.

PHONEMIC SYSTEMS

Grammatical and semantic information were apparently completely disregarded in
making phonemic analyses using either the technique of minimal pairs or the
principles of phonetic similarity, complementary distribution, and symmetrical
patterning. Considerations of meaning did arise, because we had to judge pairs of
utterances to be either similar or different in meaning. We made no other appeals
to meaning beyond that one. For a long time the reasoning behind such an
exclusion of other varieties of grammatical and semantic information appeared to
be quite simple. If the goal was to explain how a sound system carries meaning,
then meaning could not be used in describing the sound system, because doing so
would introduce undesirable circularity into the explanation. Some linguists even
argued that phonemic systems could be discovered or postulated without using
meaning at all, including differential meaning, that is, whether or not one utterance
repeated or contrasted with another. However, in practice such approaches were
always avoided as being too cumbersome and time-consuming.

Certain linguists did object to the principle that grammatical and semantic
information should be excluded in making phonemic analyses, but found little
general support for their arguments. Today, however, most linguists see the need
for using such information in their analyses. As we will show in Chapters 7 to 9, they
favor a different approach, one that holds that a linguistic system is used by
speakers to say meaningful things. They propose a model of language which
allows meaning, syntax, and phonology to function concurrently. They also argue
that if meaning, syntax, and phonology do function in that way, the three subsys-

tems will interact and strict separation cannot be justified. Furthermore, they assert that anyone who tries to set up a rather mechanical procedure, whether it requires the use of minimal pairs or of a set of principles such as phonetic similarity, complementary distribution, and symmetrical patterning, in order to discover the phonemes of a language is setting impossibly high goals. Such a procedure is not possible unless we are quite sure we know exactly what language is, how particular languages must be described, and what must be the same and different in all languages. Since there are no definitive answers to these questions (and there may never be), the construction of a discovery procedure is too strong a goal.

These last arguments are, of course, arguments against certain of the principles set forth earlier in this chapter. They do not by themselves invalidate any analysis of English presented earlier, but they suggest the limitations of such analyses. In addition, a specific analysis can be questioned because it may not cover all the known facts, or the coverage of facts that is proposed may violate certain intuitions native speakers have about their language. We should note too that the claim that an analysis of a language should conform somewhat to the intuitions of speakers of that language would not have been accepted by many of those who followed the procedures described in this chapter: they regarded such intuitions as generally unreliable.

The Trager-Smith nine-vowel system of English and the combinations of the vowels of this system with the three glides may be used to illustrate what has just been said. This analysis does not cover all the known facts, just as the concomitant four-stress system does not. It is also difficult to say what kind of unit a phoneme is within the system. If one speaker is said to pronounce *my* phonemically as /mæy/, another phonemically as /mah/, and still another phonemically as /may/, because the system demands such an interpretation, how can the observation be made that all the pronunciations are functionally the same? We could postulate some still more abstract system that all three speakers share when they speak to one another, a system which allows them all to know that /mæy/, /mah/, and /may/ are *my*; however, what would be the status of both that system and the individual phonemic notations? Stated in another way, what claims would the linguist then be making about language in general and the English language in particular?

This last point is really the crucial one. Every statement we make about language must arise from answering some question we have about language and the functions of language. The phonemic principles outlined in this chapter may be used to answer certain questions. A few of these questions no longer hold much interest; some still are of interest. In the following chapters, particularly in Chapter 8, we shall see that if we ask certain other questions about phonology, we will find some very different answers.

BIBLIOGRAPHIC NOTES

Most introductory linguistics texts contain adequate discussions of techniques for describing phonemic systems, particularly Gleason's *Introduction to Descriptive Linguistics* and Hockett's *Course in Modern Linguistics*. The Trager-Smith system is explained in Trager and Smith's *Outline of English Structure*. The system is also used at some length in both Francis' *Structure of American English* (with an accompanying workbook by McDavid and Green) and Hill's *Introduction to Linguistic Structures*. Sledd's criticism of the Trager-Smith system is found in his review of their work in *Language*.

Pike's *Phonemics* is an introductory treatment of various problems in the form of a workbook. His views on the relationship of grammar to phonology are contained in his paper "Grammatical Prerequisites to Phonemic Analysis," and his views, shared with Fries, on English vowels are contained in "On the Phonemic Status of English Diphthongs."

EXERCISES

4-1 Check to make sure that you understand each of the terms printed in **boldface** in Chapter 4.

4-2 Chapter 4 makes distinctions between certain terms. Express the distinction between the following terms as clearly as you can: *contoid* and *consonant; vocoid* and *vowel; segmental phoneme* and *suprasegmental phoneme; phonetics* and *phonemics.*

4-3 Two types of bracketing have been used in Chapters 3 and 4: [ ] and / /. Explain the difference in use of these two types of brackets.

4-4 For each of the following pairs of consonants supply a minimal pair of English words in which the contrast is made in the place indicated: initially, medially, or finally. Indicate any places where no minimal pairs exist.

1 /p/-/b/	9 /t/-/č/	17 /č/-/ž/	25 /n/-/ŋ/
2 /t/-/d/	10 /d/-/ǰ/	18 /θ/-/č/	26 /m/-/ŋ/
3 /č/-/ǰ/	11 /k/-/č/	19 /ð/-/z/	27 /r/-/l/
4 /k/-/g/	12 /g/-/ǰ/	20 /d/-/š/	28 /m/-/l/
5 /f/-/v/	13 /f/-/s/	21 /ð/-/ǰ/	29 /n/-/l/
6 /θ/-/ð/	14 /v/-/z/	22 /s/-/š/	30 /ŋ/-/l/
7 /s/-/z/	15 /č/-/š/	23 /z/-/ž/	31 /r/-/m/
8 /š/-/ž/	16 /ǰ/-/ž/	24 /m/-/n/	32 /r/-/n/

4-5 Give the Trager-Smith phonemic symbol or symbols for the underlined part or parts of the following words:

1 ache<u>d</u>	14 <u>ch</u>orus	27 <u>k</u>eep	40 ra<u>ge</u>
2 <u>a</u>loud	15 confu<u>si</u>on	28 <u>k</u>ey	41 re<u>c</u>ent
3 ba<u>the</u>	16 <u>ei</u>ther	29 k<u>i</u>tten	42 ri<u>c</u>e
4 b<u>ea</u>n	17 era<u>su</u>re	30 l<u>ie</u>d	43 ri<u>pe</u>
5 b<u>ee</u>n	18 e<u>th</u>er	31 lo<u>gs</u>	44 sea<u>so</u>n
6 bli<u>n</u>k	19 fa<u>c</u>es	32 ma<u>tt</u>er	45 si<u>ng</u>er
7 bo<u>th</u>	20 fa<u>shi</u>on	33 mea<u>su</u>re	46 <u>su</u>re
8 bou<u>ght</u>	21 <u>f</u>eet	34 na<u>ti</u>on	47 <u>th</u>ought
9 bo<u>x</u>	22 fi<u>ng</u>er	35 na<u>tu</u>re	48 <u>v</u>irgin
10 bu<u>r</u>y	23 fi<u>t</u>	36 nor<u>the</u>rn	49 wa<u>s</u>te
11 ca<u>lm</u>	24 <u>gh</u>ost	37 no<u>t</u>e	50 wi<u>sh</u>
12 ca<u>pe</u>	25 <u>h</u>ouse	38 pha<u>ses</u>	51 w<u>o</u>n't
13 <u>c</u>at	26 <u>J</u>ack	39 <u>p</u>sychology	52 w<u>oo</u>l

4-6 Transcribe the following words written in the Trager-Smith phonemic notation into their ordinary English spellings. When more than one spelling is possible, write out all the possibilities.

1 /šawt/	13 /wič/	25 /pléžər/	37 /far/
2 /vížən/	14 /miyt/	26 /howl/	38 /for/
3 /rítən/	15 /sent/	27 /čərč/	39 /bay/
4 /ayl/	16 /ləš/	28 /liykt/	40 /howm/
5 /sayt/	17 /boyz/	29 /fiš/	41 /θiŋk/
6 /tuwθ/	18 /éniy/	30 /myuwt/	42 /teypt/
7 /ðen/	19 /gərl/	31 /fir/	43 /mériy/
8 /reyn/	20 /əbáwt/	32 /wərd/	44 /hərd/
9 /yuw/	21 /sik/	33 /jəǰ/	45 /béysən/
10 /fíŋgər/	22 /wiyk/	34 /skuwl/	46 /bow/
11 /ǰæm/	23 /wiyl/	35 /pur/	47 /rič/
12 /éybəl/	24 /fǽtən/	36 /tuw/	48 /feyz/

4-7 Complete the following table by inserting the missing notation from the other transcriptional system. Record each word in a normal English spelling.

FRIES-PIKE	TRAGER-SMITH	ENGLISH SPELLING	FRIES-PIKE	TRAGER-SMITH	ENGLISH SPELLING
bit				piys	
	fit		klɪf		
kep				pleyt	
	bred		bɛg		
kul				skuwl	
	puš		fʊl		
kot				bowl	
	šawt		haʊs		
bɔɪl				toyz	
	fayt		kaɪt		

4-8 Transcribe the following words written in the Fries-Pike phonemic notation into their ordinary English spellings. When more than one spelling is possible, write out all the possibilities.

1 /ples/	7 /haul/	13 /got/	19 /smuð/
2 /fit/	8 /bɔɪz/	14 /fíbəl/	20 /wʊd/
3 /græs/	9 /kɪtən/	15 /rəš/	21 /mɪŋks/
4 /θɪn/	10 /kǽsəl/	16 /baɪt/	22 /hol/
5 /pel/	11 /hɔl/	17 /fʊt/	23 /kruz/
6 /čest/	12 /grétəl/	18 /fǽšən/	24 /brɛd/

4-9 Transcribe the following words in phonemic notation:

1 ballet	11 could	21 masseuse	31 schism
2 banquet	12 fission	22 mischief	32 sergeant
3 biscuit	13 fruit	23 music	33 spinach
4 buoy	14 height	24 other	34 Stephen
5 Caesar	15 is	25 people	35 suede
6 cause	16 island	26 plaid	36 taxi
7 cello	17 journey	27 pretty	37 tortoise
8 chute	18 kiln	28 salmon	38 veldt
9 cognac	19 Leicester	29 same	39 whimper
10 comb	20 leopard	30 saw	40 yield

4-10 Transcribe the following words containing an *r* into phonemic notation:

1 beer	9 part	17 door	25 heard
2 beard	10 heart	18 court	26 turn
3 pair	11 fire	19 sport	27 purr
4 care	12 flour	20 bar	28 jury
5 there	13 pure	21 cart	29 hurry
6 poor	14 cheery	22 bird	30 furry
7 tour	15 fairy	23 word	31 story
8 car	16 ferry	24 hurt	32 starry

4-11 The following words are often pronounced in a manner influenced by their spelling. However, each has another pronunciation which does not show this influence. Write out in phonemic notation the pronunciation which does *not* show the influence of spelling.

1 asthma	9 February	17 hiccough	25 Thames
2 boatswain	10 forecastle	18 human	26 thorough
3 bourbon (whiskey)	11 forehead	19 kiln	27 thyme
4 breeches	12 gooseberry	20 lichen	28 tortoise
5 clothes	13 Greenwich	21 Norfolk	29 toward
6 comptroller	14 gunwale	22 Norwich	30 waistcoat
7 Edinburgh	15 halfpenny	23 sieve	31 Wednesday
8 falcon	16 handkerchief	24 Southwark	32 worsted

4-12 Transcribe each of the following words in phonemic notation according to the way you pronounce each in your speech. Look out for the particular phonemic contrasts you have.

1 marry	13 egg	25 horse	37 witch
2 merry	14 collar	26 hoarse	38 which
3 Mary	15 caller	27 pin	39 grease
4 Rosa's	16 wet	28 pen	40 greasy
5 Rose's	17 get	29 aunt	41 oil
6 creak	18 root	30 class	42 earl
7 creek	19 proof	31 cot	43 about
8 wash	20 roof	32 caught	44 loud
9 water	21 do	33 horrid	45 since
10 ketch	22 due	34 orange	46 sense
11 catch	23 hog	35 with	47 cents
12 beg	24 dog	36 pith	48 push

4-13 Transcribe the consonant cluster that occurs initially in each of the following words:

1 chronic	6 schmoo	11 spume	16 svelte
2 cross	7 scream	12 squelch	17 threat
3 fleece	8 shred	13 squirt	18 three
4 growl	9 smooth	14 strange	19 throne
5 phrase	10 spray	15 stupor	20 twinge

4-14 Transcribe the consonant cluster that occurs finally in each of the following words:

1 bombed	6 farmed	11 locks	16 sang
2 box	7 fifth	12 loosed	17 sinks
3 cast	8 gorged	13 pans	18 swamped
4 cooked	9 housed	14 phased	19 things
5 false	10 laughs	15 pinch	20 tripped

4-15 Transcribe the consonant or consonants that occur medially in each of the following words:

1 able	5 assume	9 ended	13 huckster
2 acclaim	6 bitten	10 engine	14 laughter
3 address	7 bombard	11 glisten	15 order
4 aptness	8 buttress	12 hamper	16 virtue

4-16 Indicate the position of main stress in each of the following words by writing an accent mark (´) over the appropriate vowel symbol or symbols:

1 actual	13 discriminatory	25 illustrate	37 preservative
2 apple	14 divide	26 illustrative	38 responsibility
3 articulatory	15 division	27 indiscriminate	39 responsible
4 attack	16 execute	28 laconic	40 sagacity
5 baboon	17 execution	29 massage	41 universal
6 battle	18 executive	30 message	42 universality
7 behest	19 facetious	31 neurologist	43 university
8 capability	20 fashion	32 neuron	44 uvular
9 capable	21 gondola	33 photograph	45 Washington
10 caress	22 harass	34 photographic	46 Washingtonian
11 decent	23 hypertension	35 photography	47 yesterday
12 descent	24 idle	36 preservation	48 zoological

4-17 In the following data from Old English [f] is in complementary distribution with [v], [h] with [x], and [n] with [ŋ]. Explain each of the distributions.

1 bringan	[brɪŋgan]	"to bring"	10 hræfn	[hrævn̩]	"raven"
2 drincan	[drɪŋkan]	"to drink"	11 lufu	[luvʊ]	"love"
3 fæst	[fæst]	"fast"	12 mannes	[mannɛs]	"man's"
4 fīfta	[fiːfta]	"fifth"	13 mōna	[moːna]	"moon"
5 folc	[fɔlk]	"folk"	14 nīhsta	[niːxsta]	"next"
6 font	[fɔnt]	"font"	15 niht	[nɪxt]	"night"
7 hāt	[haːt]	"hot"	16 offrian	[ɔffrɪan]	"to offer"
8 hlōð	[hloːθ]	"troop"	17 ofnas	[ɔvnas]	"ovens"
9 hlyhhan	[hlyxxan]	"to laugh"	18 rūh	[ruːx]	"rough"

5

MORPHOLOGY

As we indicated in Chapter 1, each language has two systems, one of sounds and one of meanings. Chapter 4 focused on procedures for achieving some understanding of the composition and internal relationships of systems of sound. This chapter is the first of several devoted to questions of meaning, their goal being the achievement of a similar understanding of systems of meaning. This goal is much more difficult to attain.

MINIMAL UNITS OF MEANING: MORPHEMES

One possible way of beginning the endeavor is suggested by the approach followed in Chapter 4. It involves a search for minimal units of meaning and for ways of isolating such units, the basic hypothesis being that all utterances are composed of sequences of meaningful units. Chapter 4 also suggests a specific procedure that might be useful, involving the selection of pairs of utterances which are minimally different in meaning in the same way that pairs of utterances were minimally different in sound in Chapter 4. For example, if an English speaker substitutes an /r/ for the /k/ in the utterance *It's a cat,* he produces an entirely different utterance *It's a rat*. The differences are twofold: one of sound and one of meaning. *Cat* and *rat* are phonemically different; they also evoke very different responses in speakers of English, these different responses being one indication of differences in meaning. Of course, we might be tempted to ask what *cat* and *rat* mean, and what is "meaning," but the procedure does not require that answers be given to either question. All the procedure requires is that distinctions be made between utterances that are meaningful and those that are meaningless, and between utterances that are repetitions of other utterances and those that are not. Native speakers of English regard both *It's a cat* and *It's a rat* as meaningful, but as different in meaning. On the other hand, they consider *It's a dat* a "meaningless" utterance, unless it is, for example, a statement of the way in which somebody pronounced a word (*It's a* DAT, *not a* THAT), or some other such special use.

Why do *It's a cat* and *It's a rat* mean different things? In one sense the utterances differ because the former has a /k/ before the final /æt/ and the latter an /r/ before the final /æt/. No meaning can be associated with either the /k/ or the /r/, however, nor can any meaning be associated with /æt/. It violates intuitions to say that *cat* and *rat* are each composed of two meaning units so that a *cat* is a /k/ kind of /æt/ and a *rat* an /r/ kind of /æt/, even though we may find still a third example, a *bat* being a /b/ kind of /æt/. Native speakers of English reject such an analysis because they regard *cat, rat,* and *bat* as each having a unitary meaning, this meaning being different in each case and, as it were, indivisible.

We can compare the previously mentioned response with the likely response to *cats, rats,* and *bats* and to *cattle, rattle,* and *battle*. In the first set each word ends in an *s*, and this *s* does have a meaning paraphrasable as "plural." Consequently, each of the first three words may be said to consist of two meaning units: "cat," "rat," and "bat," together with "plural." On the other hand, *cattle, rattle,* and *battle* have unitary meanings, because the final /əl/ cannot be said to be a meaning unit of any kind, nor, if the /əl/ is removed in each case, can the remaining parts of the words /kæt/, /ræt/, and /bæt/ be said to have the meanings of "cat," "rat," and "bat." These parts are in fact meaningless when they are separated in this way from /əl/. Such a treatment of *cattle, rattle,* and *battle* can be compared with that of *tomcat, rattrap,* and *batman,* in which the *cat, rat,* and *bat* do have the meanings of "cat," "rat," and "bat," and *tom, trap,* and *man* occur elsewhere in utterances with similar meanings, as in *The tom was sitting on the fence, I bought a trap* and *The man left*.

The simple procedure just outlined can be used to isolate certain minimal units of meaning. These minimal units are called **morphemes.** We can also observe that these morphemic units are not equivalent to phonemes, because the examples used above indicate that a morpheme can be realized as one phoneme, such as the "plural" /s/, or more than one phoneme, such as "cat" /kæt/. Nor is a morpheme equivalent to anything we might want to call a syllable, since the "plural" /s/ is less than a syllable, "cat" /kæt/ is one syllable, and "cattle" /kætəl/ is **disyllabic.** *Alligator* and *hippopotamus* have four and five syllables respectively. As we shall see, a morpheme may even have no phonemic "content" at all, as in the "plural" *deer* in *two deer*. Finally, morphemes are not equivalent to what we conventionally regard as words, since *cats* is one word but two morphemes, "cat" and "plural." Morphemes are the minimal units of meaning out of which meaningful utterances are built.

ALLOMORPHS

If the word *dogs* is added to the set *cats, rats,* and *bats,* two further observations can be made: the first is that the final *s* in *dogs* means "plural" just as the final *s* in each of *cats, rats,* and *bats* means "plural"; the second is that this *s* is realized as /z/ in *dogs* but as /s/ in the other three words. If the word *judges* is added to the list, the "plural" meaning is now realized by /əz/, not just by /z/ alone. Therefore, the "plural" morpheme appears in at least three different phonemic shapes: /s/, /z/, and /əz/. These different phonemic shapes of a morpheme are called the **allomorphs** of the morpheme. The various allomorphs of a morpheme occur in complementary distribution with each other, just as the allophones of a phoneme occur in complementary distribution with each other: each appears in a different environment.

Phonological Conditioning of Allomorphs

In the case of the /s/, /z/, and /əz/ allomorphs of the "plural" morpheme in *cats, dogs,* and *judges,* the /s/ occurs after a /t/, the /z/ after a /g/, and the /əz/ after a /ǰ/. When the distribution of the various allomorphs can be stated in terms of their phonemic environments, the allomorphs are said to be **phonologically conditioned.** We can economically explain the distribution of the allomorphs of not only the English "plural," but also the English "possessive" (*cat's*) and the verb "third person" (*takes*) morphemes at the same time. In general, these allomorphs are all phonologically conditioned in addition to being homophonous. The usual allomorphs of the English "plural," "possessive," and "third person" morphemes are /əz/, which occurs after /s š č z ž ǰ/ (or after coronal stridents), /s/, which occurs after the remaining voiceless consonants, and /z/, which occurs elsewhere. When the "plural" morpheme is added to *church* /čərč/, the result is /čə́rčəz/, when the "possessive" morpheme is added to *snake* /sneyk/, the result is /sneyks/, and when the "third person" morpheme is added to *beg* /beg/, the result is /begz/. We can state the distributions of the phonologically conditioned allomorphs of the "plural," "possessive," and "third person" morphemes of English as follows:

"plural," "possessive," "third person"

/əz/ after coronal stridents

/s/ after voiceless consonants

/z/ elsewhere

This list is an ordered list. The final sound of *church* is /č/ and of *fish* is /š/, both voiceless coronal stridents. The above list says that since the sounds are coronal stridents then the correct allomorph is /əz/. If the first and second statements are reversed, a wrong /s/ ending would be applied to *church* and *fish*.

In another pattern of phonological conditioning the usual allomorphs of the English "past tense" and "past participle" morphemes which occur with verbs, for example in *baked,* are /əd/, which occurs after /t d/, /t/, which occurs after the remaining voiceless consonants, and /d/, which occurs elsewhere. Phonological conditioning appears to be the most general and productive kind of conditioning of morphemic variants in languages.

Morphological Conditioning of Allomorphs

In pairs such as *man-men, child-children,* and *deer-deer,* in which the second item can be said to contain the "plural" morpheme, we cannot state the variation, if any, between the two forms in terms of phonemic environments. Instead we must refer to the morphemes "man," "child," and "deer," or, alternatively, to their phonemic shapes (/mæn/, /čayld/, and /dir/), and specify the allomorph of the "plural" morpheme separately for each. This kind of variation among allomorphs is called **morphological conditioning.** The morphologically conditioned allomorphs of a morpheme are regarded as **irregular** in contrast with the phonologically conditioned allomorphs, which are regarded as **regular.** *Men, children,* and *deer* are therefore irregular English plurals, just as are *alumni, criteria, mice, women, oxen,* and *strata.* The "past tense" morpheme also has its irregular allomorphs, as in *drank, brought, swam, was, had, put, took, fled, built,* and so on; likewise, the "past participle" morpheme has irregular allomorphs, as in *drunk, brought, swum, been, broken, stood, put,* and so on.

In stating the distributions of the allomorphs of morphemes such as "plural," "past," and so on, we usually state the morphologically conditioned allomorphs first and then the phonologically conditioning environments in optimal order. The result is that "exceptions" to general rules are stated first, the narrowest phonologically conditioning environments next, and finally the most regular, or general, allomorph. This last variant may sometimes even be regarded as the phonemic "norm" of the allomorph—the most general case.

MORPHEMIC CUTTING

Since we have said that language is used to convey meaning, we could entertain the hypothesis that every utterance consists of a string of morphemes and that every phoneme in an utterance is assignable to one of the morphemes. We may want to seek confirmation of this hypothesis by inspecting an utterance such as *Bill baked two cakes and a pie* to see if it can be separated into morphemes. Such separation turns out to be relatively simple: "Bill," "bake," "past tense," "two," "cake," "plural," "and," "a," and "pie," with the phonemes assigned as /bil/, /beyk/, /t/, /tuw/, /keyk/, /s/, /ənd/, /ə/, and /pay/. The only problems that need to be solved are those of deciding how many morphemes are present in certain cases and knowing exactly where to cut between morphemes.

However, such problems may turn out to be severe, as in *Billy took his mice away.* In *Billy,* we can fairly easily decide which parts belong to which morpheme: /bil/ to the morpheme "Bill" and /iy/ to a morpheme meaning something like "diminutive." Similar divisions are far more difficult to make in *took* and *mice.* Are the consonants in *took* /tuk/ and *mice* /mays/ to be assigned with /t . . . k/ to "take" and /m . . . s/ to "mouse," and then the vowels assigned with /u/ to "past tense" and /ay/ to "plural"? Or can some other assignment be made, one perhaps more in accord with a native speaker's intuition? Some different answers to these questions will be discussed later in this chapter in the section on morpheme-allomorph relationships. *His* and *away* also raise problems in the above utterance. A connection exists among *he, his,* and *him,* and between *his* and *John's.* Therefore, *his* probably consists of two morphemes: "he" and "possessive," just as *him* consists of "he" and "object marker." *Away* also seems to consist of two morphemes, because *way* seems to resemble *way* in meaning ("way") and *a* appears to be found elsewhere in the language, as in *alive, aboard,* and *asleep,* although in this case the meaning of the morpheme is not clear—perhaps something like "state." Each phoneme in the above utterances therefore can be associated in some way with a meaning unit, and the same meaning unit occurs in other utterances in the language, although not always in the same phonemic shape.

In cutting utterances into morphemes, we try to observe a general principle that we should not be left with uniquely occurring morphemes. That is, we should be sure that the morphemes we seek to establish occur in other utterances in the language, although quite possibly in different phonemic shapes (that is, as other allomorphs). For example, the *kempt* of *unkempt* occurs as *combed,* the *ept* of *inept* occurs as *apt,* and even *couth* and *peccable* can occur (though rarely) in isolation so that *uncouth* and *impeccable* can be split. But occasionally problems do arise, as in *cranberry, gooseberry, crayfish,* and *mushroom.* In *cranberry, berry* has the same meaning as the *berry* of *blackberry* and *strawberry.* However, whereas *black* and *straw* can occur either alone or in other combinations in utterances, and are meaningful in all occurrences, until recently (when *cranapple* juice came onto the market) *cran* did not occur except with *berry.* Another kind of problem exists with the *goose* of *gooseberry,* which has a superficial resemblance to the *goose* of *Mother Goose.* We may find some difficulty in saying what the common meaning is in *gooseberry* and *Mother Goose,* but undoubtedly there is a common meaning element for many speakers of English. Historically, of course, the two *gooses* are from different sources, as we shall see in Chapter 11, but our concern at the moment is with a synchronic statement, not a diachronic one. Likewise, the *fish* in *crayfish* is historically of different origin from the *fish* of *fish and chips;* however, most speakers of English probably regard the two *fishes* as having the same meaning. Such a solution, though, puts the *cray* part of *crayfish* into the same position as the *cran* part of *cranberry,* that of being a unique occurrence. In *mushroom* neither the *mush* nor the *room* seems to be related to *mush* and *room* as these occur as independent words; consequently, *mushroom* is monomorphemic for most speakers, that is, it is a single morpheme.

Thermometer creates a problem of a different kind. Both *therm* and *meter* occur elsewhere but the *o,* phonemically /a/, does not, nor does it appear to have any meaning. If, as we have hypothesized, every phoneme must be assignable to a morpheme, the /a/ will have to be assigned somewhere. One solution is to assign the /a/ to a morpheme meaning "stemforming," if that really is a meaning. An alternative analysis would make the whole of *thermo* an allomorph of "therm" (or "heat"), so that *thermometer* would be bimorphemic in composition (*thermo-meter*) rather than trimorphemic (*therm-o-meter*), but this solution conceals the fact that the same *o* is found elsewhere in the language in the same stem-forming process: *meteor-o-graph, ped-o-meter,* and *speed-o-meter.*

The cutting process is obviously full of difficulties, and some of the cuts produce strange or awkward solutions, a few of which have just been indicated.

Several more examples are in order. We can cut up words that contain *spect* as follows: *respect* into *re* and *spect; expect* into either *ex* and *spect* or (using sound not spelling) *ek* and *spect; spectacle* into *spect* and *acle;* and so on. In each case *spect* means "look," but we cannot so easily say what *re, ex* (or *ek*), and *acle* mean or be sure that the *re* in *respect* has the same meaning as the *re* in *resolve* or *report,* or the *ex* in *expect* has the same meaning as the *ex* in *exhale,* and so on. Linguists have usually decided that all the *re*s share the same meaning and that all the *ex*s have the same meaning, but not all native speakers agree with such decisions. On the other hand, we have decided that no sameness of meaning exists in the *er* endings of *flicker, ladder, butter,* and *Peter,* and that the *fl* beginning of *flame, flicker, flit,* and *fly,* and the *sl* beginning of *slop, slurp, slob, slut,* and *slouch,* are accidentally alike phonemically, so that *fl* and *sl* are meaningless. A certain arbitrariness is therefore apparent in some of the decisions that have usually been made in morphemic cutting. It undoubtedly results from certain basic shortcomings in the approach outlined so far in this chapter.

MORPHEME-ALLOMORPH RELATIONSHIPS

In *He's an intolerable infamous individual* and *It's impossible* the negative prefix has different phonemic shapes in different environments. We may then proceed to examine the various occurrences of this negative prefix meaning "not" in the two utterances given above. There are three occurrences of the morpheme, one each at the beginning of *intolerable, infamous,* and *impossible,* with the respective pronunciations in ordinary speech being /in/, /im/, and /im/. The distribution of the different phonemic shapes of the morpheme, that is, of the allomorphs, is phonologically conditioned: the /in/ allomorph occurs before alveolars (/t/ in this case), and the /im/ allomorph occurs before labials (/f/ and /p/ in this case). We should also note that on certain occasions a word such as *infamous* may be given either a spelling pronunciation or a very careful pronunciation with an /n/ rather than an /m/. The total distribution of this "not" prefix is more complicated still, for it includes an /i/ allomorph before /r/ and /l/, as in *irrelevant* and *illegible,* and quite often an /iŋ/ allomorph before velars as in *incongruous* (/k/ in this case).

We have observed that the "not" discussed in the previous paragraph can be realized in different phonemic shapes, but the discussion so far has been rather imprecise. What do we mean by *the "not,"* by *realized,* and by *shapes?* In effect, the procedure discussed so far has resulted in the isolation of certain sequences of phonemes, the establishment of the fact that some of these sequences have the "same" meaning, the formulation of some kind of **gloss** of that "same" meaning, and a statement of the distribution of the phonemic variants of particular meaning units. The term *morpheme* has been loosely applied to both the paraphrase and the phonemic sequences which are its realizations. Since morphemes must be regarded as abstract constructs in the system of meaning (just as in Chapter 4 phonemes were regarded as abstract constructs in the system of sound), we can consider that the paraphrases provide the best representations of the meaning units. In this view, an utterance would consist of a sequence of meanings, some of which might actually be hard to specify, even by paraphrase, for example the meanings of *if, and, very,* and *the.* This sequence of meanings is realized through the phonemic system because each meaning unit, or morpheme, manifests itself in one or more phonemic shapes according to environment. For example, "not" is /in/ in one environment, /im/ in a second environment, and /iŋ/ in a third environment.

An alternative approach for discussing morphemes is to say that each morpheme has a basic phonemic shape and that this shape and the meaning are somehow inseparable. We can say that in English we have a morpheme /in/ with the meaning "not," and that this morpheme has certain variants, for example, an /im/ variant before labials and an /iŋ/ variant before velars. In this case either the most frequently occurring or the most "regular" allomorph is chosen to represent the morpheme, and all the other allomorphic variants are regarded as alternants. The various arrangements of the allomorphs according to environment exhaust the distribution of the morpheme. Alternatively, the relationships among the allomorphs may employ process-type statements, so that in the case of /in/, the /n/ is said to **assimilate** to a following labial (hence the /im/ of *impossible*), or to a following velar (hence the /iŋ/ of *incongruous*), or to drop before an /r/ or /l/ (hence the /i/ of *irrelevant* and *illegible*).

The English "plural" morpheme illustrates some of the difficulties to which reference has just been made. We can say that *cats* means "cat" plus "plural," and that *cats* is composed of two morphemes /kæt/, meaning "cat," and /s/, meaning "plural." However, is /s/ the best possible representation of the "plural"? Perhaps /z/ would be a better choice so that it is the /z/ morpheme which occurs in *cats,* but in a voiceless variety after the voiceless consonant /t/, or alternatively, that the /z/ has devoiced to /s/. The difficulties increase in describing what happens in a word like *men. Men* is "man" plus "plural." However, if morphemes are said to consist of phonemes rather than to be represented by phonemes, then we cannot easily determine what "man" and "plural" consist of in this case. Do they consist of /m-n/ and /-e-/ respectively? And, if they do, where does the /æ/ of /mæn/ fit? Or does the /e/ usurp the place of the /æ/ so that we have a **replacive allomorph** of the plural /(æ) → e/? In *two deer, deer* is a plural by analogy with *two cats* or *two boys,* but there is no overt manifestation of plurality in *deer.* The "plural" morpheme appears to have various kinds of allomorphs: an /s/ in *cats,* an /-e-/ in *men,* and a /ø/ (zero) in *deer,* and so on. We cannot easily make an economical statement of the distribution of these allomorphic variants and at the same time provide a theoretical justification for the principles that underlie the statement.

In order to avoid saying that morphemes consist of phonemes, we could simply list the various allomorphs of morphemes in the most convenient way. Consequently, the "plural" morpheme would be realized as /s/, /z/, or /əz/ in three different phonological environments, and as /-e-/ in conjunction with /m-n/, the variant of "man" that occurs with "plural." The "plural" part of *deer* /dir/ would be realized as /ø/, a **zero allomorph.** The goal in this approach is merely to list the allomorphs and state their arrangements. Consequently, the prefixed "not," referred to previously in the discussion of *intolerable, impossible,* and *illegible* is realized as /in/, /im/, and /i/ in the different phonological environments. Such an approach has sometimes seemed better than one which says that morphemes consist of phonemes, for one of the allomorphs is selected as the basic allomorph of the morpheme and all the other allomorphs are derived from that base. Alternatively, an abstract base form is set up from which all actually occurring allomorphs can be derived. The result is a set of process-type statements, and the whole approach is sometimes called a **morphophonemic** one. In the case of the "plural," /z/ is considered to be the base form, /s/ a devoiced variant in one environment, and /əz/ a variant with an inserted vowel in another environment. A zero variant of /z/ would occur in *deer* and a replacement of the vowel /æ/ by the vowel /e/ would occur in *men*. This last replacement process has one advantage in that we avoid setting up two allomorphs for "man": /mæn/ and /m-n/. However, neither approach, the arrangement statement or the process statement, is without its difficulties, a possible indication that both approaches may be missing one or more important principles.

Linguists have discussed these different ways of describing the meanings of morphemes and the distributions of the alternants of morphemes at considerable length. The ways described above represent rather different hypotheses about how the system of meaning functions and how it relates to the system of sound. Recently, discussion of such differences has lessened as attention has turned to matters which appear to be of much greater theoretical interest. Such matters will be discussed in Chapters 7 to 9.

MORPHEME TYPES

At the beginning of this chapter we hypothesized that utterances are composed of sequences of meaning units. The hypothesis seems to be acceptable in spite of some of the difficulties noted above. However, not all the meaning units apparently distribute in utterances in the same way. There appears to be some advantage in having a set of terms to describe the different types of distributions of morphemes in utterances. For example, in *cats* the order of morphemes is clearly "cat" followed by "plural." This clear ordering of morphemes in *cats* contrasts with the ordering in *men,* in which "man" and "plural" are not so clearly ordered, and with the ordering in *deer,* as in *two deer,* which contains no overt indication of the "plural" morpheme. Furthermore, in *cats* the morpheme "cat" can occur alone, for example as *cat,* but the morpheme "plural" cannot occur by itself. Likewise *tolerable,* can occur alone or with *in* (meaning "not"), as in *intolerable,* but the same *in* cannot occur alone.

Free and Bound Morphemes

A morpheme which can occur alone as an independent **word** is called a **free form;** for example, *the, cat, man, go, like, quite, alligator,* and *hippopotamus.* A free form to which other morphemes may be attached is called a **base** (or **root**). All the words in the list just given are bases. A base is not always a free form. The *dict* of *predict,* the *spect* of *spectator,* and the *spir* of *conspiracy* are not free: they are bound bases rather than free ones. Likewise, the *s* of *cats* cannot occur alone. It represents the "plural," a **bound morpheme** in English. Other examples of bound morphemes of this kind are the "past tense" morpheme in *baked,* the "negative" morpheme in *infamous,* and the "quality" morpheme in *goodness.* None of these morphemes can occur alone, except in such utterances as *What does IN mean?* or

The NESS means "quality." They are, however, **affixes,** not bases, as we shall see. A bound morpheme must cooccur with at least one other morpheme. Using examples in conventional English spelling for convenience, we see that *cats* is composed of a free form *cat* and a bound morpheme *s, goodness* of a free form *good* and a bound morpheme *ness,* and *infamous* of a free form *famous* and a bound morpheme *in.*

Some free forms never take cooccurring bound morphemes, for example *the, very,* and *quite.* On the other hand, bound morphemes need not always be attached to free forms, for they may be attached to other bound morphemes: *receive* is *re* and *ceive* and *submit* is *sub* and *mit.* Finally, free forms may be combined, as in *tomcat, briefcase, armchair,* and *showcase* to form words called **compounds.**

Affixes

Morphemes combine in certain patterns. *Cat* and *s* combine to form *cats* rather than **scat* and *in* and *famous* combine to form *infamous* rather than **famousin.* The *s* and *in* are **affixed** to *cat* and *famous* respectively but *s* is a suffix and *in* is a prefix. The affixes are sometimes written with hyphens (as *-s* and *in-*) to show their positions. Some languages have **infixes,** that is, morphemes introduced right into the middle of other morphemes. However, English does not have infixes, the nearest equivalent being the kind of situation that occurs in the "plural" form of *man* (the *-e-* in *men*) and the "past tense" form of *take* (the *-oo-* in *took*).

Affixes are added to bases or to various combinations of morphemes. Anything to which an affix can be added is called a **stem.** *Cat* is a stem because s can be **suffixed** to form *cats; tomcat* is a stem for the same reason. *Good* is a stem because *ness* can be suffixed to form *goodness; kind* is a stem because either *un* can be **prefixed** to form *unkind, ness* can be suffixed to form *kindness,* or both *un* and *ness* can be affixed to form *unkindness.* Even *unkindness* is a stem because it can occur with the "plural" suffix to form *unkindnesses.*

Inflection and Derivation

Not all affixes are alike in the effects they have on the stems to which they are affixed. Affixes may be inflectional or derivational in nature. Inflectional affixes tend to be morphemes with meanings such as "plural," "possessive," "past tense," or "feminine" and seem to occur in small sets but with a great number of stems. Each small set, or **paradigm,** of affixes may be used to define a part of speech class in the language. For example, English stems which can occur with "plural" and "possessive" **inflections** belong to the noun class and English stems which can occur with the "past tense" inflection belong to the verb class.

Quite often when we learn a new language in the traditional way, we learn words according to inflectional paradigms, particularly noun and adjective **declensions** and verb **conjugations.** For example, Latin verb forms are often listed as follows:

amo	I love
amas	you (sing.) love
amat	he (she or it) loves

amamus	we love
amātis	you (pl.) love
amant	they love

Likewise, Old English determiners and nouns are often listed as follows:

	Singular	*Plural*
nominative	se cyning	þā cyningas
accusative	þone cyning	þā cyningas
genitive	þæs cyninges	þāra cyninga
dative	þæm cyninge	þæm cyningum

Derivational affixes may also be used to define parts of speech classes to some extent, since English words ending in *ness,* such as *tallness,* and *weakness,* are nouns, but there is often a major difference in the case of derivation. The stems to which the derivational affixes are attached may belong to quite a different part of speech class from the class which the stem together with an inflectional affix defines: *tall* and *weak* are adjectives (*tall, taller, tallest,* and *weak, weaker, weakest*), but *tallness* and *weakness* are nouns. **Derivation** does not always result in a change of part of speech class. *Take* may become *retake* and *please* become *displease* without such a change, but quite often such a change occurs.

We can also observe that in English all the inflectional affixes are suffixes, as in *cats, man's, judged,* and so on. The only exception occurs in forms like *men, deer,* and *took* which either show some change in the middle of the form, as in *men* and *took* to indicate "plural" and "past tense" respectively, or show no change at all to indicate "plural," as in the *deer of two deer.*

English derivational affixes may be either prefixes or suffixes. *Retake, unbend,* and *dispossess* are words with derivational prefixes, *brighten, judgment,* and *victimize* examples of derivational suffixes, and *employment* and *unidirectional* examples of both prefixing and suffixing. We can note too that derivational affix may be added to derivational affix: *judge, judgment, judgmental* and *arm, rearm, antirearm.* Since **judgalment* and **reantiarm* are not possible, some principle of ordering exists; that is, the affixes must be attached in certain sequences.

If both derivational and inflectional suffixes occur together in English, the inflectional suffix must be the final one, so that *weaknesses* is possible but **weakesness* or **weaksness* is not allowed. Nevertheless, there is the English word *betterment.* The *er* is often regarded as an inflectional affix which along with *est* defines a part of speech class called adjective. In *betterment* the derivational suffix *ment* follows the *er,* however, in contradiction to what has just been said. We may speculate that it exists because the *good, better, best* alternation is completely irregular. Unfortunately, *bad, worse,* and *worst* is just as irregular and there is no form **worsement* in the language. But there is such a word as *worsening.*

WORDS AND IDIOMS

The preceding discussion showed how various combinations of morphemes are possible: single morphemes like *the, very, man,* and *sing;* morphemes with affixes, like *cats, unbend, deceive,* and *national;* morphemes compounded together like *briefcase, girlfriend, bulldog,* and *outlook.* A term that covers all such items is *word.* Both *a* and *antidisestablishmentarianism* are words; consequently, length differences may be considerable, as may the amount of meaning that is contained in a word: we cannot easily say what *a* means. The *s* of *cats* is not a word, however, nor is the *un* of *unbend* and the *al* of *national.* Even though the morphemes in question have meaning, they do not occur alone.

The total meaning of a word is sometimes considerably greater than the sum of the meanings of the morphemes out of which it is constituted. *Briefcase, girl-friend, bulldog,* and *outlook* above all have meanings which derive partly from the two morphemes out of which each is composed and partly from the particular arrangement, a fact which is particularly noticeable if we contrast *lookout* with *outlook, boathouse* with *houseboat, doghouse* with *housedog,* and *housecat* with *cathouse.* When the meaning of a particular morpheme or combination of morphemes in a word cannot be predicted entirely from the meanings of the individual morphemes, the word is a **lexeme.** Dictionaries also list lexemes as separate entries when words such as *cat, well,* and *rush* have several distinctively different meanings. Lexemes containing only a single morpheme may be as short as *a* or *in* or as long as *alligator* or *hippopotamus.* With more than one morpheme they may be like *into, outlook, inspection, housedog,* or even *antidisestablish-mentarianism.* When two or more words combine to form a special meaning unit with a meaning different from the sum of the individual meanings of the words, we have an **idiom.** *To tear a strip off, to get a piece of the action, to kick the bucket, to be fed up, to get on with,* and *on the other hand* are all idioms.

BIBLIOGRAPHIC NOTES

Morphology is treated in all the basic linguistics texts but generally much less adequately than phonology. Nida's *Morphology: The Descriptive Analysis of Words* is a book-length treatment in the form of a workbook. Nida also expounds his views in his paper "The Identification of Morphemes," as does Bolinger in his paper "On Defining the Morpheme." Matthews's *Morphology* is a recent treat-ment of many of the topics discussed in this chapter. A sharp attack on the concept of the morpheme is contained in Koutsoudas' "Morpheme Reconsid-ered." The most extensive description of word formation in English is Marchand's *Categories and Types of Present-Day English Word-Formation.*

EXERCISES

5-1 Check to make sure that you understand each of the terms printed in **boldface** in Chapter 5.

5-2 Chapter 5 makes distinctions between certain terms. Express the distinction between the following terms as clearly as you can: *allomorph* and *morpheme; phonological conditioning* and *morphological conditioning; regular allo-morph* and *irregular allomorph; free morpheme* and *bound morpheme; inflection* and *derivation.*

5-3 Write out the following words in phonemic notation and show the morphemic breaks with a hyphen, as follows: *received* /rə-siyv-d/.

1 abroad	**5** displacement	**9** goodness	**13** unassuming
2 antidote	**6** disregarded	**10** inducted	**14** unfolding
3 baker	**7** followers	**11** repellants	**15** wishes
4 criticized	**8** foolishness	**12** repressed	**16** witnessed

5-4 Which allomorph of the "not" prefix occurs in each of the following words? Which words may have two choices, depending on the particular style of speech that is used?

1 illegal	**4** immodest	**7** inadmissible	**10** inequitable
2 illiterate	**5** impossible	**8** incoherent	**11** irrelevant
3 illogical	**6** improbable	**9** inconceivable	**12** irreversible

5-5 The English "plural" morpheme has a variety of allomorphs. In addition, sometimes subtle changes occur in the noun to which it is affixed. State as clearly as you can how each of the following plurals is formed, that is, the "plural" allomorph which occurs and any change or changes in the noun stem.

1 boxes	**5** data	**9** men	**13** tacks
2 brethren	**6** feet	**10** mice	**14** wigs
3 children	**7** houses	**11** oxen	**15** wives
4 crises	**8** indices	**12** sheep	**16** women

5-6 The English "past tense" morpheme has a variety of allomorphs. In addition, sometimes subtle changes occur in the verb to which it is affixed. State as clearly as you can how each of the following past tenses is formed, that is, the "past tense" allomorph which occurs and any change or changes in the verb stem.

1 bent	**4** drank	**7** hit	**10** stopped
2 bled	**5** dug	**8** rose	**11** wept
3 crept	**6** grabbed	**9** spent	**12** wounded

5-7 How many morphemes does each of the following words contain? What reasons do you have for making your decision in each case?

1 bandage	**4** equate	**7** lyric	**10** trial
2 basal	**5** fallacy	**8** manual	**11** typical
3 create	**6** lunacy	**9** rustic	**12** voyage

5-8 The following words have been grouped together since each contains an *ab*-prefix. What does *ab-* mean? Can all the words easily be divided into two or more morphemes without leaving a uniquely occurring morpheme, as in the *cran-* of *cranberry*?

1 abdicate	**5** abject	**9** abolish	**13** absent
2 abduct	**6** abjure	**10** abrupt	**14** absolve
3 aberrant	**7** ablaut	**11** abscess	**15** absorb
4 abhor	**8** abnormal	**12** abscond	**16** abstract

5-9 The following sets of words have been classified as containing the meanings indicated. Do you agree with the classifications?

1 ad- ("to" or "forward")
accord, adhere, advertisement, affirm, aggregate, allude, announce, appendage, arrive, ascribe, associate, attendance
2 dis- ("apart from")
disown, displace, disqualify, disrupt, dissatisfied, dissect, dissolve, distaste, distort
3 per- ("throughout" or "completely")
perception, percussion, perennial, perfect, permeate, persist, persistence, perversion

5-10 Each of the following compounds is made up of two parts. How do the parts relate to each other? For example, a *fleabite* is a "bite from a flea," but a *birdcage* is a "cage for a bird." Indicate which words are particularly difficult to account for in this way.

1 bedside	9 heavyweight	17 paintbrush	25 strongbox
2 bypass	10 hothead	18 paleface	26 sunshine
3 comedown	11 madman	19 password	27 tenderfoot
6 crybaby	12 mailbox	20 pay dirt	28 threadbare
5 doorknob	13 nightfall	21 pigpen	29 uphold
6 frogman	14 offspring	22 put-on	30 wallflower
7 hardwood	15 outlaw	23 rainbow	31 water pipe
8 headache	16 overripe	24 smallpox	32 windowpane

5-11 It is customary to say that French feminine adjectives are derived from masculine adjectives by adding -e. However, it appears that the facts of pronunciation of certain adjectives are best explained by deriving their masculine forms from the feminine ones. Try to formulate the necessary rule from the following data:

FEMININE	MASCULINE	GLOSS
1 chaude/šod/	chaud/šo/	"hot"
2 fraîche/frɛš/	frais/frɛ/	"fresh"
3 froide/frwad/	froid/frwa/	"cold"
4 grosse/gros/	gros/gro/	"fat"
5 mauvaise/movɛz/	mauvais/movɛ/	"bad"
6 petite/ptit/	petit/pti/	"little"
7 soûle/sul/	soûl/su/	"drunk"

5-12 Try to explain the morphemic composition of the English number system. To do so, you will have to write out each number phonemically and then examine the arrangements of any morphemes you wish to postulate.

5-13 The following pairs of words appear to be related in some way. In which cases is the relationship one that can easily be expressed morphologically? What problems are there in the other cases?

1 act, active	6 in, inning
2 broad, breadth	7 people, popular
3 crumb, crumble	8 point, punctual
4 dead, death	9 slow, sloth
5 devil, diabolic	10 young, youth

6

CONSTITUENTS AND PATTERNS

Chapter 5 provided an entry point into questions of meaning by describing ways in which meaning units can be identified. The chapter also introduced the concept of the word as a minimal unit of meaning that is freely pronounceable by itself in a language. Nevertheless, in no language do utterances consist of words strung together in random order. Certain important constraints exist concerning how words fit together in utterances. For example, a pair of English words like *the* and *boy* seem to fit together better as *the boy* than as *boy the,* and *John kissed Mary* is a more intuitively satisfying arrangement of these three words than is *John Mary kissed.* Both *boy the* and *John Mary kissed* can occur as sequences in English, as in *He was the boy the man wanted* and *It was John Mary kissed,* but such sequences can exist only within longer sequences and have no meaning apart from the longer sequences. What we require is some principle that allows us to make interesting claims about the arrangements of words in these utterances and to distinguish between sequences such as *the boy* and *boy the.*

CONSTITUENTS AND CONSTRUCTIONS

In an utterance such as *the boy jumped* a closer relationship exists between *the* and *boy* than between *boy* and *jumped.* For example, if native speakers of English are asked to divide *the boy jumped* into two parts, they will almost certainly choose to make the division between *the boy* and *jumped,* as follows:

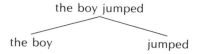

They will proceed to divide *the boy* between *the* and *boy* so that the whole utterance will be subdivided as follows:

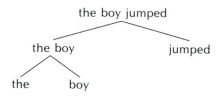

The above method of diagraming suggests that we must make the first division between *the boy* and *jumped* and a second division between *the* and *boy*. The divisions are ordered in importance within a very simple hierarchy.

We use **constituent** to refer to any word or group of words that appears at the bottom of one of the lines in diagrams such as those used above. When two constituents are joined together by two lines in a diagram, these constituents are said to be in construction with each other. A **construction** is a relationship between constituents. Actually, this explanation neatly reverses the claim that is being made: the existence of constituents and constructions allows us to draw diagrams such as those above; consequently, the diagraming represents constituents and constructions rather than determines them. In the last diagram *the* and *boy* are constituents in construction with each other, *the boy* and *jumped* are constituents in construction with each other, and *the boy jumped* is an independent constituent, therefore a total utterance.

Many linguists believe that a great number of interesting observations can be made about languages using the terms *constituent* and *construction*. They hypothesize that utterances in any language are made up of constituents in construction with each other and that these constructions occur in hierarchies such as the one shown above. According to such a hypothesis, utterances are not composed of sequences of words in a simple linear, additive fashion. Instead, utterances have a kind of depth, because the claim that they are composed of hierarchies of constructions means that utterances must have an additional dimension to their obvious linear dimension. The remainder of this chapter examines several aspects of this concept of the syntactic depth of utterances.

Constituents of Words

We could make still another division in *the boy jumped* if we wanted to cut below the level of the word, because *jumped* can be divided into *jump* and *-ed*. This construction can be diagramed in several ways, as follows:

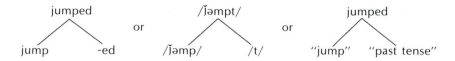

Each of the three diagrams reveals the constituents of *jumped* differently: by their spelling, by their phonemic realization, and by their meaning. Each diagram therefore suggests something different about the constituent structure of *jumped*. A roughly similar approach to the constituent structure of the word *men* shows the differences even more clearly:

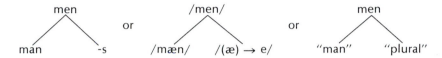

Using conventional spelling, we can show the constituents of the word *unhappy* to be *un-* and *happy*:

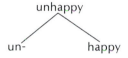

However, not all words containing affixes are as easy to analyze into their constituent parts as *unhappy*. More complicated words require a hierarchical ordering of constructions. For example, *unhappiness* and *playboys* must be analyzed into the following hierarchies:

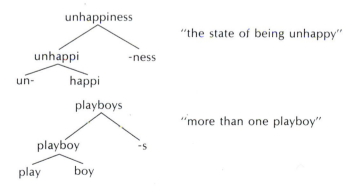

The meanings given to the right of each diagram are those that are most appropriate for each word for speakers of English. The meaning of *unhappiness* is something like "the state of being unhappy"; it is not something like "the opposite of happiness," even though *unhappiness* may indeed be used as an antonym for *happiness*. Hence the following diagram would be incorrect for *unhappiness*:

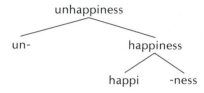

A speaker using the word *unhappiness* is more concerned with the state of being unhappy than with specifying the opposite of the state of being happy. The constituent structure shown in the above diagram captures this concern. Likewise, *playboys* does not mean "boys who play" but "more than one playboy," *playboy* being a pluralized stem in this case.

Disrespectful is a more difficult example to analyze. Alternative solutions are possible:

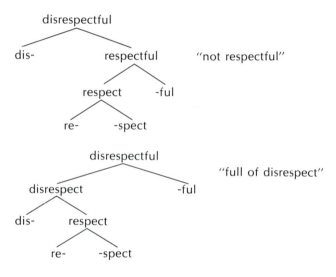

A *disrespectful* person or gesture is one that is either "not respectful" or "full of disrespect." Possibly the second interpretation is better than the first, for a *disdainful* person is someone who is "full of disdain" for someone or something rather than someone who is "not dainful." This last interpretation is meaningless because *dainful* does not occur in English.

Constituents of Word Groups

The kinds of problems just exemplified multiply when attempts are made to show the constituent structures of utterances, or parts of utterances. For example, each of the following utterances creates a different problem: *very pretty girls; two young girls; I can go; I can't go; Are you ready?; Did he go?*; and *Jack and Jill.* We will look at each of these examples in turn.

Ignoring for the moment the peculiar problem associated with the **bi-**

morphemic word *girls,* we can propose two different analyses for *very pretty girls,* as follows:

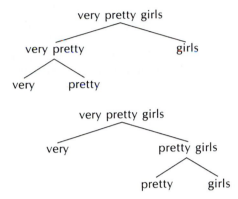

The first interpretation accords with the native speaker's intuition, for *very pretty girls* are "girls who are very pretty" rather than "pretty girls who are very," which is quite meaningless. We can compare this analysis of *very pretty girls* with that of *two young girls,* the correct analysis for which appears to be as follows:

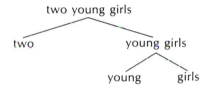

This last analysis brings sharply into focus the problem that was momentarily ignored in *very pretty girls,* that of the analysis of *girls.* An obvious relationship exists between *two* and the plural *-s* of *girls.* However, the following analysis, which goes below the word level, does not show that relationship:

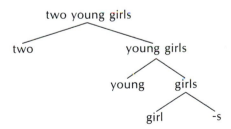

Perhaps such a failure is unimportant. On the other hand though, the failure might indicate that this kind of analysis by successive **binary** cutting, that is cutting into two parts, has certain deficiencies. We will return to this point shortly.

A constituent analysis of *I can go* seems to be straightforward:

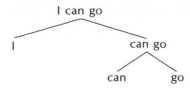

The following alternative analysis can be rejected as not according with the intuition of native speakers of English:

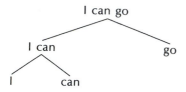

If we try to substitute single-word constituents within the two structures in place of *can go* in the first and *I can* in the second, we observe that the words that can be substituted for *can go* differ in an important way from those that can be substituted for *I can:*

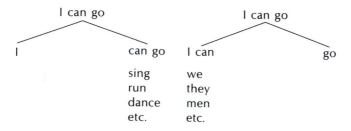

Sing, run, and *dance* are like *can go* in that they are all verbs or verb phrases forming a sentence predicate; however, *we, they,* and *men,* being all nouns or pronouns, differ from *I can,* which is a pronoun plus a **modal** verb. There is no structural similarity between *we, they,* and *men* and *I can* in this case.

I can't go raises a problem not unlike the one that occurred with *two young girls.* One analysis of *I can't go* is as follows:

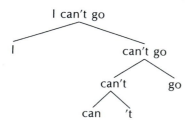

However, *I can't go* is a negation of *I can go;* consequently, an alternative analysis can be proposed, as follows:

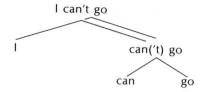

This last analysis shows the constituents of *I can't go* to be *I can go* and *'t*. However, there is something very different about such an analysis: the diagram shows that one constituent *'t* ("negative") appears to be inserted into another constituent *I can go*. It is as though the sentence is basically *I can go* plus *'t* or *I can go* plus "negative," as in the following diagram:

In this case, the broken line represents a more abstract structure than the one which the actual sentence has in its realization in words.

A similar kind of observation can be made about *Are you ready?* Two of the constituents appear to be *you* and *are ready*, with *you* inserted between *are* and *ready*. *You* is one constituent and *are ready* is another, and the two constituents form an interrogative construction when *you* and *are* are inverted. A constituent such as *are ready*, the parts of which are separated by another constituent, is called a **discontinuous constituent.** An alternative "abstract" diagraming of *Are you ready?* is:

It may be of interest to ask what kinds of discontinuity occur in languages, and then to ask what the best procedures are for handling such discontinuities within constituent analysis.

Did he go? is even more of a problem than *Are you ready?* in that it bears less resemblance to the related statement form *He went* than *Are you ready?* bears to its related statement form *You are ready.* However, such an analysis does not deal satisfactorily with the occurrence of the past tense form of the verb *do* in the question. We can also maintain that the proper constituents of *Did he go?* are *he went* and "question," not *He* and *did go,* since *Did he go?* is the question form of *He went.*

Multiple Constituents

So far the number of constituents in any construction has always been two, even though problems have arisen in certain cases in connection with determining the actual constituents, particularly if discontinuity is to be avoided wherever possible. However, an example such as *Jack and Jill* seems to be a counterexample to the observation that constructions are always binary, unless *Jack and Jill* contains a discontinuous constituent. Such an analysis, however, makes *Jack Jill* a strange kind of discontinuous constituent and establishes a relationship between *Jack Jill* and *and* that is of a completely different order from the relationship of *the* and *boy* in *the boy* or *dogs* and *bark* in *dogs bark.* On the other hand, if *Jack and Jill* is analyzed as consisting of three parts, we cannot claim that all constructions are binary:

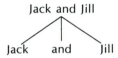

Of course, constructions employing such words as *and, but,* and *or* may be regarded as exceptions to the principle that constructions are binary. An alternative procedure is to treat such words as *and, but,* and *or* as though they did not actually occur in constructions as constituents. *Jack and Jill* could then be diagramed as follows, with *and* encircled to show that it marks a particular type of construction rather than that it is itself a constituent in a construction:

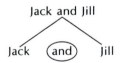

However, when three or more constituents are joined together, as in *Peter, Paul, and Mary* or *I came, I saw, I conquered,* an exception must still be made to the principle that all constructions are binary.

Constituent Analysis

Even though certain difficulties arise, constituent analysis appears to be a useful approach to describing how morphemes and words relate to each other in utterances. Whole utterances may be diagramed in depth using this kind of analysis; the resulting diagrams are called **constituent structures.** The constituent structures of the following sentences are diagramed down to the word level only, with intermediate constituents omitted:

The boy chased the dog.

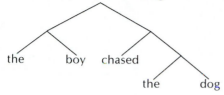

The old dog lay down.

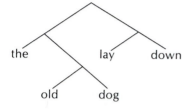

Suddenly, Jack ran to the back.

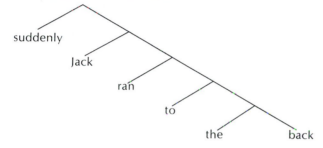

He took his umbrella because it was raining.

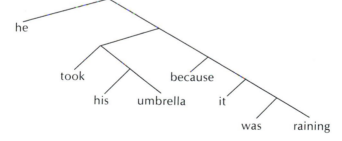

He ran up a bill.

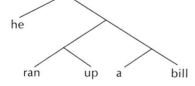

He ran up a hill.

Jack, Fred, and Peter went.

This analytic technique obviously has a wide usefulness, for it allows us to represent the structure of a sentence as a hierarchical array of constructions which are usually binary. It is not so useful with certain types of sentences not illustrated above for reasons already hinted at. For example, negative and question sentences create problems because of discontinuity. Even sentences such as those immediately above can be troublesome if any serious attempt is made to deal with problems such as tense and number. A still more difficult question to resolve is that of explaining how one analysis appears to be better than another. Since justification of the preferred analysis often seems to depend on intuition, we may be overlooking an important source of data when we do not acknowledge how important such intuition is in preferring one analysis to another.

CONSTRUCTION TYPES

Modification

An analysis of the constructions that occur in sentences reveals patterns of similarity. For example, there is a recurrent pattern in which one of the constituents seems to be a head (H) of some kind and the other constituent a modifier (M):

old man

```
        old man
        /      \
    (M)         (H)
    old         man
```

In this case the modifier *old* is an adjective and the head *man* is a noun.

```
      runs slowly
      /        \
  (H)           (M)
  runs          slowly
```

In this case the modifier *slowly* is an adverb and the head *runs* a verb.

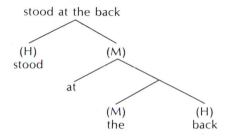

stood at the back

(H)
stood

(M)

at

(M)
the

(H)
back

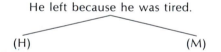

Slowly, he stood up.

(M)
slowly

(H)

he

(H)
stood

(M)
up

The above two examples contain two additional kinds of modifiers: *at the back* is a prepositional phrase serving as an adverbial modifier of *stood,* and *slowly* is an adverb which modifies the whole clause *he stood up.* The next sentence contains a whole clause *because he was tired* serving as a modifier of another clause, *he left:*

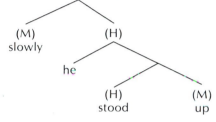

He left because he was tired.

(H)
he left

(M)
because he was tired

This kind of construction is called a structure of **modification.** It is also sometimes called an **endocentric construction** because the total construction (H plus M, or M plus H) has the same distributional characteristics as the head constituent (H): *The man came, The old man came; He runs, He runs slowly;* and *He stood, tall and upright, He stood at the back, tall and upright.*

Predication

A structure of **predication** contains two constituents: a subject (Sb) and a predicate (P):

John sang.

(Sb)
John

(P)
sang

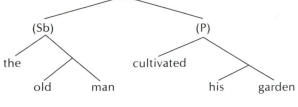

The old man cultivated his garden.

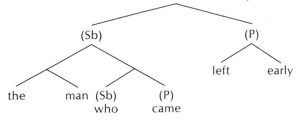

The man who came left early.

Different kinds of subjects and predicates are illustrated in the above examples: a noun and verb in *John* and *sang;* a noun phrase and verb plus object in *the old man* and *cultivated his garden;* a pronoun and verb in *who* and *came;* and a noun phrase which includes a relative clause and verb plus adverb in *the man who came* and *left early.*

Complementation

A structure of **complementation** contains a verbal (V) and a complement (C):

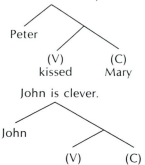

Peter kissed Mary.

John is clever.

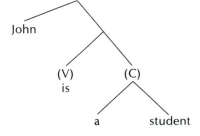

John is a student

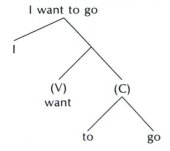

The four **complements** illustrated are a noun (*Mary*), used as an object of a transitive verb, an adjective (*clever*) and a noun phrase (a *student*) used as complements of *is*, and an infinitive (*to go*) used as a verb complement.

Subordination

A structure of **subordination** contains a subordinator (Sub), which is either a preposition, a particle, or a subordinating conjunction (a word like *in, over, to, after, because,* and so on), and a dependent unit (D):

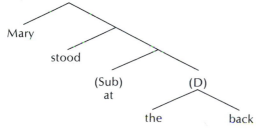

In this example *at* is a preposition and *at the back* is a prepositional phrase.

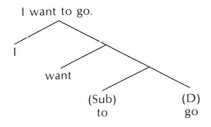

To is the marker of the infinitive verb *to go* rather than a preposition; such markers are sometimes referred to as particles.

She cried when she fell down.

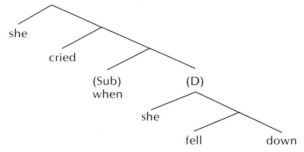

When is a subordinating conjunction which precedes the full clause *she fell down*.

Coordination

A structure of **coordination** contains a marker or coordinator (Co) and two or more independent units (I). These independent units can be words, as in the first two examples below (*Jack, John,* etc.), phrases, or even whole sentences, as in the third example (*Jack sings, Mary dances*).

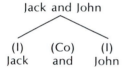

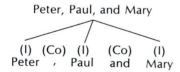

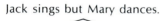
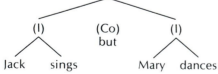

HIERARCHIES OF CONSTRUCTIONS

We are now in a position to diagram sentences showing not only their constituent elements but also the kinds of constructions in which these elements are arranged hierarchically, as follows:

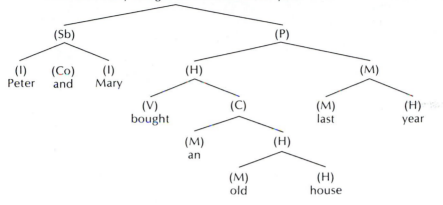

Peter and Mary bought an old house last year.

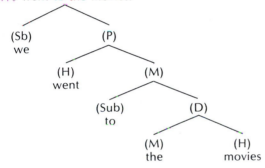

We went to the movies.

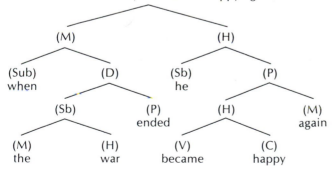

When the war ended, he became happy again.

A sentence such as *He asked what I wanted* may be analyzed as having *what* as a subordinator (Sub) and *I wanted* as a dependent (D) to avoid discontinuity:

He asked what I wanted.

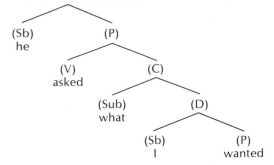

Such an analysis is not entirely satisfactory, however, because there is a sense in which *what* is in a complement relationship to *wanted* and the diagram above gives no hint of this fact. On the other hand, in a sentence such as *John is old* the diagraming suggests that *old* is a complement of *is;* however, *old* is also a modifier of *John,* a fact the analysis fails to indicate. Such weaknesses may be a further indication that it is necessary to analyze sentences at some greater "depth" than that of **surface structure** alone.

Forms and Functions

Constituent analysis enables us to distinguish between linguistic forms and linguistic functions. As we have indicated in the preceding pages, different linguistic forms can function alike. For example, a structure of modification can have different parts of speech or structural groups for its constituents:

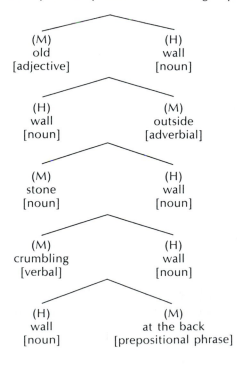

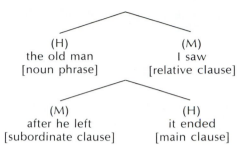

(H)
the old man
[noun phrase]

(M)
I saw
[relative clause]

(M)
after he left
[subordinate clause]

(H)
it ended
[main clause]

Likewise, a structure of coordination can conjoin a variety of forms: nouns (*men and women*); verbs (*sing and dance*); clauses (*after the war ended but before the peace treaty was signed*); and so on. Each branching in the tree shows a relationship, or construction, but numerous possible combinations of linguistic units are available to "fill" each relationship. The relationship is a functional one in each case: modification, coordination, and so on. However, the relationship is expressed through linguistic forms: nouns, verbs, verb phrases, clauses, and so on.

SENTENCE PATTERNS

As we have indicated, numerous problems arise in making constituent analyses of sentences, and arbitrary decisions must sometimes be made. Partly for this reason an alternative approach to sentence analysis through using sentence patterns has been proposed. This approach holds that the sentences in any language are constructed from a rather small set of basic structural patterns and through certain processes involving the expansion or transformation of these basic patterns.

Each of the following English sentences exemplifies a different sentence pattern.

1 Dogs bark.   noun + verb

2 Dogs chase cats.   noun^1 + verb + noun^2

3 Dogs are animals.   noun^1 + *be* + noun^1

Sentence 1, with its noun + verb arrangement is an example of a subject, **intransitive**-predicate sentence pattern. Sentence 2, with its noun^1 + verb + noun^2 arrangement (in which the superscripted numerals indicate that the nouns do not have a common reference) is an example of a subject, **transitive**-predicate, direct-object sentence pattern. Sentence 3, with its noun^1 + *be* + noun^1 arrangement (the nouns of which have a common reference) is an example of a subject, **copula,** noun-complement sentence pattern. We can describe a variety of English patterns in addition to the three given above:

4 Dogs are nice.   noun + *be* + adjective (subject, copula, adjective complement)

5 Dogs make John happy.   noun^1 + verb + noun^2 + adjective (subject, transitive predicate, direct object, object-adjective complement)

6 John gave Fred money.	noun^1 + verb + noun^2 + noun^3 (subject, transitive predicate, indirect object, direct object)
7 We elected Joan president.	noun^1 + verb + noun^2 + noun^2 (subject, transitive predicate, direct object, object-noun complement)
8 John is here.	noun + *be* + adverbial (subject, copula, adverb)

In addition to these patterns, other frequently occurring patterns in English are:

9 It's raining.	*it* + *be* + weather or time expression
10 There's a man outside.	*there* + inverted clause containing an indefinite subject
11 It's good that you said so.	*it* + *be* + adjective + *that* + clause

Undoubtedly still other patterns exist. For example, not all verbs which take objects are like *Dogs chase cats.* Sentences like *John has three sisters* and *The book weighs two pounds* cannot be made into passives (* *Three sisters are had by John* and * *Two pounds are weighed by the book*), unlike *Dogs chase cats* (*Cats are chased by dogs*). So sentences with verbs such as *have* and *weigh* must be sentences which conform to some other pattern. However, the eleven patterns given above are used over and over again in English sentences.

Nearly all the patterns have been described in two ways: first according to the linguistic forms that are usually present (noun, verb, adjective, and so on), and secondly according to the functions of these forms (subject, transitive predicate, adjective complement, and so on). The patterns are also all affirmative, active, statement patterns, for no negative, question, request, or passive patterns are included in the list.

Expansions and Transformations

Only a limited number of such patterns are available in English, and longer and more complicated sentences can best be described as being made up from expansions and transformations of the patterns given previously:

Our two old dogs were chasing the neighbors' cats.
       (Dogs chase cats.)

In this case expansion is achieved through extensive modification: *our two old* modifying *dogs, were* and *-ing* modifying *chase,* and *the neighbors'* modifying *cats.* A similar use of expansion occurs in the following sentence:

The award for bravery made John's sister extremely happy last night.
       (Award made sister happy.)

However, the next sentence raises several problems:

The little boy was where his mother had left him.
            (Boy was there.)

The last example contains two **finite verbs,** that is, verbs which show time as either present or past tense; in this case *was* and *had* both indicate past tense. (In the above sentence *left* is the past participle of *leave* not the past tense form of that verb.) The sentence *The little boy was where his mother had left him* is made up of two patterns which have been combined: *boy was* [*there*] and *mother left him,* with the second of these patterns actually used as an expansion of part of the first pattern, of the [*there*] in the first pattern to be exact:

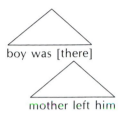

boy was [there]

mother left him

This diagram also introduces a useful convention for presenting grammatical information, the triangle. A triangle represents a total construction (here a grammatical construction with its own subject and predicate) without specifying its internal structure and components. It is useful for showing the interrelationships of the various constructions when two or more occur in some larger construction, as in the above example. A fuller diagraming of the whole sentence is as follows:

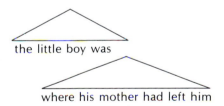

the little boy was

where his mother had left him

Further complications arise in such sentences as *He asked to go to hear the lecture,* with its long complement structure *to go to hear the lecture,* and, of course, in negative, question, request, and passive sentences and combinations of these. *He asked to go to hear the lecture* contains only one finite verb *ask* so the pattern resembles a subject, transitive-predicate, direct-object pattern with an expanded direct object. However, such a solution is almost certainly counterintuitive. Certainly no passive sentence can be made out of the above sentence, for * *To go to hear the lecture was asked by him* is unacceptable, and *to go to hear the lecture* has a different relationship to *He asked* in the above sentence than does *John* to *He asked* in *He asked John.* We can see the difference if we use triangles to diagram the possible clauses in the sentence:

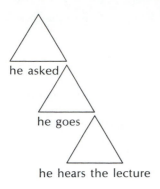

he asked

he goes

he hears the lecture

The sentence-pattern approach to sentences containing sequences of nonfinite verbs (that is, verbs that do not indicate time) is not altogether a very satisfactory one, producing, as it does, ad hoc solutions.

We could establish separate sets of patterns for negative, question, request, and passive sentences, and for combinations of these, so that each of the above eleven types of sentence would exhibit a more or less full set of patterns of its own, just as does *Dogs chase cats* in the examples which follow:

Dogs chase cats.	(Affirmative)
Dogs don't chase cats.	(Negative)
Cats are chased by dogs.	(Passive)
Cats aren't chased by dogs.	(Negative-passive)
Chase cats!	(Request)
Don't chase cats!	(Negative-request)
Be chased by dogs!	(Passive-request)
Don't be chased by dogs!	(Negative-passive-request)
Do dogs chase cats?	(Question)
Don't dogs chase cats?	(Negative-question)
Are cats chased by dogs?	(Passive-question)
Aren't cats chased by dogs?	(Negative-passive-question)

Alternatively, *Dogs chase cats* could be said to exhibit some kind of basic pattern and the other sentence types could be regarded as **transformations** of this basic pattern: negative, question, passive-request, negative-passive-question, and so on. Such a solution avoids a proliferation of patterns and captures certain facts known to speakers of English: active sentences have passive counterparts; affirmative sentences have negative counterparts; any statement can be rearranged to demand a *yes* or *no* answer; and so on. However, not only should the optimal grammatical system for English account for this intuitive knowledge that speakers have, but it should also accomplish this goal in a principled way. This chapter has tried to find such principles but without any great success. For example, we have felt a constant need to get below the surface structure of sentences to look at deeper relationships and a still further need to show relationships among sentences. The next chapter has such principles as its central concern.

BIBLIOGRAPHIC NOTES

The topics covered in this chapter are covered in Fries' *Structure of English* and in two books which owe much to Fries' work, Francis' *Structure of American English* (with an accompanying workbook by McDavid and Green) and Roberts' *Patterns of English*. Two technical papers on problems of constituent analysis are Wells' "Immediate Constituents" and Longacre's "String Constituent Analysis."

EXERCISES

6-1 Check to make sure that you understand each of the terms printed in **boldface** in Chapter 6.

6-2 Chapter 6 makes distinctions between certain terms. Express the distinction between the following terms as clearly as you can: *constituent* and *construction; form* and *function; expansion* and *transformation; active* and *passive; finite verb* and *nonfinite verb; transitive* and *intransitive.*

6-3 Diagram the constituent structure of each of the following words, phrases, and sentences. Explain the cuts you make when an explanation appears to be necessary.

1 dehumanize
2 retractable
3 antiwar movements
4 free traders
5 a very old brick house down the street
6 He might have done it.
7 His young friend arrived yesterday.
8 Last night the boys went to the movies.
9 Can you see what I see?
10 Jack and Jill went up the hill, a fact we should all remember.

6-4 Diagram the constituent structure of each of the following sentences and label the constructions as structures of modification, predication, and so on:

1 The two boys left early.
2 I left when the show ended.
3 He bought some bread and cheese.
4 I cannot understand what she is saying.
5 Did you do that? Certainly not!

6-5 Use constituent-structure diagrams to resolve the ambiguities of the following sentences or newspaper headlines. In which cases do you need some further labeling of the structures to resolve the ambiguity?

1 Flying planes can be dangerous.
2 They have injured people there.
3 NIAGARA FALLS AT LAST

   4 He went to a criminal lawyer.
   5 It's too hot to eat.
   6 Call me a cab.
   7 MENTALLY RETARDED TEACHERS SOUGHT BY EDUCATION DEPARTMENT
   8 I like John's picture.
   9 GIRL HUNTER SAYS FATHER SETS EXAMPLE
   10 The police stopped fighting after dark.

6-6 Rewrite each of the ten sentences in 6-5 in two different ways so as to remove the ambiguity.   Make as few changes as possible in doing so.

6-7 Describe the basic sentence pattern used in each of the following sentences:

   1 The boy is big.
   2 The dog chased the cat.
   3 They elected him president.
   4 The men are all friends.
   5 We gave him a gift.
   6 The girls go quite often.
   7 We appointed him secretary of the group.
   8 We sent her a bouquet of roses.
   9 The soldiers were very unhappy.
   10 All cats are animals.
   11 All the students wrote very good papers.
   12 The gift made her very happy.
   13 John seems happy.
   14 Your friend is at the door.
   15 The book John gave him is very good.
   16 After the war ended, they presented the medal to him.
   17 They will leave when you send him the answer.
   18 We gave him five dollars because he had lost his money.
   19 What I want is none of your business.
   20 I know where he is.

6-8 The following sentences exhibit patterns some of which are variations of those in 6-7.   However, there are certain new patterns.   Which patterns are the variations, and which are new?   Describe the variations.

   1 Ouch!
   2 Send her some roses.
   3 Who gave him that idea?
   4 Are they working steadily?
   5 The dog didn't chase the cat.
   6 The cat was chased by the dog.
   7 Chasing cats is fun for dogs.
   8 Cats run, jump, chase, and scratch.
   9 I don't know what happened to him.
   10 I promise I won't do it again.
   11 To understand is to forgive.
   12 Tell her I love her.
   13 There's a fly in my soup.
   14 It's raining.
   15 It's good that he did it.

GENERATIVE-
TRANSFORMATIONAL
GRAMMAR

Chapter 6 outlined a method that could be used to represent the structure of a sentence as a kind of inverted tree with labeled branches. For example, we can diagram the structure of a sentence like *The boy ran to the park* as follows to show the linguistic forms out of which it is constituted:

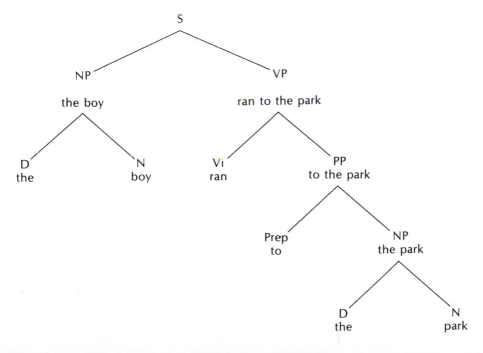

In this diagram the various constituents are labeled as follows: S for sentence; NP for noun phrase; VP for verb phrase; D for determiner; N for noun; Vi for intransitive verb; PP for prepositional phrase; and Prep for preposition.

Chapter 6 raised the problem of how it is that native speakers of English are able to assign such a structure to the sentence. One possible answer is that they can do so because, as native speakers, they have access to a set of rules which constrain them to produce grammatical sentences and to avoid ungrammatical sentences. Can we recast the above diagram in the form of a set of rules? If so, what are the consequences?

We might also ask that our rules help us account for the fact that native speakers of English perceive that the two sentences *This boy reads well* and *This book reads well* express different relationships between *boy* and *reads* and *book* and *reads*. The boy actually reads and does so with skill, but some unspecified person reads the book and does so easily because the book is well written. How can our rules capture such a perception?

We should note that sentences such as *I promised Fred to quit, I persuaded Fred to quit,* and *I expected Fred to quit* express different ideas as to who is to quit and between the first verb in each sentence and what follows. With the verb *promise* it is *I* who will quit, but with the verb *persuade* it is *Fred* who will quit. Fred is also the object of both *promised* and *persuaded,* but not of *expected.* These differences can be seen in the following diagrams:

How can rules help us state such facts about this kind of knowledge of their language which native speakers of English possess? This chapter and the two that follow seek answers to that question.

GENERATIVE GRAMMARS

Let us begin by recasting the diagram at the beginning of this chapter in the form of a set of rules that will produce, or **generate,** the diagram. For example, an alternative way of expressing the relationships among the topmost branches:

is as follows:

S → NP + VP

Such a rule states that a sentence (S) consists of (→) a noun phrase (NP) and (+) a verb phrase (VP). The same procedure may be used to express the relationship among the verb phrase (VP), intransitive verb (Vi), and prepositional phrase (PP):

The following rule expresses the relationship:

VP → Vi + PP

This rule states that a verb phrase (VP) consists of (→) an intransitive verb (Vi) and (+) a prepositional phrase (PP). The total set of rules, called **phrase-structure rules,** required to express all the relationships in the diagram for the sentence *The boy ran to the park* is as follows:

S → NP + VP
VP → Vi + PP
PP → Prep + NP
NP → D + N
D → *the*
N → *boy, park*
Vi → *ran*
Prep → *to*

Such a set of rules, or grammar, requires interpretation; consequently, we must have a set of conventions for interpreting the rules. For example, are the rules ordered or not, that is, must we proceed through the rules in a certain way? (The answer is that they are not ordered except for convenience of statement.) May an individual rule be changed at will or used only in part, or may only certain rules be used and the rest ignored? (The answer is that no change can be made in a rule if it is chosen, but not all rules need be chosen.) What claims about the nature of language and its users do the rules make? (The answer, as we shall see, is very powerful claims.) All these questions are not of equal importance, but none is unimportant. The last question about the nature of language and of language users is far more important to linguists than any of the other questions, because linguists are interested in finding out as much as possible about the phenomenon of language. Only by asking questions of the kind just indicated can they formulate hypotheses to be tested so that competing claims about language can be evaluated.

Sentence Basis

One generalization apparently captured by a set of rules of this kind is that a language consists of a set of sentences. Such a generalization is captured by the very first symbol, S, which stands for sentence. The initial S indicates that the grammar is to be about Ss and that the grammar is to be a grammar of sentences. Consequently, sentences are acknowledged to be the basic constituents of the language. A "language" is, therefore, a set of sentences, and a "sentence" itself is anything that is produced by the grammar. As we have previously indicated, the arrow means "consists of," so that an S consists of an NP and a VP, that is, a "noun phrase" and a "verb phrase," two further grammatical constituents. The relationship among the three units, S, NP, and VP, is also specified in that the S dominates both the NP and VP; that is, it includes both of these constituents. Because the NP also precedes the VP when the S is resolved into its constituents, the rule also specifies the linear arrangement of these constituents.

The fact that the rules show that S consists of an NP and a VP indicates that both the NP and the VP must be present in a sentence. If we also want to describe sentences without subjects or predicates, then we must either rewrite the rule S → NP + VP or we must rewrite the second rule to delete either the NP or the VP of the first rule as required. The rules are ordered to the extent that it is more convenient to state some facts before others, for example, to state the need for PPs or VPs *before* stating what either of these consists of. Proceeding through a set of rules sequentially is much more economical than proceeding through a set in some random manner.

Generativeness

The set of rules given above for the sentence *The boy ran to the park* is extremely limited in a variety of ways. For example, the set can be used to produce only a finite number of sentences, actually only four sentences:

1 The boy ran to the park.

2 The boy ran to the boy.

3 The park ran to the boy.

4 The park ran to the park.

Two of these sentences, sentences 3 and 4, turn out to be rather strange, and the second sentence is a little peculiar with its twofold occurrence of *boy*. Almost certainly an adequate grammar of English should not generate sentences such as 3 and 4, or, if it does, should indicate in some way that these sentences are less acceptable than sentences 1 and 2. However, we may experience some difficulty in deciding which alternative is better.

Much more serious at the moment, though, is the fact that this grammar generates so few sentences. A native speaker of a language can generate infinitely many sentences. What we need is a grammar that will generate any sentence in the language and no sentence which is not in the language; that is, the grammar should generate *all and only* sentences of whatever language it is the grammar of, just as a native speaker does. In the sense used here "to generate" means to produce possible sentences and, in so doing, to produce grammatical descriptions of these sentences. A grammar should not produce sentences which native speakers clearly reject, for such sentences, being ungrammatical, will deviate from the rules. In practice, however, in discussing sentences, we often find no sharp dichotomy between grammatical and ungrammatical but rather a continuum on a scale of grammaticality with clearly grammatical sentences (*The dog chased the cat*) at one end, clearly ungrammatical sentences (**Dog the the chased cat*) at the other, and various degrees of grammaticality in between (?*Colorless green ideas sleep furiously; ?The tree groaned in the wind*).

The last principle, that the grammar should generate only the sentences of a language and nothing which is not a sentence in the language, is clearly an important principle to be observed in writing rules. Writing a set of rules to generate *all* English sentences would not be a difficult task, but writing a set of rules to generate all English sentences *and only English sentences* has so far proved to be impossible. For example, a computer could be programmed to print out random strings of English words drawn from an unabridged English dictionary, the strings to be of any length. The result would be the occasional production of an acceptable English sentence, but the cost in terms of the production of unacceptable sentences would be prohibitive. It would be possible to refine the program in various ways, but so far no such refinement has come near to producing *all and only* English sentences. Yet a native speaker has just such an ability to produce all and only English sentences, and it should be our task to characterize that ability in any grammar that we write.

Types of Rules

We must make certain changes in the previous set of phrase-structure rules if it is to generate even the following four additional sentences: *The boy ran, The boy was young, The girl won a prize,* and *The girl won.* The goal now is to write one set of rules that will generate all five sentences; however, the set of rules, that is, the grammar, should not produce ungrammatical sentences like *The girl won to the park* or *The boy ate young*. The following set of rules suffices:

S → NP + VP

VP → $\begin{Bmatrix} \text{Vi} + \text{(PP)} \\ \text{Vt} + \text{(NP)} \\ \text{be} + \text{Adj} \end{Bmatrix}$

PP → Prep + NP

NP → D + N

D → the, a

N → boy, girl, park, prize

Vi → ran

Vt → won

be → was

Prep → to

Adj → young

The additional labels are Vt for transitive verb and Adj for adjective.

We can observe that two additional conventions for writing rules are employed in this last set. Both occur in the following rule:

VP → $\begin{Bmatrix} \text{Vi} + \text{(PP)} \\ \text{Vt} + \text{(NP)} \\ \text{be} + \text{Adj} \end{Bmatrix}$

The first convention is the use of **braces** { }. This convention requires one of the lines to be chosen from out of the braces. In the above case the braces indicate that a VP consists of any one of Vi + (PP), Vt + (NP), or be + Adj. One of the three must be chosen to rewrite any particular VP. The second convention is the use of **parentheses** ( ) to indicate an option: the unit within the parentheses may or may not be chosen as one pleases. That is, a Vt may occur alone or with an NP. In the above case, a VP may be said to consist of Vi or Vi + PP, or Vt or Vt + NP, or be + Adj. However, all of Vi, Vi + PP, Vt, Vt + NP, and be + Adj are VPs, or predicates of S. The rule allows for the five different predicates we have in the sentences: *ran* (Vi); *ran to the park* (Vi + PP); *won* (Vt); *won a prize* (Vt + NP); and *was young* (be + Adj).

This set of rules will generate many other sentences in addition to the five for which it was devised, for example, *The girl ran, A boy won a prize, The apple ran, A prize won the girl,* and *The park was young.* Some of these sentences are strange; consequently, the rules are not yet exact enough, nor do they account for any but a very few English sentences. We may hypothesize though that we could expand and refine the above set of rules so that the expanded refined set would generate all and only the sentences of English. This set would then be a very explicit grammar of the language. We might then claim that speakers of the language produce sentences by drawing upon just such a set of rules, for that set prescribes the form their utterances must take. Language learning in such a case would be the task of internalizing this same set of phrase-structure rules.

Of further interest are questions concerning the kinds of rules that are necessary in order to write a complete grammar of a language. The grammar given above employs braces and parentheses. The use of such devices represents a claim about the possible kinds of rules a grammar can have. The claim is that a grammar allows for certain choices and that these choices are of two kinds: the braces { } represent an obligatory choice, and the parentheses ( ) represent an optional choice. We are obligated to choose a predicate of one kind or another, but we may choose not to give objects to certain transitive verbs. Linguists are not interested in using ad hoc rules and devices to cover data in a language: they are vitally interested in what kinds of claims their rules seem to make about language in general, about speakers, and about such processes as language acquisition.

The set of rules given above could be expanded to account for many additional sentences, but even an expanded set might not be as revealing as we would like it to be. It might not make any very interesting claims about language in general or English in particular or it might not make claims we would seek to make. For example, native speakers of English know that the sentences *The old house fell down* and *The house which was old fell down* are related to each other; however, we cannot easily express such a relationship through a set of rules. Native speakers also know that *The boy chased the girl* and *The girl was chased by the boy* are related, but again we cannot easily write a set of rules of this kind to demonstrate that relationship and at the same time say something interesting about the structure of language in general and English in particular. They also know that *He needed the money more than Mary* is ambiguous ("He needed the money more than Mary needed the money" or "He needed the money more than he needed Mary"). Our rules should allow us to show the ambiguity in some way.

Such requirements have prompted many linguists to develop this model of linguistic description in various ways. The sets of rules given so far in this chapter are little more than explicit reformulations of one kind of constituent analysis of sentences. The reformulations do add the notions of rule, generation, and explicitness to what was discussed in Chapter 6, but they too do not succeed in the kinds of tasks in which constituent analysis failed.

DEEP AND SURFACE STRUCTURES

One possible way in which we might develop this model is to allow for rules which describe two kinds of structure for each sentence. One structure would be that of the sentence as it is actually produced and the other structure would contain all the units and relationships that are necessary for interpreting the meaning of the sentence. Consequently, a sentence such as *The old house fell down* might be said to have two structures: one is the structure of the sentence as it is pronounced or written, and the other is a more abstract structure that allows a native speaker of English to know that this sentence means both *The house fell down* and *The house was old*. In the same way, a native speaker of English knows that both *The boy chased the girl* and *The girl was chased by the boy* have similar meanings; consequently, we might seek to provide both sentences with much the same abstract structure, but to provide this abstract structure with two different realized structures because the actually produced sentences are different. An ambiguous sentence like *He needed the money more than Mary* should have different abstract structures because it has two clearly distinct meanings.

We can use the terms **deep structure** and **surface structure** to refer respectively to the abstract structure and to the actually produced structure. A crucial problem arises in stating the relationship of deep structure to surface structure, or vice versa. The term *transformational* will be used to refer to the relationship. Since the relationship is usually a complex one, we can best use *transformational* to apply to all the steps in the relationship, that is, to the total process of relating deep to surface structures. We can then employ **transformation** as a term for each step in the transformational process.

The transformational relationship between deep and surface structures and the transformations which relate the two kinds of structures can be illustrated by reference to the sentences given previously. The sentence *The old house fell down* is derived from a deep structure presented schematically with each triangle representing a clause (or S) as follows:

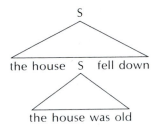

The following set of rules generates the above deep structure:

$$S \rightarrow NP + VP$$
$$VP \rightarrow \begin{Bmatrix} be + Adj \\ Vi + Adv \end{Bmatrix}$$
$$NP \rightarrow NP + (S)$$
$$NP \rightarrow D + N$$
$$D \rightarrow the$$
$$N \rightarrow house$$
$$Vi \rightarrow fell$$
$$Adj \rightarrow old$$
$$Adv \rightarrow down$$
$$be \rightarrow was$$

The above schematic drawing can now be replaced by the following representation of the deep structure:

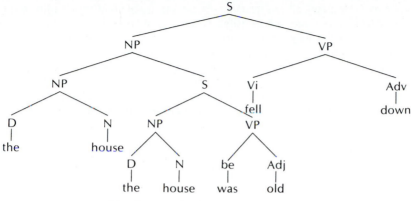

[the house [the house was old] fell down]

Recursion

One very important difference exists between the set of phrase-structure rules which generates such a deep structure and any previous set of rules we have used: In the last set of rules an S constituent appears both to the left of the rewriting symbol (S → NP + VP) and to the right of that symbol (NP → NP + (S)). When a constituent that has been rewritten by being used to the left of the rewriting symbol is used in the same or in a later rule to the right of the rewriting symbol, the rules take on a property called **recursion.** The rules become a recursive set, that is, a set that permits an infinite expansion. The following diagram illustrates such a possibility from a rule of the form NP → NP + (S):

Recursive rules of this kind allow us to expand a noun phrase by adding clauses, as in the nursery rhyme "The House that Jack Built": *This is the farmer . . . that kept the cook . . . that waked the priest . . . that married the man . . . that kissed the maiden . . . that milked the cow . . . that tossed the dog that worried the cat that killed the rat that ate the malt. . . .* Recursion allows clauses to be embedded within clauses (to form complex constructions) and to be conjoined to other clauses (to form compound constructions). Every language has this recursive property, for each language allows its users the possibility of creating an infinite set of sentences from the finite set of rules which speakers employ. The set of sentences is infinite because, among other things, it is always possible to add additional modifiers to any sentence. A nursery rhyme like "The House that Jack Built" could go on forever—the only limitations are human, not linguistic. The type of rule just illustrated, therefore, captures one critical generalization about language that we seek to make: The sentences of a language form an infinite set as a result of the recursive property of the rules that generate the set.

TRANSFORMATIONS

The next problem is that of deriving *The old house fell down* from *the house [the house was old] fell down* and of showing how *The old house fell down* is also related to *The house which was old fell down*. A grammar of a language contains one set of rules, the phrase-structure rules, which produce deep structures such as *the house [the house was old] fell down*. It also contains a set of transformational rules to turn deep structures into surface structures, that is, into actually produced sentences. One transformational rule states that if an NP + S sequence occurs dominated by an NP, and if that S dominates an NP whose referent is the same as the NP in the NP + S sequence, then the dominated NP ultimately becomes either *who* or *which*. This rule is called the relative transformation.

The house which was old fell down.

A further optional rule is the deletion transformation (*be*-deletion transformation) which allows for the removal of the *who* or *which* together with any form of the verb *be* that follows, giving *the house* [*old*] *fell down*.   Still another rule (adjective movement transformation) moves any resulting single adjective between the D and the N, that is, between *the* and *house* in this case to produce *The old house fell down*.

An alternative way of showing these transformations and the relationship of deep to surface structures is as follows:

Deep structure   [the house [the house was old] fell down]

■

relative transformation

➡

[the house [which was old] fell down]

■

be-deletion transformation

➡

[the house   [old]   fell down]

■

adjective movement transformation

➡

Surface structure   The old house fell down

We can observe that the transformational process also relates *The old house fell down* to *The house which was old fell down* since it derives the former through the latter in the process of going from deep to surface structure.   The difference between the two sentences resides in the fact that the *be*-deletion transformation applies in the first case but not in the second.

The grammar also helps us to see how the sentences *The boy chased the girl* and *The girl was chased by the boy* are related.   However, the second sentence is not a transformation of the first.   Transformations do not change one sentence into another; they change one structure into another, often a deep structure into a surface structure.   These two sentences have slightly different deep structures. The similarity in their meanings arises from the fact that the difference between the deep structures is slight, being almost entirely stylistic in nature.   We can note that a verb such as *chase* may be active or passive, depending on which noun phrase is brought into first position in the sentence.   In order to account for the occurrence of the passive we include a rule to expand the VP in the previous set of rules, as follows:

VP → (passive) + Vt + NP

If this optional passive constituent is chosen in going through the phrase-structure rules to produce a deep structure, then the passive transformation must be applied to this deep structure to turn it into a surface structure.   This transformation exchanges the NPs and introduces a form of the verb *be* before the Vt and *by* before the second NP, as follows:

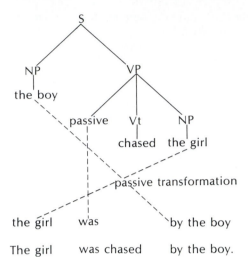

The girl   was chased   by the boy.

Using the graphical device of the triangle, we can illustrate the difference between the two sentences *The boy chased the girl* and *The girl was chased by the boy* as follows:

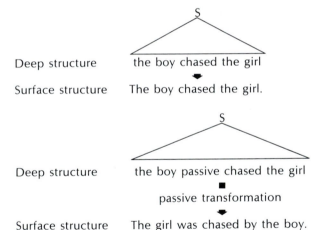

Deep structure   the boy chased the girl

Surface structure   The boy chased the girl.

Deep structure   the boy passive chased the girl

passive transformation

Surface structure   The girl was chased by the boy.

We can postulate that *He needed the money more than Mary* derives from alternative deep structures, as follows:

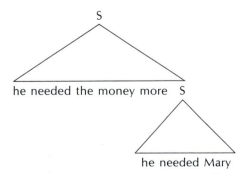

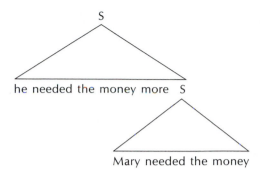

The comparison transformation which incorporates the lower sentence into the higher sentence by deleting part of the lower sentence realizes both deep structures in the same surface structure through the intermediate *He needed the money more than he needed Mary* and *He needed the money more than Mary needed the money.* These deep structures and the necessary transformational apparatus are undoubtedly inadequately expressed here, but the principle is correct—sentences with different meanings (including ambiguous sentences) derive from different deep structures.

GENERATIVE-TRANSFORMATIONAL GRAMMARS

A **generative-transformational grammar** contains two sets of rules. One set of rules, called **phrase-structure rules,** generates deep structures, and the other set of rules, called **transformational rules,** changes these deep structures into surface structures. Hence we employ the term *generative-transformational* for the grammar as a whole. The rules must be economical because scientific method dictates that if two systems cover the same data, the more economical system is to be preferred over the less economical. They must be plausible, in the sense of being natural or intuitively correct, because language is a natural human phenomenon. This last criterion is a lot more controversial to apply, however, being considerably more subjective than the first.

The rules must also be stated in a form which is not unique to a particular language. Languages are different (English is not Japanese and Tagalog is not Mixtec), but similarities do exist among languages. These similarities are sometimes referred to as linguistic **universals.** The grammar of any language would ideally show which features of that language are universal and which are specific to the language. A generative-transformational grammar accomplishes this task through the claim that certain conventions such as the "consists of" (rewriting) convention (→), parentheses and braces, rule-ordering, and transformations operating on structures must be employed in the description of all languages. On the other hand, the facts that in English N is rewritten as *book, dog, house,* and so on, or that the English subject NP precedes the English object NP, or that the English passive transformation switches the subject and object and introduces a form of *be,* past participle, and *by* into the surface structure, are facts peculiar to English, and therefore not universal.

The rules of a generative-transformational grammar also define various grammatical constituents such as noun phrase, verb phrase, noun, verb, and so on. Each of these terms covers a set of which the members have the same function in at least one linguistic process. Of course, since there are many linguistic processes, a need exists to specify a great many additional categories. However, the same principle applies in every case: if NP may be rewritten as either NP + S or D + N, then sentences must occur in which both NP + S and D + N function alike, as in the two passive sentences *He was attacked by the bear which killed the horse* and *He was attacked by the bear*. In these sentences *the bear which killed the horse* and *the bear* are subject NPs in the deep structures of the respective sentences. The passive transformation has moved them after the verb and *by*.

Various relations in the phrase-structure trees may also be labeled. For example, an NP immediately under or dominated by an S is the **subject** of that S:

$$S$$
$$|$$
$$NP$$

An NP immediately dominated by a VP is the **object** of that VP:

$$VP$$
$$|$$
$$NP$$

Consequently, constituents such as S, NP, VP, and so on, and functions of constituents such as subject and object, are given definitions and distinguished from each other in a generative-transformational grammar.

A generative-transformational grammar is a grammar of sentences. The S, for sentence, is an axiomatic starting point. Sentences themselves are the products of the grammar, so that one definition of a sentence in a language is anything that the grammar of that language generates. The grammar therefore encapsulates the claims that speakers of a language speak in sentences and that sentences are the basic units of linguistic communication. One possible further claim is that little or no need exists for grammarians to be concerned with any higher level unit than the sentence, for example, some kind of discourse or paragraph unit. These claims are no more than claims, or hypotheses, and as such, are subject to proof or disproof just as are all hypotheses put forward by scientists. They are not articles of faith.

The rules postulated by grammarians are also not meant to be rules that describe the mental processes of speakers of a language. No claim is being made that the rules and transformations of the grammarian are psychologically real, or that they have been internalized in some way by speakers, even though at times it may be tempting to make just that claim. Linguists do not know how the human mind works. Their interest is focused on language. We must be aware that no really adequate description of any language exists; consequently, no one can claim to know exactly what must be internalized. We must also acknowledge that in language learning and language use, human beings need not necessarily employ devices which linguists consider to be optimal from the viewpoint of language description.

BIBLIOGRAPHIC NOTES

This chapter is based on the ideas of Noam Chomsky as expounded in such books as *Syntactic Structures, Aspects of the Theory of Syntax,* and *Language and Mind.* Lyons' *Noam Chomsky* contains an interesting appraisal of Chomsky's work. Bach's *Syntactic Theory* is a recent comprehensive discussion of many fundamental issues in generative-transformational theory.

EXERCISES

7-1 Check to make sure that you understand each of the terms printed in **boldface** in Chapter 7.

7-2 Chapter 7 makes distinctions between certain terms. Explain the distinction between the following terms as clearly as you can: *deep structure* and *surface structure; phrase-structure rules* and *transformational rules.*

7-3 The following symbolic conventions are used in Chapter 7. Explain the meaning and use of each, giving an example: S; →; +; ( ); { }.

7-4 Write out all the "sentences" each of the following grammars generates. If this is not possible, indicate why not.

1 A → B C
   B → D (F)
   $D \to G \begin{Bmatrix} H \\ I \end{Bmatrix}$
   F → J K

2 A → B (C)
   $B \to D \begin{Bmatrix} E \\ F \end{Bmatrix}$
   F → G (HI)

3 A → (B) C D
   $C \to \begin{Bmatrix} E \\ F \end{Bmatrix}$
   E → D (G)
   F → (A) H
   $D \to \begin{Bmatrix} I \\ B \end{Bmatrix}$

7-5 Write out ten acceptable English sentences which the following grammatical rules generate. Write out ten unacceptable sentences which the rules generate. Why are they unacceptable? Write five acceptable sentences which the rules do not generate.

S → NP + VP

$VP \to \begin{Bmatrix} Vt + NP \\ Vi \end{Bmatrix}$ (Adv)

$Adv \to \begin{Bmatrix} Time \\ Place \end{Bmatrix}$

NP → (D) + N

Vt → stopped, stole, took, lost, moved

Vi → stood, fell, rushed, died

Time → yesterday, recently

Place → outside, behind

D → this, a, much

N → boy, dog, apples, cars, cake, cows, money

7-6 Write a simple set of rules that employs the conventions of Chapter 7 to generate the following sentences:

1 John ate an apple regularly.
2 The boy bought a pear.
3 A girl found his sandwich.
4 John stole sometimes.
5 The girl drank her coke.
6 John was there.

7-7 Write out five additional acceptable sentences that the grammar you composed for 7-6 generates. Write out five unacceptable sentences that the grammar you composed for 7-6 generates. In what ways would you have to modify that grammar in order to prevent such sentences from being generated?

7-8 Each of the following sentences has a part which is missing from its surface structure, but which can be understood from that structure. What is this part of the deep structure that is missing in each case? Write out a full sentence which contains the understood part.

1 I can do it if you can.
2 I expect her to go but not him.
3 Drink up!
4 Mary is prettier than Joan.
5 John must have seen it and Peter too.
6 Mary bought a pretty red dress and a green one.
7 If you are going to speak to him, I'm not.
8 He ate some mushrooms, but she didn't.
9 John and Mary kissed.
10 John and Fred married Sue and Mary respectively.
11 John is going to make one for Fred, and vice versa.
12 I couldn't have gone last week, nor could Peter.

8

ENGLISH SENTENCE TRANSFORMATIONS

This chapter is concerned with showing the deep structures of selected English sentences and the transformations required to change these into surface structures. The discussion will focus on various problems, from how a particular transformation works to the relative ordering of transformations, and from the interpretation of ambiguous sentences to reasons for the ungrammaticality of other sentences. Throughout the chapter the emphasis will be on general principles rather than on specific details. In fact, some specific details given in the chapter may well be incorrect, since generative-transformational grammar is a rapidly changing field of inquiry within linguistics; however, many of the general principles discussed in the chapter are likely to remain valid for some time.

PHRASE-STRUCTURE RULES

The phrase-structure rules given in Chapter 7 for certain English sentences must be expanded considerably if they are to cover any variety of English sentences at all. Figure 8-1 contains a set of phrase-structure rules which, though by no means complete, will provide most of the deep structures that are necessary for the

S → S(S)

S → (Pre S) NP Aux VP (Adv)

Pre S → $\left(\left\{ \begin{matrix} Q \\ Imp \end{matrix} \right\} \right)$ (Neg)

VP → $\left\{ \begin{matrix} \text{(Passive) Vt NP} \\ \text{Vi} \\ \text{be Pred} \end{matrix} \right\}$

Pred → $\left\{ \begin{matrix} \text{Adv} \\ \text{NP} \\ \text{Adj} \end{matrix} \right\}$

NP → $\left\{ \begin{matrix} \text{NP (S)} \\ \text{(D) N (S)} \end{matrix} \right\}$

Adv → (Time) (Place) (Manner) (Reason)

Aux → Tense (M) (Perf) (Prog)

Tense → $\left\{ \begin{matrix} \text{pres} \\ \text{past} \end{matrix} \right\}$

M → *can, may, shall, will*

Perf → *have + en*

Prog → *be + ing*

Passive → *be + en*

Time → *sometime, yesterday, afterward, early, now,* SOMETIME, ...

Place → *someplace, there, outside, here,* SOMEPLACE, ...

Manner → *somehow, quietly, suddenly,* SOMEHOW, ...

Reason → SOMEREASON

D → *the, a, this, that, some,* SOME, ...

N → *boy, girl, cake, soap, bus, money, fact, idea, hope, something, someone, book, hill, John, Mary, son, they, you,* SOMETHING, SOMEONE, ...

Vt → *eat, shoot, sell, bake, search, catch, do, hurt, kill, like, please, wash, wound,* . . . .

Vi → *go, come, sleep, die, get up, leave, live,* . . . .

Adj → *rich, slow, red, happy, alive, old, little, poor, young,* . . . .

KEY:

Adj	Adjective	Pred	Predicate
Adv	Adverb	pres	Present
Aux	Auxiliary	Pre S	Pre sentence
D	Determiner	Prog	Progressive
Imp	Imperative	Q	Question
M	Modal	S	Sentence
N	Noun	Vi	Intransitive verb
Neg	Negative	VP	Verb phrase
NP	Noun phrase	Vt	Transitive verb
Perf	Perfect		

FIGURE 8-1 Some phrase-structure rules for English.

transformations that follow in this chapter. Most of the + symbols used in Chapter 7 are omitted from the rules to avoid a profusion of symbols.

The phrase-structure rules given in Figure 8-1 employ only the conventions discussed previously in Chapter 7. However, two additional observations should be made. The third rule:

$$\text{Pre S} \rightarrow \left(\left\{ \begin{matrix} Q \\ Imp \end{matrix} \right\} \right) \text{(Neg)}$$

is of interest because both constituents to the right of the rule are shown as optional. In such a case the Pre S constituent can be rewritten as Q Neg, Imp Neg, Q, Imp, Neg, or nothing at all. In the last case there would actually be no Pre S constituent in the deep structure which results from application of the rule. The rule itself is meant to capture such generalizations as the facts that sentences can be negative as well as affirmative, can be questions or imperatives as well as statements, or can be certain combinations of these, but cannot, of course, be questions and imperatives at the same time.

A second observation concerns the rewriting rules for such constituents as Time and Place. Time and Place are rewritten as *afterward* and *there* and also as *sometime* and *someplace*. These last two words also appear in the rules written in uppercase letters: SOMETIME and SOMEPLACE. This typographic distinction is used to distinguish between genuine adverbs, written in lowercase italics (*sometime* and *someplace*), and PRO adverbs, written in uppercase forms. A **PRO constituent** is one that is not fully specified; rather it is specified only in terms of certain grammatical properties, that is, as an adverb of time rather than as a specific adverb of time such as *afterward* or *sometime*. If Q and SOMETIME cooccur in the same deep structure, a transformation will ultimately produce a question beginning with the question word *when,* just as the cooccurrence of Q with SOMEPLACE will ultimately produce a question beginning with *where.*

TRANSFORMATIONS

Affix Transformation (T_{affix})

One transformation that must be used in the generation of almost every English sentence is the affix transformation, or T_{affix} to use a convenient abbreviation. The rules given in Figure 8-1 always generate affixes before verbs, as follows:

1 past *go*

2 pres *be + ing eat*

3 past *have + en shoot*

4 pres *have + en be + ing sell*

5 past *have + en be + en search*

6 past *may go*

7 past *can be + ing die*

The T$_{affix}$ is a transformation that switches affixes and verbs. The transformation can apply only once to any affix, so the transformational rule is written as follows:

T$_{affix}$

    Affix Verb ▶ Verb Affix #

The heavy arrow ▶ distinguishes a transformational rule from a phrase-structure rule (→), and the # in the rule is provided to prohibit any further movement of the affix, which otherwise would be possible whenever a sentence has more than one affix. Examples 8 through 14 are transformations of 1 through 7 above:

  8 *go* past # (= *went*)
  9 *be* pres # *eat ing* # (= *is eating*)
10 *have* past # *shoot en* # (= *had shot*)
11 *have* pres # *be en* # *sell ing* # (= *has been selling*)
12 *have* past # *be en* # *search en* # (= *had been searched*)
13 *may* past # *go* (= *might go*)
14 *can* past # *be die ing* # (= *could be dying*)

    Without the presence of # in the transformational rule the affix transformation would apply to example 5 more than once, as follows:

5 past *have* + *en be* + *en search*
   have past *be en search en*
   * *have be* past *search en en*
   * *have be search* past *en en*

The result would be the placing of all the verbs at the left and all the affixes at the right. However, such an arrangement does not occur in English. Consequently, the last two verb phrases are starred (*) to show that they are ungrammatical.

Negative, Question, Tag, and Emphasis Transformations (T$_{negative}$, T$_{question}$, T$_{tag}$, and T$_{emphasis}$)

There are sentences of the following kind in English which show certain very marked similarities:

1a He can go.
 b He can't go.
 c Can he go?
 d He can go, can't he?
 e He cán go.

2a He has gone.
 b He hasn't gone.
 c Has he gone?
 d He has gone, hasn't he?
 e He hás gone.

3a He is going.
 b He isn't going.
 c Is he going?
 d He is going, isn't he?
 e He ís going.

4a He is here.
 b He isn't here.
 c Is he here?
 d He is here, isn't he?
 e He ís here.

5a He sleeps.
 b He doesn't sleep.
 c Does he sleep?
 d He sleeps, doesn't he?
 e He doés sleep.

6a He has a son.
 b He hasn't a son. *OR* He doesn't have a son.
 c Has he a son? *OR* Does he have a son?
 d He has a son, hasn't he? *OR* He has a son, doesn't he?
 e He hás a son. *OR* He doés have a son.

In each of the above sets (1 through 6) the differences among the member sentences result from the presence of Neg and Q in the deep structures underlying the *b* and *c* sentences respectively, both of which constituents are given in the rules in Figure 8-1 at the beginning of this chapter. In the *d* and *e* sentences the presence of Tag and Emphasis constituents in their respective deep structures, neither of which is given in the rules in Figure 8-1, results in the particular surface structures of these sentences.

The presence of the Neg, Q, Tag, and Emphasis constituents in the deep structures requires the use of the negative, question, tag, and emphasis transformations ($T_{negative}$, $T_{question}$, T_{tag}, and $T_{emphasis}$). These transformations can be stated as follows:

$T_{negative}$

$$\text{Neg NP Tense} \left(\left\{ \begin{matrix} have \\ be \\ M \end{matrix} \right\} \right) \blacktriangleright \text{NP Tense} \left(\left\{ \begin{matrix} have \\ be \\ M \end{matrix} \right\} \right) n't$$

$T_{question}$

$$\text{Q NP Tense} \left(\left\{ \begin{matrix} have \\ be \\ M \end{matrix} \right\} \right) (n't) \blacktriangleright \text{Tense} \left(\left\{ \begin{matrix} have \\ be \\ M \end{matrix} \right\} \right) (n't) \text{ NP}$$

T_{tag}

$$\text{Tag NP}^1 \text{ Tense} \left(\left\{ \begin{matrix} have \\ be \\ M \end{matrix} \right\} \right) \left\{ \begin{matrix} n't \\ \varnothing \end{matrix} \right\} \ldots \# \blacktriangleright$$

$$\text{NP}^1 \text{ Tense} \left(\left\{ \begin{matrix} have \\ be \\ M \end{matrix} \right\} \right) \left\{ \begin{matrix} n't \\ \varnothing \end{matrix} \right\} \ldots \# \text{ Tense} \left(\left\{ \begin{matrix} have \\ be \\ M \end{matrix} \right\} \right) \left\{ \begin{matrix} \varnothing \\ n't \end{matrix} \right\} \text{Pro}^1$$

T_{emphasis}

$$\text{Emphasis NP Tense} \left(\left\{ \begin{matrix} have \\ be \\ M \end{matrix} \right\} \right) \ \blacklozenge \ \text{NP Tense} \left(\left\{ \begin{matrix} have \\ be \\ M \end{matrix} \right\} \right)'$$

In general, these transformations affect a structure of a tense morpheme plus any following *have, be,* or modal verb. The negative transformation deletes Neg and inserts *n't* after this structure; the question transformation deletes Q and inverts the subject NP and this structure; the tag transformation deletes Tag and copies this structure at the end of the clause, changes an affirmative to a negative (or vice versa), and adds a Pro (pronoun) to match the subject NP; and the emphasis transformation adds a stress morpheme (') after this structure.

Examples 1*b*, 2*c*, 3*d*, and 4*e* will now be described in some detail to show how each of the four transformations applies to a deep structure to turn it into a surface structure:

1b Neg *he* pres *can go*

■

T_{negative}
↓

he pres *can n't go*

■

T_{affix}
↓

he can pres# *n't go*

He can't go.

Neg is deleted and *n't* is added after pres *can*. Then the affix transformation applies.

2c Q *he* pres *have + en go*

■

T_{question}
↓

pres *have he en go*

■

T_{affix}
↓

have pres# *he go en#*

Has he gone?

Q is deleted and *he* and pres *have* are inverted. Then the affix transformation applies.

3d Tag *he* pres *be + ing go*

■

T_{tag}
↓

he pres *be + ing go#* pres *be n't he*

■

T~affix~

he be pres# *go ing# # be* pres# *n't he*

He is going, isn't he?

Tag is deleted, pres *be* is copied at the end of the clause, *n't* is added to change the affirmative to a negative, and *he* is added to match the first *he*.   Then the affix transformation applies twice, once in the main clause and once in the tag clause.

4e Emphasis *he* pres *be here*

T~emphasis~

he pres *be ' here*

T~affix~

he be pres# *' here*

He is here.

Emphasis is deleted and the stress morpheme (') is placed after pres *be*.   Then the affix transformation applies.

Do-support Transformation (T*~do~*)

Sentences 5*b* through 5*e* and 6*b* through 6*e* show certain peculiarities not observed in sets 1 through 4.   Sentences 5*b* through 5*e* follow the transformational rules exactly; however, in each case no structure exists to which the T~affix~ can apply, since each of the other transformations (negative in 5b, question in 5c, tag in 5d, and emphasis in 5e) produces an isolated affix.   In such cases *do* is inserted after this isolated affix by the *do*-support transformation (T*~do~*) to provide a verb for the affix transformation (T~affix~).

5b Neg *he* pres *sleep*

T~negative~

he pres *n't sleep*

T*~do~*

he pres *do n't sleep*

T~affix~

he do pres# *n't sleep*

He doesn't sleep.

5c Q *he* pres *sleep*
■

T_{question}
→

pres *he sleep*
■

T*_{do}*
→

pres *do he sleep*
■

T_{affix}
→

do pres# *he sleep*

Does he sleep?

5d Tag *he* pres *sleep*
■

T_{tag}
→

he pres *sleep#* pres *n't he*
■

T*_{do}*
→

he pres *sleep#* pres *do n't he*
■

T_{affix}
→

he sleep pres# # *do* pres# *n't he*

He sleeps, doesn't he?

5e Emphasis *he* pres *sleep*
■

T_{emphasis}
→

he pres ' *sleep*
■

T*_{do}*
→

he pres *do* ' *sleep*
■

T_{affix}
→

he do pres# ' *sleep*

He doés sleep.

Sentences 6*b* through 6*e* show a dialect variation. In one dialect one set of sentences is used and in the other dialect, the other set. The difference arises when one dialect treats *have* as the same kind of verb as *sleep*. In such a case the *do*-support transformation is required, so sentences such as *He doesn't have a son* and *Does he have a son?* result. The first of these sentences is derived as follows:

6b Neg *he* pres *have a son*

■

T~negative~

⬇

he pres *n't have a son*

■

T~*do*~

⬇

he pres *do n't have a son*

■

T~affix~

⬇

he do pres# *n't have a son*

He doesn't have a son.

However, in the other dialect with *He hasn't a son* the *have* is treated just like the *have* of *have* + *en* so that the *do*-support transformation is not required. Therefore, we have the following alternative derivation from the same deep structure:

6b Neg *he* pres *have a son*

■

T~negative~

⬇

he pres *have n't a son*

■

T~affix~

⬇

he have pres# *n't a son*

He hasn't a son.

We should also note that in the first dialect the *do*-support transformation is required in *He has a dollar, doesn't he?* but not in *He has gone, hasn't he?* in which the *have* is part of *have* + *en* and not a full verb like *sleep*. Speakers who use *do*-support with *have* do not therefore produce sentences such as **He has gone, doesn't he?*

Wh- Transformation (T~*wh*~)

Other kinds of questions exist in addition to those requiring a *yes* or *no* answer. Questions requiring a *yes* or *no* answer result from deep structures containing a Q or Tag. There are also questions like those in sentences 7 through 11:

  7 Where is he going?

  8 What do you eat?

  9 Who left?

 10 Which book do you want?

 11 Why did you do that?

What are the deep structures of each of these sentences? Each deep structure contains both Q and a PRO constituent, the latter being a constituent that is never fully specified as *man, book,* and *this* are specified. $T_{question}$ is applied to any deep structure that contains a Q, and then the presence of the PRO constituent requires the application of the *wh-* transformation (T_{wh}). This transformation moves the PRO constituent (such as SOMEONE or SOMETHING) to the front of the total deep structure and attaches *wh-* to it. The *wh-*PRO constituent is then rewritten as a question word according to the particular PRO constituent that is involved in the movement, as follows:

*wh-*SOMEPLACE   ▶ *where*

*wh-*SOMETHING   ▶ *what*

*wh-*SOMEONE   ▶ *who*

*wh-*SOME   ▶ *which*

*wh-*SOMEREASON ▶ *why*

*wh-*SOMEMEANS ▶ *how*

*wh-*SOME noun   ▶ *which* noun

    We can now represent the deep structures and transformations for sentences 7 through 11 as follows:

7 Q *he* pres *be + ing go* SOMEPLACE

        ■

        $T_{question}$
        ▼

pres *be he ing go* SOMEPLACE

        ■

        T_{wh}
        ▼

*wh-*SOMEPLACE pres *be he ing go*

        ■

        T_{affix}
        ▼

*wh-*SOMEPLACE *be* pres# *he go ing*#

      Where is he going?

8 Q *you* pres *eat* SOMETHING

        ■

        $T_{question}$
        ▼

pres *you eat* SOMETHING

        ■

        T_{wh}
        ▼

*wh-*SOMETHING pres *you eat*

        ■

        T_{do}
        ▼

*wh-*SOMETHING pres *do you eat*

        ■

T_{affix}

wh-SOMETHING *do* pres# *you eat*

What do you eat?

9 Q SOMEONE past *leave*

$T_{question}$

past SOMEONE *leave*

T_{wh}

wh-SOMEONE past *leave*

T_{affix}

wh-SOMEONE *leave* past#

Who left?

10 Q *you* pres *want* SOME *book*

$T_{question}$

pres *you want* SOME *book*

T_{wh}

wh-SOME *book* pres *you want*

T_{do}

wh-SOME *book* pres *do you want*

T_{affix}

wh-SOME *book do* pres# *you want*

Which book do you want?

11 Q *you* past *do that* SOMEREASON

$T_{question}$

past *you do that* SOMEREASON

T_{wh}

wh-SOMEREASON past *you do that*

T_{do}

wh-SOMEREASON past *do you do that*

T_{affix}

wh-SOMEREASON *do* past# *you do that*

Why did you do that?

It is important to note that questions which begin with *wh-* words (*where, when, which, what, why,* and *how*) undergo both the question and *wh-* transformations in that order.

Passive Transformation (T_{passive})

Passive sentences have deep structures that contain Passive rewritten as *be + en,* as in the following deep structure:

John past *be + en catch Mary*

When there is a *be + en* in the deep structure, the passive transformation (T_{passive}) applies to switch the subject and direct object NPs of that structure and to introduce *by* in front of the direct object NP of the surface structure:

T_{passive}

NP¹ . . . *be + en* VT NP² ▶ NP² . . . *be + en* VT *by* NP¹

The deep structure just given becomes sentence 12 as follows:

12 *John* past *be + en catch Mary*

T_{passive}

Mary past *be + en catch by John*

T_{affix}

Mary be past# *catch en#* *by John*

Mary was caught by John.

As I indicated in Chapter 6, verbs such as *have* and *weigh* (and also such others as *cost, measure, resemble,* and *suit*) are not Vts. They cannot undergo the passive transformation.

Agent Deletion Transformation (T_{deletion})

Sentence 13 has a different derivation from sentence 12:

13 Mary was caught.

In this case the sentence does not tell us who caught Mary; consequently, the deep structure should reflect this fact. The following deep structure and transformational derivation, which employs the agent deletion transformation ($T_{deletion}$), accounts for sentence 13:

13 SOMEONE past *be + en catch Mary*

∎

$T_{passive}$

Mary past *be + en catch by* SOMEONE

∎

$T_{deletion}$

Mary past *be + en catch*

∎

T_{affix}

Mary be past# *catch en*#

Mary was caught.

We can observe that the agent deletion transformation applies when the agent is not specified in a deep structure that contains the Passive constituent, that is, when the agent is a PRO constituent.

Reflexive Transformation ($T_{reflexive}$)

The reflexive transformation ($T_{reflexive}$) applies when the deep subject and direct object of a transitive verb are identical in reference. The reflexive transformation substitutes a pronoun for the direct object and adds *self* or *selves* to that pronoun. The remaining examples in this chapter will ignore irrelevant aspects of the deep structures of the sentences under discussion and illustrate only the transformation or transformations of immediate concern, as in the following examples:

14 John[1] hurt John[1]

∎

$T_{reflexive}$

John hurt himself.

15 Sarah[1] washed Sarah[1]

∎

$T_{reflexive}$

Sarah washed herself.

16 the boys[1] amused the boys[1]

∎

$T_{reflexive}$

The boys amused themselves.

In sentence 14, the two *Johns* must be considered to refer to the same person, for if sentence 17 ever actually occurred, we must interpret it as referring to two different people by the name of John:

17 John hurt John.

Reflexive pronouns must be distinguished from other pronouns. *John helped him* contains an **anaphoric pronoun,** one that refers to someone or something already mentioned or known. The *himself* in *John hurt himself* is a **reflexive pronoun** and the *himself* in *John himself said it* is an **emphatic pronoun.** Pronouns such as *each other* and *one another* are **reciprocal pronouns.** *The boys helped themselves* and *The boys helped one another* are quite different in meaning. Pronouns, of course, replace noun phrases not just nouns. In *The young man I met last week hurt himself yesterday,* the *him* of *himself* replaces all of *the young man I met last week.*

Imperative Transformation (T$_{imperative}$)

In deep structure Imp may occur with *you* pres *will,* an expansion of the subject NP and of Aux. The imperative transformation (T$_{imperative}$) deletes Imp *you* pres *will* when this sequence occurs:

T$_{imperative}$
       Imp *you* pres *will* ▶ ø

The only subject pronoun and auxiliary that can occur in English commands are *you* and *will* respectively, as in sentences 18 through 23:

18 Get up, *will* you!

19 Get up, *won't* you!

20 Wash *your*self!

21 *You,* get up right now!

22 Get up, *you!*

23 Jack, *you* get up right now!

Sentences 24 through 29 are all unacceptable in English:

24 * Get up, *would* you!

25 * Get up, *wouldn't* you!

26 * Wash *him*self!

27 * *He,* get up right now!

28 * Get up, *they!*

29 * Jack, *he* get up right now!

The acceptability of sentences 18 through 23 and the unacceptability of sentences 24 through 29 requires the presence not only of the constituent Imp but also of the constituents *you* pres *will* in the deep structures of commands in English.

Relative Transformation (T$_{relative}$)

All the transformations so far discussed operate on underlying structures deriving from a single S. However, the recursive property mentioned in Chapter 7 and incorporated into the rules in Figure 8-1 allows for more than one occurrence of S in a deep structure. It allows a structure of the following kind as part of the deep structure of a sentence:

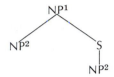

This structure contains three different NPs, two of which are marked as similar in reference (NP^2). When such a structure occurs, the relative transformation (T$_{relative}$) applies. This transformation moves the NP^2 below the S to the front of that S and substitutes the appropriate **relativizer** (*who, whom, which,* and so on) for the NP^2. Sentences 30 through 32 illustrate the transformation:

30 the boy^2 [the boy^2 was poor] left

T$_{relative}$

The boy who was poor left.

31 the boy^2 [I like the boy^2] left

T$_{relative}$

The boy whom I like left.

32 the place^2 [I live at the place^2] is over there

T$_{relative}$

The place where I live is over there.

English has rules allowing for a variation between *that* and *whom, who,* or *which* in certain cases, as in sentences 30 (*The boy that was poor left*) and 31 (*The boy that I like left*), for the deletion of *whom, that,* or *which,* as in sentence 31 (*The boy I like left*), and for a possible alternation between *whom* and *who,* as in sentence 31 (*The boy who I like left*).

Be-deletion and Adjective Movement Transformations (T$_{be\text{-}deletion}$ and T$_{Adj\ Movt}$)

If the verb in the relative clause in the relative transformation is a form of *be,* then the relative pronoun and *be* may be deleted by the *be*-deletion transformation (T$_{be\text{-}deletion}$), as in sentence 33:

33 the boy² [the boy² was at the back] left

$T_{relative}$

the boy who was at the back left

$T_{be\text{-}deletion}$

The boy at the back left.

If only a single adjective is left in the relative clause after the application of $T_{be\text{-}deletion}$, it must be moved in front of the noun it modifies by the adjective movement transformation ($T_{Adj\ Movt}$), as in sentence 34:

34 the boy² [the boy² was poor] left

$T_{relative}$

the boy who was poor left

$T_{be\text{-}deletion}$

the boy poor left

$T_{Adj\ Movt}$

The poor boy left.

Sentences 35 and 36 are both ungrammatical because in sentence 35 $T_{Adj\ Movt}$ has not been applied when it was required, and in sentence 36 a movement transformation has been applied when it should not have been, since only a single word can be moved and not a phrase containing two or more words:

35 *The boy poor left.

36 *The at the back boy left.

Noun Complement Transformation ($T_{Noun\ Comp}$)

We can also use the rules given in Figure 8-1 to rewrite an NP as follows:

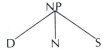

The result is a different deep-structure configuration from that underlying relative clauses and a different surface structure. The consequence is a set of noun complements because the noun complement transformation ($T_{Noun\ Comp}$) applies to the deep structure to produce sentences such as 37 to 40:

37 The fact that you came pleased me.

38 I didn't like the idea that he would go alone.

39 Any hope that John was still alive faded.

40 It pleased me that you came.

We should also note that sentence 40 has undergone an additional extraposition transformation from a deep structure like the following:

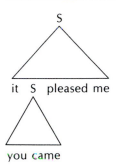

The *you came* has been moved after the verb and the complementizer *that* has been added as a result of this extraposition transformation. The embedded clause of such a construction can often be moved around the main verb by extraposition. For example, sentence 39 can undergo extraposition to *Any hope faded that John was still alive.*

Sentences 37 and 38 can be compared with sentences 41 and 42, which contain relative clauses deriving from deep structures like those discussed earlier in this chapter in connection with the relative transformation.

41 The fact that you discovered pleased me.

42 I didn't like the idea that he expounded to me.

A word about **complementizers** is in order. Complementizers are particles which appear when one clause is embedded in another, for example, TO, THAT, 'S-ING, and FOR TO in the following sentences: *I want* TO *go; The fact* THAT *he did it angered me; John's strik*ING *out hurt us;* and FOR *him* TO *try to do it was crazy.*

Adverbial Transformations

Sentences containing what have traditionally been called subordinate adverbial clauses are derived from deep structures in which the constituent Adv has been rewritten as S, as in sentences 43 through 45:

43 he went SOMEREASON [I asked him something]

He went because I asked him.

44 he left SOMETIME [the show ended then]

He left when the show ended.

45 he lived SOMEPLACE [I was born there]

He lived where I was born.

The embedded clause in each case is incorporated into the main clause by means of the appropriate subordinating conjunction: *because, when,* and *where* in these examples.

Verb Complement Transformations

It is traditional to call sentences such as *I want to go* and *He expected me to do it* simple sentences because each sentence contains a single finite verb, that is, a verb capable of showing tense. In a generative-transformational grammar such sentences must be treated as deriving from two Ss, by verb complement transformations, as in sentences 46 and 47:

46 I want SOMETHING [I go]

I want to go.

47 he expected SOMETHING [I do it]

He expected me to do it.

We can compare *He expected me to do it* and *He expected to do it.* If the subject of the embedded clause is identical with that of the main clause, then the second pronoun does not appear in the surface structure. A sentence such as *He expected him to do it* must have different referents for the *he* and the *him.* When a subject from an embedded clause becomes a constituent in the structure of a higher clause—for example, the main clause—we have a phenomenon known as **subject raising.** For example, *Fred believed [Sally was here]* results in *Sally* being raised to become the object of *believed* in *Fred believed Sally to be here.* This structure can then undergo the passive transformation to become *Sally was believed by Fred to be here.* In this case the subject of the embedded clause has actually become the surface subject of the main clause.

Coordination Transformations

Still another kind of structure that is possible from the phrase-structure rules in Figure 8-1 is the coordinate one shown as SS. When certain parts of the two or more sentences are alike in structure, the sentences can be conjoined by one of the coordination transformations, as in sentences 48 through 50, which employ the coordinators *and, but,* and *nor:*

48 [Jack went up the hill] [Jill went up the hill]

Jack and Jill went up the hill.

49 [he left] [I stayed]

He left but I stayed.

50 [Peter didn't go] [Fred didn't go]

Neither Peter nor Fred went.

Numerous problems arise in connection with conjoining. For example, some pairs of sentences can be conjoined in any order so that *He smoked* and *He drank* can be conjoined to form either *He smoked and drank* or *He drank and smoked*. But *He left and ate* and *He ate and left* (both conjoinings of *He left* and *He ate*) indicate different sequential arrangements of events. *And* has different "meanings" depending on what it conjoins. Still another problem deserves mention. Sentences 51 and 52 are different in meaning:

51 The girls, who wore raincoats, left early.

52 The girls who wore raincoats left early.

These sentences have different meanings, as we can see if we relate them to sentences 53 and 54:

53 The girls left early and they were wearing raincoats.

54 The girls wearing raincoats left early, but the ones wearing swimsuits stayed.

The difference in meaning arises from the fact that sentence 51 derives from an underlying SS structure:

[the girls left early] [the girls wore raincoats]

On the other hand, sentence 52 derives from an underlying relative clause structure:

the girls² [the girls² wore raincoats] left early

SCOPE OF TRANSFORMATIONS

The preceding pages have drawn attention to only a small number of English transformations, none of which has been stated with full explicitness. Many more transformations are necessary in a comprehensive grammar of English, each of which must be stated completely explicitly in terms of the structure on which it operates and the structural changes it produces. Transformations apply to the kinds of structures produced by rules such as those in Figure 8-1; they do not apply to words or to sentences. Transformations change one structure into another through processes such as addition, deletion, or rearrangement. For example, the passive transformation ($T_{passive}$) adds *by* before the surface structure object NP, the imperative transformation ($T_{imperative}$) deletes Imp *you* pres *will*, and the question transformation ($T_{question}$) moves Tense$\left(\begin{Bmatrix} have \\ be \\ M \end{Bmatrix} \right)$($n't$) to a position before the subject NP. We must also note that if a particular structure meets the structural requirements of a transformation, then that transformation must be applied. Consequently, a structure containing an Imp *you* pres *will* must undergo $T_{imperative}$, one containing a *be* + *en* must undergo $T_{passive}$, and one containing a PRO constituent must undergo some kind of deletion or replacement transformation, for example $T_{deletion}$ or T_{wh}.

Most transformations are obligatory; optional transformations produce only stylistic changes, as, for example, the changes that occur in the following sentences:

55 John gave Peter the book.
John gave the book to Peter.

56 Who did you give it to?
To whom did you give it?

57 He looked up the date.
He looked the date up.

In example 55 the two noun phrases after the verb can occur in either order with a *to* required before the second noun phrase in the second order. Example 56 contains a less "formal" variant first and a more "formal" variant second. Example 57 illustrates the possibility of moving certain particles to the ends of sentences in which they appear. We should note that if the object is a pronoun, for example, *it,* this particle movement transformation is obligatory, so that *He looked it up* results. **He looked up it* is unacceptable with this meaning.

ORDERING OF TRANSFORMATIONS

In this chapter transformations have been presented in a particular order when more than one transformation has been involved in changing a deep structure into a surface structure. Transformations are ordered relative to each other. For example, $T_{negative}$ must apply before $T_{question}$ so that *n't* can be moved in front of the subject NP along with Tense $\left(\begin{Bmatrix} have \\ be \\ M \end{Bmatrix}\right)$. $T_{passive}$ must apply before $T_{reflexive}$ so as to produce a sentence like 58, which, even though inelegant, is a possible English sentence:

58 John was hurt by himself.

and to avoid a sentence like 59:

59 *Himself was hurt by John.

Sentence 58 is derived as follows:

58 *John^1 past be + en hurt John^1*
■

$T_{passive}$
⬇

John^1 past be + en hurt by John^1
■

$T_{reflexive}$
⬇

John past be + en hurt by himself
■

T_{affix}

John be past# hurt en# by himself

John was hurt by himself.

If T_{reflexive} were to apply before T_{passive,} the following derivation would occur:

59 *John¹ past be + en hurt John¹*

T_{reflexive}

John past be + en hurt himself

T_{passive}

himself past be + en hurt by John

T_{affix}

himself be past# hurt en# by John

*Himself was hurt by John.

T_{reflexive} must also precede T_{imperative} in order to produce the *yourself* in commands, as in sentence 60:

60 Wash yourself!

If T_{imperative} were to apply first, it would delete the subject NP, *you* in this case, and remove part of the structure required for the operation of T_{reflexive} so as to produce *yourself*. Therefore, transformations must be ordered relative to each other. Furthermore, when one S is included in another S, all the transformations required in the embedded S apply before the transformations in the matrix S and before conjoining transformations.

SOME COMPLICATED DERIVATIONS

We will now use sentences 61 through 64 to illustrate some of the principles illustrated so far in this chapter:

61 Don't go now!

62 Why was the young man given the reward?

63 What did Peter expect to be given?

64 The little old lady who lived in the shoe didn't look after herself.

Not all the sentences will be treated alike, nor are the derivations given in the same form. The purpose is to illustrate the processes and principles that have been mentioned, not insignificant details.

61 Imp Neg *you* pres *will go now*
■
$T_{negative}$
↓

Imp *you* pres *will n't go now*
■
$T_{imperative}$
↓
n't go now
■
T_{do}
↓
do n't go now

Don't go now!

Sentence 61 shows us that *do* is provided for affixes like *n't* as well as for verbal affixes.

62 Q SOMEONE past *be + en give the reward the man*[2] [*the man*[2] past *be young*] SOMEREASON
■
$T_{relative}$
↓

Q SOMEONE past *be + en give the reward the man* [*who past be young*] SOMEREASON
■
$T_{be\text{-}deletion}$
↓

Q SOMEONE past *be + en give the reward the man* [*young*] SOMEREASON
■
$T_{Adj\ Movt}$
↓

Q SOMEONE past *be + en give the reward the young man* SOMEREASON
■
$T_{passive}$
↓

Q *the young man* past *be + en give the reward by* SOMEONE SOMEREASON
■
$T_{deletion}$
↓

Q *the young man* past *be + en give the reward* SOMEREASON
■
$T_{question}$
↓

past *be the young man en give the reward* SOMEREASON
■
T_{wh}
↓

⬆

wh-SOMEREASON past *be the young man en give the reward*

■

T_{affix}

⬇

wh-SOMEREASON *be* past# *the young man give en*# *the reward*

Why was the young man given the reward?

63

S

Q *Peter* past *expect* SOMETHING S

SOMEONE past *be + en give* SOMETHING *Peter*

Q *Peter* past *expect* SOMETHING [SOMEONE past *be + en give* SOMETHING *Peter*]

■

T_{passive}

⬇

Q *Peter* past *expect* SOMETHING [SOMETHING past *be + en give by* SOMEONE *Peter*]

■

T_{deletion}

⬇

Q *Peter* past *expect* SOMETHING [SOMETHING past *be + en give Peter*]

■

$T_{\textit{to}\text{-incorporation}}$

⬇

Q *Peter* past *expect* SOMETHING *to be + en give Peter*

■

$T_{\text{pronominalization}}$

⬇

Q *Peter* past *expect* SOMETHING *to be + en give him*

■

$T_{\text{pronoun deletion}}$

⬇

Q *Peter* past *expect* SOMETHING *to be + en give*

■

T_{question}

⬇

past *Peter expect* SOMETHING *to be + en give*

■

T_{wh}

⬇

wh-SOMETHING past *Peter expect to be + en give*

■

■
T_{do}
↓

wh-SOMETHING past *do Peter expect to be* + *en give*

■
T_{affix}
↓

wh-SOMETHING *do* past# *Peter expect to be give en*#

What did Peter expect to be given?

64 [Neg *the lady*[1] . . . .
    [*the lady*[1] past *be little*]
    [*the lady*[1] past *be old*]
    [*the lady*[1] past *live in the shoe*]

          . . . . past *look after the lady*[1]]
           [*the lady*[1] past *be little*]
           [*the lady*[1] past *be old*]
           [*the lady*[1] past *live in the shoe*]

■
$T_{relative}$
↓
$T_{be\text{-}deletion}$
↓
$T_{Adj\ Movt}$
↓

Neg *the little old lady*[1] *who* past *live in the shoe* past *look after the little old lady*[1] *who* past *live in the shoe*

■
$T_{reflexive}$
↓

Neg *the little old lady who* past *live in the shoe* past *look after herself*

■
$T_{negative}$
↓

the little old lady who past *live in the shoe* past *n't look after herself*

■
T_{do}
↓

the little old lady who past *live in the shoe* past *do n't look after herself*

■
T_{affix}
↓

the little old lady who live past# *in the shoe do* past# *n't look after herself*

The little old lady who lived in the shoe didn't look after herself.

AMBIGUITY

Sentences like 65 and 66 are ambiguous:

65 What annoyed John was being ignored by everyone.

66 He likes entertaining guests.

These sentences are ambiguous because each of sentences 65 and 66 can be derived from a pair of different deep structures. Sentence 65 can be derived from a deep structure that would also produce *John was annoyed because everyone was ignoring him* if the passive transformation were not applied:

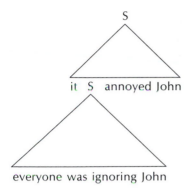

or from a deep structure that would also produce *Everyone was ignoring the thing that annoyed John* (again with the passive transformation):

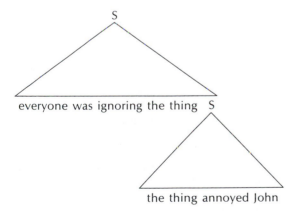

Sentence 66 can be derived from a deep structure that would also produce *He likes to entertain guests:*

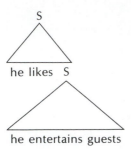

or from a deep structure that would also produce *He likes guests who are entertaining:*

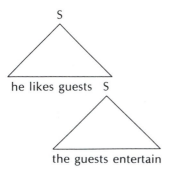

Sentences which have different meanings have different deep structures; therefore, ambiguous sentences must derive from pairs, or even triples, quadruples, and so on, of different deep structures which become alike in surface structure through undergoing certain transformations.

UNGRAMMATICALITY

Sentences like 67 through 69 are ungrammatical:

67 *He was died by the bullet.

68 *Stand up and are you going?

69 *He can had gone there.

The various phrase-structure and transformational rules given earlier in this chapter will not generate sentences 67 through 69. The verb *die* in sentence 67 is an intransitive verb (Vi), not a transitive verb (Vt). Since *die* is a Vi, it cannot be generated along with the Passive constituent in the phrase-structure rules. No conjoining transformation allows for the conjunction of sentences one of which contains Imp and the other Q; consequently, sentence 68 is disallowed. Sentence 69 contains either two tense affixes, on *can* and *had,* or one tense affix but on *had* rather than on *can.* No string deriving from a single S can contain either two tense affixes or a tense affix in any other place than on the first verb in the Aux part of the derivation. Therefore, the rules reflect our intuitions about what is grammatical and what is ungrammatical.

SENTENCE PRONUNCIATION

Two important aspects of language have not been discussed within the genera-tive-transformational model outlined so far. One concerns the treatment of meaning and the other the treatment of sound. The following chapter will focus on certain problems of meaning, but a few observations will be made about the treatment of sound at this point, that is, about the treatment of phonology in a generative-transformational grammar.

We will assume that somehow the right words are introduced into sentences at some point in their generation so that the surface structures contain words. One basic requirement of a generative-transformational grammar is a set of instructions, or rules, detailing how surface structures are to be pronounced. Such an approach requires a rather different method of describing sounds from the way outlined in general in Chapter 4. This different approach allows the use of semantic and syntactic information in writing phonological rules. The emphasis in the different approach is on rules, because a language is considered to be rule-governed and generative in its phonology as well as in its syntax. In addition to a generative syntax we must therefore have a **generative phonology.**

Features

Rules, of course, must have something to operate on. In the case of phonology, they operate on phonological segments or successions of such segments. Each segment [   ] comprises a set of features, selected from distinctive features such as voice, vocalic, strident, and so on, as indicated at the end of Chapter 3. A distinctive-features approach has always seemed to be more suitable for genera-tive-transformational grammar than one which employs either the International Phonetic Alphabet or a traditional phonemic system.

Only features not predictable by rules need be specified for the underlying forms of words. For example, the first segment of English *nip* need be specified only [+nasal, +coronal]; such features as [+voice, +consonantal] are predictable from these. In *scream* the first segment need be specified only as [+consonantal], the second as [+consonantal, +high], and the third as [+consonantal, −anteri-or]. An initial English cluster containing three consonants must have [s] as its first consonant, one of [p], [t], or [k] as its second consonant, and either [r] or [l] as its third consonant. The features that can be predicted—for example, the voicing in the [n] of *nip* and the voicelessness of the [sk], the stridency of the [s], and the stop quality of the [k] in the [skr] of *scream*—can be predicted by morpheme-structure rules that add features to the underlying forms. Such morpheme-structure rules can be stated once for the grammar as a whole; they do not have to be repeated for each example. Phonological rules themselves are transformational in that they add, delete, and change features and segments in the underlying forms of words.

Rules

A generative-transformational grammar of English would contain a set of rules for the "plural" morpheme that would at some point rewrite the "plural" as a voiced coronal strident, basically a [z] sound, as explained in Chapter 3:

$$\text{plural} \rightarrow \begin{bmatrix} +\text{continuant} \\ +\text{voice} \\ +\text{coronal} \\ +\text{strident} \end{bmatrix}$$

However, not all instances of the "plural" morpheme in English are pronounced as voiced coronal stridents [z]. There are also instances of [əz] and [s] pronunciations, as in *churches* and *cats*. Consequently, further rules are required to produce such instances. The first rule requires that if the final segment of the morpheme to which the "plural" is to be attached is itself [+coronal, +strident], then the [z] is added together with a schwa [ə] to produce [əz] endings, as in *judges* and *churches* ([ǰəǰəz] and [čárčəz]). A second rule matches the voicing feature of the "plural" to that of the final segment of the morpheme to which it is attached in all remaining cases. That is, the [+voice] of the [z] becomes [−voice] (hence [s]) if that final segment is [−voice]: *cats* ([kæts]). But of course [+voice] in the final segment leads to an unchanged [z] "plural": *dogs* ([dagz]).

These rules state that the voiced coronal strident "plural" morpheme, basically a [z], becomes a central vowel [ə] plus [z], or [əz], after any kind of coronal strident. Since *batch, judge, pass, maze, wish,* and *garage* all end in coronal stridents, [č], [ǰ], [s], [z], [š], and [ž] respectively, this rule provides the correct plural for each of these words. The second rule applies *after* the first. The second rule "devoices" the [z] to [s] after any remaining voiceless segments, for example, after after [p], [t], [k], [f], or [θ], as in *cap, cat, sack, cliff,* and *faith*. These rules account for all the regular English plurals; another special set of rules, which would apply *before* this set applies, accounts for irregular plurals such as *men, deer,* and *geese.*

Abstractness

Definite similarities exist between this type of phonology and the type of syntax outlined in the earlier part of the chapter. The units involved are abstract units called **systematic phonemes** which can undergo changes, or transformations, as a result of the application of rules. Consequently, we can postulate underlying "sounds" for words that are rather different from the sounds in the words as they are actually pronounced. For example, it is sometimes desirable to show that the following pairs of words really have the same vowels in the underlying phonology: *bite* and *bitten* [ī]; *meter* and *metric* [ē]; *sane* and *sanity* [æ]; and *phone* and *phonic* [ɔ]. In the *bite–bitten* pair the [ī] would diphthongize in the first case to produce the pronunciation [baɪt] and would shorten in the second case to produce [bɪtn̩]. Vowel raising would occur in *meter* ([ē] to [ī]), *sane* ([æ] to [ē]), and *phone* ([ɔ] to [ō]), and vowel shortening in *metric* ([ē] to [ɛ]), *sanity* ([æ] to [æ]), and *phonic* ([ɔ] to [ɔ] or [a]). The particular type of change, for example, diphthongization, raising, shortening, and so on, would depend on general phonological processes in the language. Establishing similarities and phonological processes of these kinds leads to a more economical statement of phonological rules than insisting either that no similarity exists between such pairs of words, or that the similarity is a historical one only and therefore to be disregarded by the writer of a synchronic description.

Naturalness

Even though underlying phonological forms are abstract in the sense that they may differ considerably from the actual pronunciations that occur, they must be real in the sense of being phonetically possible. The underlying phonological forms must be natural, as must the processes that operate to change these forms into observed pronunciations. Natural means that the forms and processes must be in accord with the forms and processes that are actually observed to occur in languages. For example, [ī] can shorten to [ɪ] or diphthongize to [aɪ], but it cannot change to [o]. Then, too, the changes or processes which occur will tend to apply to classes of segments which share one or more distinctive features. English nouns ending in coronal stridents (therefore all [+coronal, +strident] in the final segment) behave alike so far as pluralization is concerned, as do the remaining English nouns ending in voiceless consonants. In the first case we get [əz] "plural" endings; in the second case we get the "devoiced" [s] plural. Ad hoc forms and processes are ruled out if they violate this naturalness criterion, even though they might provide elegant solutions to certain problems.

BIBLIOGRAPHIC NOTES

Liles' *Introductory Transformational Grammar* and *Introduction to Linguistics* provide introductory material on several of the topics covered in this chapter. Two readable book-length treatments of English generative-transformational grammar are Grinder and Elgin's *Guide to Transformational Grammar* and Jacobs and Rosenbaum's *English Transformational Grammar*. Langendoen's *Study of Syntax* provides a different introductory approach. Fodor and Katz' *Structure of Language* and Reibel and Schane's *Modern Studies in English* are both collections of technical papers on generative-transformational grammar which cover a wide variety of topics. Burt's *From Deep to Surface Structure* discusses many different transformations and some of the complexities involved in making decisions about the form and ordering of rules.

Halle's "Phonology in Generative Grammar" is a very satisfactory short introduction to that topic. Schane's *Generative Phonology* and Harms' *Introduction to Phonological Theory* are much more technical treatments, and Postal's *Aspects of Phonological Theory* is somewhat discursive and polemical. Hyman's *Phonology: Theory and Analysis* is the best general treatment of issues. The most comprehensive treatment of English phonology within generative-transformational theory is contained in Chomsky and Halle's *Sound Pattern of English*.

EXERCISES

8-1 Check to make sure that you understand each of the terms printed in **boldface** in Chapter 8.

8-2 Chapter 8 makes distinctions between certain terms. Explain the distinction between the following terms as clearly as you can: SOMETIME and *sometime; yes-no question* and *wh- question; main clause* and *embedded clause; noun complement* and *verb complement; obligatory transformation* and *optional transformation.*

8-3 Apply the indicated transformations to the string:

    1 past *can have+en be+ing go* (affix)
    2 Neg *John* pres *can go* (negative)
    3 Q *you* pres *be+ing leave* (question)
    4 Emphasis *they* pres *have+en go* (emphasis)
    5 pres *he know Peter* (do)
    6 past SOMEONE *say that* (wh-)
    7 pres *can you see* SOMETHING (wh-)
    8 *John* past *be+en take the book* (passive)
    9 *the boy who* past *be at the back* past *leave* (*be*-deletion)
    10 *the boy*[1] past *injure the boy*[1] (reflexive)
    11 Imp *you* pres *will sit down* (imperative)
    12 *the car red* past *speed away* (adjective movement)

8-4 Each of the following simplified deep structures will produce a sentence. Write out each sentence.

    1 *John* past *stand outside*
    2 *Mary* pres *have+en be+ing eat candy again*
    3 *they* pres *must have+en hide the book*
    4 Neg *we* pres *be+ing go to the movies*
    5 *the company* past *be+en notify Fred*
    6 Q *you* pres *must do that*
    7 Q SOMEONE pres *have+en notify John*
    8 Q Neg SOMEONE pres *have+en be to a game yet*
    9 Q *you* pres *want* SOMETHING
    10 Q *you* past *get that hat* SOMEPLACE
    11 Imp Neg *you* pres *will ask me*
    12 Q *John*[1] past *buy* SOMETHING *for John*[1]

8-5 Write out the complete transformational derivations of sentences 7 through 12 in the previous exercise. Indicate the transformations you use.

8-6 Each of the following sentences or headlines is ambiguous. Consequently, each must have at least two deep structures. Indicate two possible deep structures for each sentence, and for each deep structure an alternate surface structure.

    1 Flying planes can be dangerous.
    2 GIRL HUNTER SAYS FATHER SETS EXAMPLE
    3 I asked to go at five o'clock.
    4 This lamb is too hot to eat.
    5 Please stop hurrying people.
    6 I had a car stolen.

8-7 Each of the following "sentences" is ungrammatical. Attempt to explain the ungrammaticality of each in terms of rule violation.

  1 *Did go he in not?
  2 *He must can go.
  3 *The boy with the drawings you requested from the children are outside.
  4 *The book I want the book is over there.
  5 *Don't wash himself!
  6 *Himself was hurt by Peter.
  7 *Are you going and I don't want to.
  8 *I expect me to go.
  9 *What and why did they do?
  10 *She's an ill girl.

8-8 The following sentences are acceptable in certain dialects of English or certain styles of speech. Examine each sentence carefully: if you would not use the sentence, try to say how the rules in the other dialect differ from those in your dialect.

  1 Has he any?
  2 It ain't gonna rain no more.
  3 I might could do it.
  4 I seen him yesterday.
  5 He be real sick.
  6 To whom am I speaking?
  7 Those kind of things hurt.
  8 Give me those ones.
  9 He can't hardly do it.
  10 Be not afraid.

9

MEANING

Although any language is a system for expressing meanings through sounds, the study of meaning itself, that is, **semantics,** has been one of the most neglected areas in linguistics, for only recently has a serious interest been taken in its various problems. Such neglect is understandable, because many serious difficulties arise in discussing meaning.

MEANING: SOME DIFFICULTIES

Philosophers have long puzzled over what words mean, or what they represent, or how they relate to reality, whatever reality is. In what ways do words refer to the things they name? Do they actually substitute in some way for those things? The "wise men" of Swift's Grand Academy of Lagado in *Gulliver's Travels* preferred to carry around objects on their bodies rather than words in their heads so that they could make direct reference. Are words themselves referential in some sense, names of some kind? *Noun* comes from the Latin *nomen,* "name." If so, what do *unicorn, God, sad, democracy,* and the *square root of minus one* refer to or name? And why do we have alternative means of reference, such as both *George Wash-*

ington and *the first president of the United States of America?* Of course, meanings may be more abstract than this. Are they concepts: "home" rather than
home? Or is the meaning of *home* for a particular speaker that speaker's individual disposition to respond to the word as a result of all the speaker's experiences
with that word? Is meaning contextual rather than conceptual or referential?

Dictionary makers face considerable problems in dealing with meaning. A
simple word like *table* can create all kinds of problems. One may ask whether
words do have essential meanings, so that *table,* for example, can be said to have
some essential meaning basic to the accidental meanings associated with it in
particular contexts. However, *table* may have no essential meaning, but rather
have multiple distinct meanings. For example, *table* appears to have distinctly
different meanings in *water table, dining table,* and *table an amendment.* May
these then not be three homophonous words *table* with distinctly different
meanings, therefore, three **homonyms?** Are *oculist, eye doctor,* and *ophthalmol-
ogist* **synonyms?** *Myopic* and *nearsighted? Sphere* and *globe? Bachelor* and
unmarried male? How does one define synonymy? **Antonyms** are words of
opposite meaning, for example, *large* and *small.* But what does *opposite* itself
mean? It means something different in pairs such as *dead-alive* (mutually exclu-
sive) and *hot-cold* (ends of a continuum). *Buy-sell* are also antonyms, but in this
case the words show a reciprocal relationship. Furthermore, to return to *large* and
small, a large insect is still small but a small whale is very large. So antonyms
require some kind of reference to use and context too.

A word like *good* creates even more problems. What shared meaning does
good have in *good beating, good book, good knife, good idea, good race, good
reason, good water,* and *good woman?* What does *good* mean and how does a
speaker of English ever learn to use the word correctly? Even a word such as *left* in
the expressions *the left arm of a chair* and *the left drawer of a bureau* may be said to
have different meanings, because *left* is used in relation to a speaker's position as
he uses these objects. The left arm of a chair requires *left* to refer to the left side of
a person as he sits in the chair, but the left drawer of a bureau requires *left* to refer
to the left side of the bureau as a person faces the bureau. How can such facts
about essential meanings, multiple meanings, and real-world conditions be taken
into account in a comprehensive theory of meaning that recognizes the systematic
nature of language? This question is being asked more frequently.

The connotative uses of words add further complications to any theorizings
about meaning, particularly their uses in metaphoric and poetic language. Any
understanding of connotation, metaphor, and poetic language must be based on an
understanding of what may be called the "normal use of language." A serious
problem, of course, arises in determining where the norm is located. Is it located
in speakers, in the language itself, or in the contexts in which communication takes
place? If the norm is located in the speakers of a language, how does the
philosopher, psychologist, or linguist gain access to it? If the norm is located in
the language itself, how do speakers learn the norm, and what kind of claim is it
that the norm is somehow independent of its users? If the norm is located in the
contexts in which communication takes place, exactly what kind of process is
communication, and what are its distinctive characteristics?

Many different answers have been proposed to the questions just asked.
Psychologists have tried to assess the availability of certain kinds of responses to

objects, to experiences, and to words themselves, particularly in laboratory experiments using verbal stimuli. Philosophers have proposed a variety of systems and theories to account for the data that interest them. Communications experts have developed information theory so that they can use mathematical models to explain exactly what is predictable and what is not predictable when messages are channeled through various kinds of communication networks. From these varying approaches a bewildering array of conceptions of meaning emerges; however, few of these conceptions are relevant to linguistic concerns.

LINGUISTS AND MEANING

Most linguists make no attempt to understand how ideas or words arise in the mind. They are much more concerned with how ideas are expressed in words and combinations of words once they do arise. Nor are they really interested in the quantity and quality of responses to various kinds of verbal and nonverbal stimuli and in the mathematics of information theory. However, certain problems of meaning are of interest: for example, such problems as the role of syntax in meaning, the nature of synonymy (how utterances can be said to have the same meaning), and the question of semantic universals (what characteristics of meaning are common to all languages).

Additional reasons exist for this noticeable reluctance to deal with certain kinds of problems. For a long time, students of language intermingled statements about linguistic forms with statements about meanings: nouns were said to be naming words, sentences to be groups of words that made sense, and interrogatives to be groups of words that asked questions. Many structural linguists decided to cut a way through the resulting jungle of confusion by removing considerations of meaning as far as possible from their work with linguistic forms and systems. They argued with considerable conviction that since a language is a system of forms used to convey meaning, an investigator who uses meaning to describe the properties of the system cannot hope to come to an adequate understanding of either the formal system of a language or meaning itself, nor to escape circularity and **tautology.** Consequently, the prevailing methodological approach to linguistic analysis dictated that the phonological system of a language be described first, and that this description be done without appeal to syntactic or semantic information. Any syntactic description would follow the phonological one, and finally some attempt could be made at observations about meaning.

In such circumstances we should not be surprised to find that very little progress was made in coming to any understanding of meaning. Meaning was important only insofar as knowledge concerning whether or not two utterances had the same meanings helped linguists to decide questions about morphemic cutting and grouping; however, they ignored most other aspects of meaning or uses of meaning in their work. Much linguistic work in the 1940s and 1950s was of this kind, and even the Chomskyan revolution of the late 1950s did little initially to change the emphasis. However, a dramatic shift did occur in the mid-1960s, and in the last decade or so questions of meaning have come to the forefront in linguistic investigation.

SETS, COLLOCATIONS, AND REGISTERS

Sets

A central problem in discussing meaning must be one of finding interesting questions to answer. One such question might be phrased as follows: Do the meanings of English words differ in any noticeable way according to their grammatical characteristics? In answer to this question we can note that the following words may be assigned to two distinct sets: *cat, a, ran, stairs, the, down.* The two sets are *cat, ran, stairs* and *a, the, down.* The two sets can, of course, be combined, and at least one sequence of the members of both sets forms a grammatical sentence: *A cat ran down the stairs.* However, several differences exist between the two sets. The first difference is that the first set (*cat, ran, stairs*) is one of **content words,** that is, words that refer to "things," "actions," or "events" in the real world, whereas the second set (*a, the, down*) does not have this quality. It is a set of **structure words.** No one can point to an instance of an "a," "the," or "down." The second difference is that the first set contains words that can take inflections of the kind discussed in Chapter 5. The members of the set belong to parts of speech classes that can be inflected: *cat* and *stair* for "plural" (*cats* and *stairs*) and *run* for "past tense" (*ran*). On the other hand, *a, the,* and *down* cannot be inflected. The third difference is that the first set is an "open" set whereas the second set is a "closed" set: words capable of taking inflections are being added to the language continually as new nouns and verbs are created; however, no new determiners (*a, the*) or prepositions (*down*) are being created in the same way.

Structure words, along with inflections on the content words, provide much of the grammatical framework of English. We can observe how this is the case in such a poem as Lewis Carroll's "Jabberwocky," here printed with the structure words and inflections in boldface:

> **'Twas** brillig, **and the** slithy toves
> **Did** gyre **and** gimble **in the** wabe:
> **All** mimsy **were the** borogoves,
> **And the** mome raths outgrabe.

We need not be surprised that the poem filled Alice's head with ideas but that she was not at all clear what those ideas were.

Collocations

We can ask further questions about the relationships of words that cooccur in a discourse. For example, what kinds of words cooccur in sentences? The word *soldier* is more likely to be found in context with words such as *war, guarded, army,* and *weapon* than with *blackboard, coiffure,* and *brocade. Seminar* is also much more likely to cooccur with *professor* and *books* than it is with *yacht* or *wardrobe.* However, we will find some difficulty in establishing such related sets of words, sometimes called **collocations,** in a principled way. Just how does one draw the bounds around a particular set? For example, which words collocate in this paragraph? *Collocations, collocate, relationships, cooccur, discourse, related, sets,* *words, principled, study, data, paragraph, linguistic* perhaps do. But what is so special about the set, except that it is unique, occurring only in this paragraph? What wider generalizations are possible?

The insights to be gained from a well-developed study of collocation have intrigued a number of linguists. However, many are skeptical about collocation in the absence of systematic ways of handling data. Consequently, the study of collocation tends to remain almost virgin territory within linguistics, for it is territory perhaps more suitable to exploration by rhetoricians and psychologists than to exploration by linguists.

Registers

One can also study **registers,** the particular vocabulary choices made by an individual or a group to fulfill the variety of language functions that add up to communication. There are technical registers, social registers, and perhaps even regional registers. A professor uses a certain kind of language, or register, with an academic peer, another with a son or daughter, and still another with a friend at a football game. The professor, the parent, and the football fan are the same person, but the particular words and expressions used vary considerably according to the context and audience. The study of registers raises questions additional to those raised by the study of collocations, because with registers a subtle interplay of syntax and meaning occurs that is extremely difficult to investigate. Linguists have tended to focus their attention more on questions of dialect differences than of register differences, having devised techniques to handle the former, as we shall see in Chapter 12. Consequently, those aspects of register which can be subsumed under dialect tend to be explored and the others ignored. Again this consequence follows from the absence of a well-defined theory of register.

MORPHOLOGY

Most linguists have discussed questions of meaning almost entirely within the study of morphology, that is, the study of minimal meaning units and the possible combinations of these in a language, as outlined in Chapter 5. Many problems have arisen in such study, some of which appear to resist solution. For example, there are questions concerning the actual specification of the meanings of morphemes. *Good* might be said to have the meaning of "good," except that such a definition is really no more than a tautology. However, where is the meaning "good" in *better* or *best?* And how are the other morphemes in these two words best described within a consistent system? Are they "more" and "most" respectively, and are these the same "more" and "most" that occur in *more money* and *most unwise?* Even this last solution is not without its own difficulties because we can factor out a common meaning element from "more" and "most." Might we not also say that *bad* is "not good," so that both *good* and *bad* contain a common morpheme? And if we do this for *good* and *bad,* should we not do the same for all antonyms that have obviously polar meanings: *hot* and *cold, old* and *young,* and *large* and *small?* But are the meanings only polar out of context, as with *large insect* and *small whale?*

Does *goose* in *gooseberry* have the same meaning as *goose* in *goose and gander,* does *green* mean the same in both *greenhouse* and *green and gold,* and what does *cran* mean in *cranberry?* Any investigator who takes almost any English sentence and attempts to analyze that sentence into its ultimate constituent morphemes according to the procedures outlined in Chapter 5 will experience difficulty in deciding what many of these ultimate constituents "mean." The investigator may well conclude that the study of morphology is more concerned with discovering meaning units called *morphemes* than with saying anything very important about meaning itself.

Componential Analysis

Fortunately, within the traditional morphological framework at least two rather interesting approaches to meaning have been developed. One of these employs a technique called **componential analysis.** Componential analysis is an attempt to discover the ultimate meaning units out of which a particular set of words appears to be composed in some systematic way. Certain segments of vocabulary lend themselves to such analysis better than others, for example, kinship systems, pronoun systems, color terms, systems of folk medicine, and sometimes words for discussing various kinds of flora and fauna. Through componential analysis, we can seek to find out how speakers use the vocabulary of a language in order to classify reality by referring to certain parameters of meaning.

By examining such a system as the words a speaker uses to name various relatives, we can establish how parameters such as sex, age, sanguinity, and generation are used to provide component meanings for the system. The distribution of such meanings in the system is likely to correlate with certain social patterns. For example, if a large set of terms exists for relationships through the mother's side of the family and for female relationships in general and a correspondingly small set for equivalent male relationships, this evidence would suggest the existence of a matriarchal system among the speakers. In English *aunt* can refer to four different relationships: father's sister, mother's sister, father's brother's wife, or mother's brother's wife. This evidence suggests that the exact identification of aunts is not very important for speakers of English and that aunts are not really very important people in family structures. Although English has a poor vocabulary for expressing membership in any kind of "extended" family, most speakers of English do not consider this poverty to be a deficiency because they live in "nuclear" rather than extended families.

The technique of componential analysis is severely limited, and its usefulness outside quite small closed sets of words, such as those referring to certain family and social groups, pronoun systems, and folk-type classifications, or taxonomies, of certain natural phenomena, may be questioned. Nevertheless, the technique is much more sophisticated than any developed so far for solving problems of collocation and register, and anthropological linguists in particular have found it useful in their work.

Markedness

The concept of markedness in linguistics derives from the work of a number of European linguists. It has also been developed and used more in investigations into phonology and syntax than into semantics. The concept holds that many linguistic units are best described as members of pairs of units, one member of the pair being **marked** and the other member **unmarked** for a certain feature. For example, in the phonological systems of some languages, English being an example, units such as /b/ and /p/ are marked and unmarked respectively. In this case the marking is manifested by the feature of [+voice] associated with /b/ but lacking with /p/. In syntactic systems the marked member of a pair of grammatical units contains a feature not present in the unmarked member, and this feature provides the distinctive contrast between the two. In English we may consider *cats* to be marked for "plural" in contrast to unmarked *cat, runs* to be marked for "third person" in contrast to unmarked *run, baked* to be marked for "past tense" in contrast to unmarked *bake,* and *best* to be marked for "superlative" in contrast to unmarked *good.*

However, the example of *good* and *best* raises what appears to be a serious problem in connection with markedness. The use of the two terms *marked* and *unmarked* implies the presence of a binary system, but *good, better, best* appears to be a ternary system. We could argue that the sequence *good, better, best* displays a hierarchy of binary systems rather than a ternary system: *good* is unmarked, *better* and *best* are both marked for "comparison," and in addition, *best* is marked for "superlative." Consequently, *best* is "superlative comparative," *better* is "comparative," and *good* is unmarked.

A similar technique may be used in other areas of meaning because certain pairs of words exist, the members of which appear to be in an unmarked-marked relationship. For example, many animal names are unmarked as to the sex of the animal: *dog, sheep, pig, horse,* and so on. But there are also marked varieties if "male" and "female" need to be specified (with gaps, of course): *dog* (————, *bitch*), *sheep* (*ram, ewe*), *pig* (*boar, sow*), and *horse* (*stallion, mare*). We are all aware too that "man includes woman," so that generic *man* is unmarked and "sexless," whereas generic *woman* is always "female." Likewise, "day includes night," making *night* the marked member of that pair. In the pair *man* and *bachelor* the second word is marked for "unmarried," just as is *spinster* in the pair *woman* and *spinster.* In the pairs *long* and *short* and *wide* and *narrow* we use the unmarked words *long* and *wide* for ordinary measuring purposes: *a foot long* and *two yards wide.* We use *short* and *narrow* only with length and width understood: *It's short* ("not long") and *It's too narrow* ("not wide enough"). Hence *short* and *narrow* are marked and *long* and *wide* are unmarked. The concept of "markedness" obviously has some usefulness in revealing distinctions between pairs of vocabulary items and in isolating initial differences in meaning.

MEANING AND GENERATIVE-TRANSFORMATIONAL GRAMMAR

Both componential analysis and studies of marking reveal a concern with finding ultimate semantic units or components for use in studies of meaning. A similar kind of concern arises in attempts to deal with meaning within generative-transformational theory. The discussion of that theory and the parts of a possible grammar of English in Chapters 7 and 8 ignored virtually all problems associated with meaning. We did note that a generative-transformational grammar relates meaning to sounds through a syntactic system. The two preceding chapters were concerned with that syntactic system and, briefly, at the end of the previous chapter, with related phonological issues. We said little about the meanings of sentences and assumed that together the deep syntactic structure of a sentence and the meanings of the words used in that structure represent the total meaning of the sentence. This total meaning would presumably be derived through a set of rules for combining the meanings of the various words according to the syntactic structures in which they occur. What we need now is some understanding of those words and that set of rules, that is, some understanding of the semantic system, or the semantic component, of a **generative-transformational grammar.**

We are therefore assuming a model of generative-transformational grammar which has a syntactic component as its central component and two "interpretative" components (semantic and phonological) on its periphery. The syntactic component, together with the words which are somehow "fitted" into it, provides both a deep structure (derived from the phrase-structure rules) and a surface structure (derived through the transformational rules). This surface structure is given a semantic interpretation through the semantic component and a phonological realization through the phonological component.

Semantic Features

One of the first difficulties that arises in any attempt to spell out the details of a possible semantic component of a generative-transformational grammar is that of deciding how best to represent the units of meaning that we wish to introduce into deep syntactic structures. One solution is to introduce words as complete units, for example *hope, house, cat, man,* and so on, along with additional information concerning the syntactic category (noun, verb, adjective, and so on). We can also provide the basic phonological information which will later allow us to derive the actual pronunciation once all the necessary phonological rules have applied.

However, if we do not impose any restrictions, except gross grammatical ones, on what can occur with what in the deep structure, we would permit our grammar to generate the sentences in both the *a* and *b* series that follow:

a That's a fond hope.   b * That's a red hope.
   The house remained empty.   * The house breathed.
   The cat died.   * The cat spoke.
   The man spoke.   * The man which came spoke.

We cannot fail to observe that the sentences in the *b* series are somehow anomalous. We would almost certainly want to write rules that would prevent our grammar from generating such sentences. The problem seems to be one of specifying permissible relationships among words, these relationships being more subtle than simple noun-verb or adjective-noun relationships since they require classifying these various parts of speech according to certain semantic components. The rules would then recognize these additional classifications so as to disallow *hope* to be *red, houses* to *breathe, cats* to *speak,* or *man* to be referred to by *which.*

A solution to the difficulty might reside in specifying certain **semantic features** for words whenever these features have important syntactic correlates, the ignoring of which results in anomalous sentences. Consequently, we may choose to assign at least the following semantic features to the nouns given above:

$$
\begin{bmatrix} hope \\ +\text{noun} \\ -\text{concrete} \\ -\text{animate} \\ -\text{human} \end{bmatrix}
\begin{bmatrix} house \\ +\text{noun} \\ +\text{concrete} \\ -\text{animate} \\ -\text{human} \end{bmatrix}
\begin{bmatrix} cat \\ +\text{noun} \\ +\text{concrete} \\ +\text{animate} \\ -\text{human} \end{bmatrix}
\begin{bmatrix} man \\ +\text{noun} \\ +\text{concrete} \\ +\text{animate} \\ +\text{human} \end{bmatrix}
$$

The phrase-structure rules would permit an adjective such as *red,* specified among other things for the semantic feature [+concrete], to be used as a modifier of a noun specified also as [+concrete] but not of a noun specified as [−concrete]; consequently, *red hope* would not be allowed. Likewise, the verb *breathe* would require cooccurrence with a subject specified as [+animate]; therefore, *house breathed* would not be allowed. The verb *speak* would require a subject specified as [+human], but, since *cat* is [−human], *cat spoke* would be disallowed. The pronoun *which* replaces noun phrases, the head nouns of which must be specified as [−human]; however, *man* in *man which* is clearly a head noun that is [+human].

The problem of specifying the total set of features that is required for a language, or for languages in general, is an enormous one. One difficulty is knowing how far to go in specifying features. Since almost every word differs from every other word in meaning, we might argue that as many features are necessary as there are words, in which case little advantage seems to be gained in specifying features at all. In addition, certain verbs require specific kinds of subjects or objects. The verb *speak* requires a subject specified as [+human]. Likewise, the verb *doff* requires an object specified as [+outer cover] and [+upper body], since we can doff hats, coats, and jackets, but not boots and shirts. *Elapsed* requires a subject which is specified as [+time]. *Hours, days,* and *years* elapse, but not *cars, hope,* and *oranges.* In these examples the problem of the seemingly endless recursion necessary to specify all relevant features becomes apparent. Verbs like *scatter* and *disperse* are still more complicated because either the subject or the object must be specified as [+numerous], since each of sentences 1 through 6 is possible:

1 The crowd scattered.
2 The farmer scattered the seed.
3 The airplane scattered the spectators.
4 The mob dispersed.
5 The emperor dispersed the crowd.
6 The gas dispersed the platoon.

However, sentences 7 through 10 are not possible:

7 *The farmer scattered.
8 *The farmer scattered the tree.

9 *The emperor dispersed.

10 *The gas dispersed the boy.

Sentences 1 and 2 are also useful for distinguishing semantic plurality from syntactic plurality. *Crowd* in sentence 1 and *seed* in sentence 2 are semantically plural, or [+numerous], but syntactically singular. These sentences differ in meaning from sentences 11 and 12, in which *crowds* and *seeds* are syntactically plural, a fact indicated by the presence of the "plural" morpheme, spelled *s* in this case:

11 The crowds scattered.

12 The farmer scattered the seeds.

Still another difference exists between *crowd* and *seed:* we can say *much seed,* but *much crowd* is not possible. The feature [count] is required to show this difference. *Seed* may be specified as either [−count] or [+count] giving both *much seed* and *many seeds;* however, *crowd* must be specified as [+count], for, while *many crowds* is possible, *much crowd* is not. *Many* and *much* seem to cooccur with the [+count] and [−count] features respectively in specifying quantities: we can compare *many men,* in which *men* is [+count], and *much milk,* in which *milk* is [−count].

Features and Transformations

If the problem of the apparently excessive regression of feature specification can be solved, we could specify not only certain important common meaning elements for vocabulary items but also cooccurrence restrictions. A feature system would also enable us to reduce the amount of tree diagraming required to represent the deep structures of sentences at a cost, of course, of specifying features and extra transformations. For example, we could account for different kinds of determiners and singularity and plurality in noun phrases by specifying nouns for such features as [definite] and [singular], as follows:

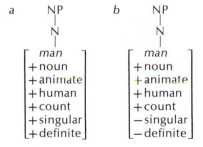

Then transformations would automatically rewrite the above structures to give new structures by copying the appropriate [+definite] or [−definite] and [+singular] or [−singular] features, as follows:

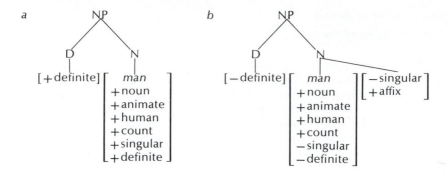

Further rules would introduce *the* as the appropriate determiner in *a* to produce *the man* as the NP and *some* as the appropriate determiner in *b* to produce *some men* as the NP.

Still another example may be useful in showing how we can use features and transformations to reduce deep-structure diagraming by increasing the quantity of information included in the semantic segments of the deep structure. Sentence 13 provides such an example:

13 The children have been going to the park.

In addition to the specifications which we have already discussed for NPs we can specify tense as [±past], that is, as either [+past] or [−past], and the Vi of the verb phrase as [+perfect] and [+progressive]. We can also specify the Adv as a noun (*park*) with certain features, among which is the preposition *to*:

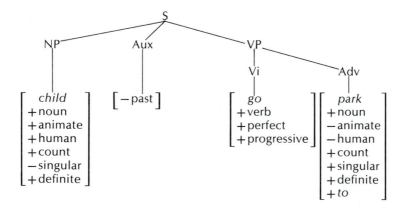

Various transformations applying to the segments allow us to rewrite the [+definite] and [−singular] features under NP, as follows:

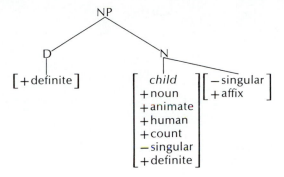

The rewriting of the features under Adv results in the following structure:

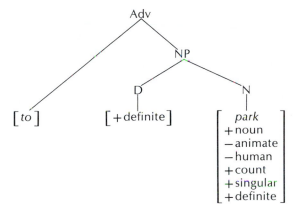

The rewriting of the remaining features under VP is more complicated. First of all, the [+perfect] and [+progressive] features result in new segments, with [+perfect] moved to the "left" of [+progressive]:

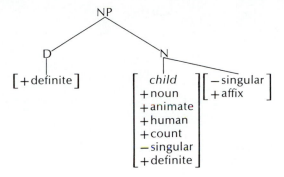

Another transformation assigns the affixes which accompany [+perfect] and [+progressive] and automatically "hops" them, just as the affix transformation did in the previous chapter:

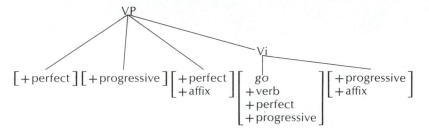

A later transformation moves the leftmost of these segments under Aux:

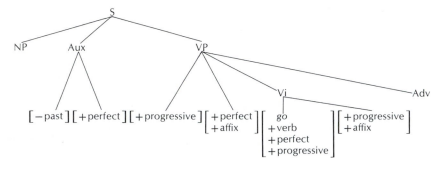

The final surface structure results after all the necessary words and affixes are introduced and the affixes are attached to words by still other transformations:

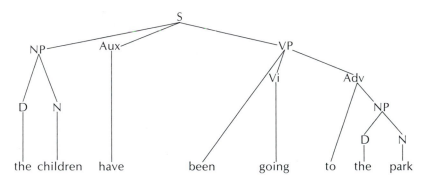

The children have been going to the park.

The transformations manifest the features that are present in any deep structure as either full words or inflections on these words, and arrange these in their proper positions in the surface structure. At each point the structures intermediate between the deep and surface structures are preserved because transformations apply to structures, syntactic structures, or segment structures, but not to the actual words or features themselves. Transformations are both structure-preserving and meaning-preserving.

Semantic Readings

Feature notation leaves many problems unsolved. One of them is that of specifying how the meanings of individual features and words somehow add up to produce the meanings of the total sentences. Some linguists have postulated the need for a set of rules to accomplish this goal. Such a set would specify the combinatorial possibilities of individual meanings and offer interpretations for the possible combinations. The rules, called **semantic projection rules,** would provide semantic interpretations for syntactic structures into which meaning units had been inserted at some point or points. The meaning units themselves would be introduced directly, in the form of words, as were *go, child,* and *park* above, or in the form of features, as were [+perfect] and [−singular] above, or in the form of idioms, as for example, *kick the bucket, way out,* and *fast and loose.* The syntax is the central generative component of the whole grammar, and this semantic component merely synthesizes the meaning, just as the phonological component provides the sound.

Within linguistics the above approach has often been called an interpretative approach. Since one of its principal advocates is Noam Chomsky, the originator of generative-transformational theory, it is sometimes referred to as either the *extended standard theory* or *interpretative semantics.*

GENERATIVE SEMANTICS

An alternative approach to making semantics interpretative is possible. It is to make semantics generative. Such a solution makes the semantic component the generative component and the syntactic component interpretative. Consequently, the deep structure of a sentence is a semantic structure rather than a syntactic one and syntactic restrictions and arrangements are completely determined by the semantic structure. This approach is known as **generative semantics.**

Such an arrangement has several advantages. The first advantage is the intuitive appeal of such a system: speakers put meanings into sentence form, and the meanings they want to express may be said to determine the specific sentence forms that are chosen, rather than vice versa. A further weakness of keeping the syntax central is the generation of deep structures which cannot be allowed to become surface structures, for example, deep structures containing Imp but not *you* or *will.* Such structures must be prevented from becoming sentences by rules which reject, or block, the structures. Making the semantics generative has the advantage of avoiding a counterintuitive "blocking." The final advantage is that certain paraphrase relationships are stated rather easily within a generative semantics but not at all or only with considerable virtuosity within a generative syntax. For example, sentences 14 and 15 have the same meaning:

14 His resistance to the idea surprised me.

15 It surprised me that he resisted the idea.

In interpretative semantics it might be possible to show the similarity in meaning by allowing alternative stylistic variations from a single deep structure. However, such a solution is difficult to advance for sentences 16 and 17, which have quite different surface forms but the same meaning:

16 His operation was a success.

17 He operated successfully.

Sentences 18 and 19 are different in meaning from sentence 17 but show another possible meaning for 16:

18 The operation on him was a success.

19 He was operated on successfully.

Sentences 18 and 19 are also synonymous. What seem to be required are two abstract semantic structures which express the semantic relationships, one of sentences 16 and 17 and the other of sentences 16 (other reading), 18, and 19. These abstract semantic structures can then be realized syntactically in different ways.

CASE GRAMMAR

Sentences 20 to 23 can be used to illustrate some of the possibilities of another approach, known as **case grammar:**

20 The janitor opened the door.

21 The key opened the door.

22 The janitor opened the door with the key.

23 The door opened.

From sentences 20 to 23 we note that the verb *open* can cooccur with certain nouns and some indication of time (or modality). A sentence, therefore, may be considered to have three elements: modality, one or more nouns (or roles) in a propositional relationship to a verb, and that verb:

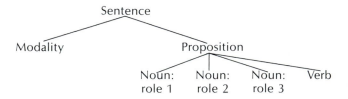

In sentences 20 through 23 *janitor* fills an agent role, *door* an object role, and *key* an instrument role in conjunction with "past" modality and the verb *open*. The verb *open* required the object role to be filled but does not require the other roles to be filled: something must open or be opened. If only the object role is filled, then sentence 23 results. If both the agent and object roles are filled, then either sentence 20 or sentence 24 results.

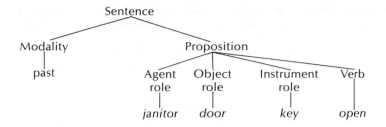

24 The door was opened by the janitor.

If only the object and instrument roles are filled, then sentence 21 results. If all three roles are filled, either sentence 22 or sentence 25 results:

25 The door was opened with the key by the janitor.

This approach produces some interesting problems. For example, one problem involves the relationship between roles and grammatical functions. Although *janitor* is in an agent role in 20 and 22 and *key* is in an instrument role in 21, both are the grammatical subjects of *opened,* as is *door,* in an object role, in 23. The grammatical-subject function, therefore, can be filled by very different roles. Sentences 26 and 27 contain still another role in the subject function:

26 The dog died.
27 John left.

Neither *dog* nor *John* is an agent: instead each is an animate noun somehow affected by the action of the verb, a role sometimes called the dative role. We can compare *John* in sentence 27 with *John* in sentence 28, in which it is in an agent role:

28 John tore the book.

Only a few of the possible roles have been illustrated here. How many roles are necessary is still undecided, but investigations have shown that certain interesting restrictions occur among the roles that are known to exist. For example, sentence 29 can be interpreted only as meaning that both John and the brick broke the window by both coming into contact with it, even though sentences 30 and 31 are possible:

29 John and the brick broke the window.
30 John broke the window.
31 The brick broke the window.

Consequently, in sentence 29 both *John* and *brick* must have the same role, in this case instrument; *John* cannot be agent and *brick* instrument in this sentence.
Another interesting problem arises in connection with the prepositions that

occur with the various roles. If the agent is made the grammatical object of a sentence, it is preceded by *by,* as in sentence 24. If both object and instrument roles are filled, regardless of whether the agent is present or not, and the object role is the grammatical subject, as in sentence 25, then the instrument is preceded by *with.* A definite system of relationships appears to exist among particular prepositions, particular roles, and particular grammatical functions in surface structures.

This kind of grammar can be used to reveal similarities among certain words, for example between *die* and *kill.* *Die* allows for only a single dative role, as in sentence 26: *The dog died.* However, the requirements for *kill* are obligatorily a dative and optionally an agent and an instrument, as in sentences 32 to 37:

32 The dog was killed. (dative)

33 The dog was killed with a knife. (dative, instrument)

34 The man killed the dog. (agent, dative)

35 The dog was killed by the man. (dative, agent)

36 The man killed the dog with a knife. (agent, dative, instrument)

37 The dog was killed with a knife by the man. (dative, instrument, agent)

Causation

Kill can also be said to mean "cause to die" so we may consider *kill* to be the causative form of *die.* *Kill* is a **causative verb.** We can then account for the difference in distribution between *die* and *kill* by the presence of the semantic element [+cause] in *kill* but not in *die* and possibly even understand why sentences 38 to 45 are synonymous:

38 Smoking caused Peter to die.

39 Smoking caused Peter's death.

40 Smoking killed Peter.

41 Peter's death was caused by smoking.

42 Peter was killed by smoking.

43 Peter's smoking killed him.

44 Peter died from smoking.

45 Peter smoked himself to death.

The word *possibly* is deliberately used, because it is not easy to find principles which clearly demarcate where postulating interesting and productive structural similarities ends and creating scholastic monstrosities begins.

However, the causative-noncausative distinction is useful in describing how many verbs work. Verbs like *lengthen, shorten,* and *widen* even have an overt causative marker in the *-en* suffix, as in a sentence such as *He shortened the rope.* If someone flies a plane, the plane flies because that person "causes" it to fly. This applies also to verbs like *burn* (a book), *sink* (a ship), *open* (a door), *fill* (a can), *bounce* (*a ball*), and *stop* (*a fight*). But if someone sweeps a floor, the floor does not sweep. Likewise, with *take* (*a book*), *toss* (*a ball*), *strike* (*a wall*), and *open* (*a box*). Whereas *He opened the door and the window* is satisfactory (The door opened, The window opened), *He opened the door and the box* is somewhat bizarre because of the conjunction of a causative construction (The door opened) and a noncausative construction (* The box opened).

Such explanatory possibilities are in many cases extremely valuable. For example, sentences 46 and 47 are possible, but sentences 48 and 49 are not:

46 The boy is sad.

47 The movie is sad.

48 * The boy and the movie are sad.

49 * The boy is as sad as the movie he saw.

Sentence 47 contains a causative verb because *The movie is sad* means something like "The movie causes people to be sad." Sentence 48 is disallowed because a causative construction is once more conjoined to a noncausative one, and sentence 49 is disallowed because a comparison construction does not allow for the conjoining of two such disparate constructions.

Negation

A multitude of other problems exists in connection with any study of meaning. A few further examples will serve to show some of the variety of these problems. Sentence 50 is ambiguous:

50 John doesn't beat his wife because he loves her.

Sentence 50 can mean either that John doesn't beat his wife at all being too much in love with her to do so, or that he does beat her, but for a reason other than that he loves her. The ambiguity resides in what may be called the "scope of the negative," that is, in what exactly is being negated in the sentence. We should note that the corresponding positive sentence 51 is unambiguous: in sentence 51 either John, or his wife, or both, need psychiatric help:

51 John beats his wife because he loves her.

Sentence 52, containing a negative, is likewise ambiguous, but the corresponding positive sentence 53 is unambiguous:

52 John won't speak until ten o'clock
   (because Fred will be speaking until then).
   (because he has to finish at 9:45).

53 John will speak until ten o'clock.

We should also note that the negative sentence 54 does not have a corresponding positive sentence like 55:

54 John didn't die until five o'clock.

55 *John died until five o'clock.

Likewise, there is no *John budged to match John didn't budge. Negation, particularly as it concerns the scope of negatives, would appear to be an interesting area in which to investigate problems of meaning.

Presupposition

A sentence such as 56 presupposes that the team in question played in the World Series in 1975:

56 The Yankees lost the 1975 World Series.

However, sentence 57 contains no such presupposition:

57 The Yankees didn't lose the 1975 World Series.

In this case, the problem does not involve the scope of the negation but concerns the real-world conditions that must exist to make the sentences acceptable in meaning. Sentence 56 can be used only if the Yankees played in the 1975 World Series, but sentence 57 can be used whether or not they played. Sentence 56 means the Yankees played and lost, but sentence 57 can mean either that they played in and won the 1975 World Series or that they did not lose the 1975 World Series because they did not play in it. This area of presupposition is also of interest to some linguists because the acceptability of sentences depends to some extent on the claims that sentences must be making about the world because of their structures. A person cannot confess to something that was never done or never felt by someone to have been done, or for someone else's doing something; consequently, sentences 58 and 59 must be rejected:

58 *I confessed to being 250 years old.

59 *I confessed to John's committing the crime.

Nor can one answer the question in 60 unless he agrees with the basic presupposition that he has indeed been beating his wife:

60 Have you stopped beating your wife?

A CONCLUDING NOTE

In Chapters 7 and 8, we postulated that the syntactic component of a grammar provided the apparatus necessary to generate an infinite set of sentences. We assumed that an additional semantic component would provide for the interpretation of these sentences. In this chapter some examples and arguments have been presented to indicate a few of the apparent inadequacies of such an approach. This chapter outlined parts of other approaches in which the semantic component is made generative and the syntactic component merely produces the observed sentences from the meanings that are generated. At the moment, possibly the most interesting question in linguistics concerns which of these two approaches to meaning and syntax is likely to produce more insights into the structure of language and to stimulate further productive investigations.

Two important principles are generally recognized: the first that sentences must be interpreted in context; the second that some of the restrictions on the meanings of sentences are cognitive ones. Context disambiguates sentences. We must remember that most sentences are ambiguous out of context if for no other reason than that the exact referents of many of the words are unknown. But context also makes sentences appropriate or inappropriate, as in the "requests" contained in sentences 61 to 65:

61 Shut the door!

62 Please shut the door!

63 Would you mind shutting the door for me?

64 I wonder if you would mind shutting the door for me.

65 It's cold in here!

More and more it appears that pragmatic considerations, such as the actual contexts in which words and sentences are used, have important linguistic consequences.

Because speakers and listeners use language, their cognitive abilities are also important. What speakers and listeners can remember, produce, and process takes on significance. A sentence such as 66:

66 The halfback the coach the students revered liked scored a touchdown.

is hard to understand because of the way in which the clauses are embedded within each other. However, the addition of a pair of *that's* helps to break up the three initial NPs, as in 67:

67 The halfback that the coach that the students revered liked scored a touchdown.

These pronouns help the listener understand what is going on in the sentence by reducing the cognitive burden of the structure. Apparently, human cognitive limitations lead to languages "employing" such devices as relative pronouns and restrictions on the variety of different types of surface structure. Certain syntactic constraints therefore have a cognitive basis: only certain linguistic possibilities exist because people could not possibly cope with anything and everything that might be possible.

BIBLIOGRAPHIC NOTES

Questions of meaning have been approached from many directions, and Brown's *Words and Things* ranges over many of the approaches. Three philosophical works of interest are Austin's *How to Do Things with Words,* Quine's *Word and Object,* and Ziff's *Semantic Analysis;* the first of these books has been particularly influential in linguistics in recent years. Three entirely different approaches to meaning from these, and from each other, are those from general semantics, represented by Hayakawa's *Language in Thought and Action,* from literature and symbolism, represented by Ogden and Richards' *Meaning of Meaning,* and from psychology, represented by Osgood, Suci, and Tannenbaum's *Measurement of Meaning.*

Information theory is discussed in Cherry's *Human Communication,* Miller's *Language and Communication,* and Shannon and Weaver's *Mathematical Theory of Communication.* Chapter 23 of Gleason's *Introduction to Descriptive Linguistics* contains a brief introduction to this topic.

Componential analysis is the subject of some of the early chapters in Burling's *Man's Many Voices,* Lounsbury's "Semantic Analysis of the Pawnee Kinship Usage," and Goodenough's "Componential Analysis and the Study of Meaning." Form classes and function words are discussed in Fries' *Structure of English* and Roberts' *Patterns of English.* No comprehensive, easily readable treatment of marking exists.

Semantics within a generative-transformational grammar is the concern of Katz and Fodor's "Structure of a Semantic Theory" and of Katz' *Philosophy of Language* and his *Semantic Theory.* Bolinger's "Atomization of Meaning" and Weinreich's "Explorations in Semantic Theory" are critiques of their views. General problems of meaning within current linguistics are discussed by a number of writers in Bach and Harms' *Universals in Linguistic Theory* (particularly the papers by Fillmore and McCawley), in Fillmore and Langendoen's *Studies in Linguistic Semantics,* in Jacobs and Rosenbaum's *Readings in English Transformational Grammar* (particularly Parts 2 and 3), and in Steinberg and Jakobovits' *Semantics.* Lakoff's *Irregularity in Syntax* is a critique of many ideas usually associated with generative-transformational theory and Langendoen's *Essentials of English Grammar* is an attempt to incorporate many recent linguistic ideas into a post-Chomskyan sketch of English grammar. Chafe's *Meaning and the Structure of Language* describes a semantically oriented grammar. A general introduction to the various problems discussed in this chapter is Leech's *Semantics.*

EXERCISES

9-1 Check to make sure that you understand each of the terms printed in **boldface** in Chapter 9.

9-2 Chapter 9 makes distinctions between certain terms. Explain the distinction between the following terms as clearly as you can: *content words* and *structure words; generative syntax* and *generative semantics; agent* and *dative; object* and *instrument.*

9-3 Each of the following adjectives has at least two antonyms: *bright, fair, light, rich, right, tender.* Use each adjective in two sentences which show its different meanings. Then use the antonyms of each meaning in two further sentences.

9-4 In Chapter 8 adjectives modifying nouns such as *old* in *old man* were derived from relative clauses: Man [man is old] → man [who is old] → man [old] → old man. Explain any problems you see in connection with the derivation of the following phrases. What solutions can you propose?

1 the former president	6 my civil rights
2 the right side	7 a beautiful soprano
3 an old friend	8 a good friend
4 the late George Smith	9 a poor sport
5 a second Christ	10 the poor guy

9-5 What does *good* mean in each of the following expressions?

1 good assignment	9 good rate
2 good beating	10 good reason
3 good book	11 good results
4 good knife	12 good water
5 good idea	13 good woman
6 good music	14 a good win
7 good parents	15 a good cup of coffee
8 good tickets	16 good wine

9-6 Place the words in the following paragraph into two groups: (1) content words and (2) structure words. Are there any problems in assignment?

People have long been interested in language, in such matters as its origin, its nature, and its uses, whether in persuasion, poetry, or prayer. Language has always been something of a mystery, not unlike the mysteries of creation, the origin of the sun, and the coming of fire. As such, it has provided people with such a rich source of myth that even today much of the mystery of language prevails.

9-7 Explain how the members of the following pairs of words differ from each other in their semantic composition. Write a sentence for each word such that the other word cannot be used as a replacement.

1 skin, flesh	6 wife, widow
2 boot, shoe	7 arm, hand
3 ice, water	8 cow, bull
4 shirt, jacket	9 mare, foal
5 meat, fish	10 twig, branch

9-8 What phrase or sentence results from each of the following?

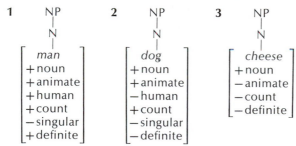

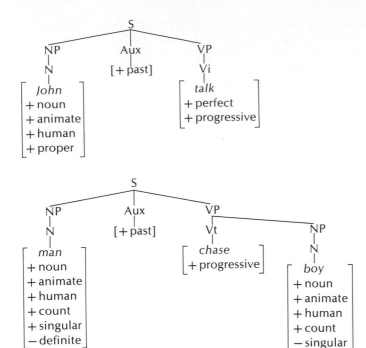

9-9 What role does each of the italicized phrases play in the following sentences? You will have to specify some roles not mentioned in Chapter 9.

1 *Mr. Smith* died *last week.*
2 *John* broke *the window with a brick.*
3 *John* hit *Fred with a brick.*
4 *The brick* broke *the window.*
5 *John* hit *Fred* and *the window at the same time.*
6 *John* hit *the floor.*
7 *The vase* was broken *by John.*
8 *John* made *a vase.*
9 *The news* was broken *by John.*
10 *John* heard *the news.*

9-10 What presupposition is behind each of the following sentences?

1 Have you stopped beating your wife?
2 Even Mary has done it.
3 I forgave him for his insult.
4 John is tall even for a basketball player.
5 I pronounce you man and wife.
6 John is in tenth grade, but he can spell.
7 Smith has been here before.
8 I sentence you to fifteen years' hard labor.
9 My neighbor had a miscarriage.
10 He reported the crime.

9-11 Why is each of the following sentences strange, probably to the point of being ungrammatical?

   1 (?) Be pretty!
   2 (?) His father was believed by the boy.
   3 (?) The boy and the accident stopped the bus.
   4 (?) John is as sad as the movie he saw.
   5 (?) John is as sad as Mary is old.
   6 (?) The dog believed his master would return.
   7 (?) He wrote the novel I stole from the library.
   8 (?) The door is open and wide.

9-12 Explain how each of the following sentences is ambiguous.

   1 John won't speak until ten o'clock.
   2 John doesn't beat his wife because he loves her.
   3 John loves his wife and so do I.
   4 John and Mary went to New York last week.
   5 John left his sister to paint in Paris.
   6 It didn't budge.
   7 They certainly can win.
   8 He must know that.
   9 Books are amusing friends.

10

HISTORICAL-COMPARATIVE LINGUISTICS

Chapters 1 through 9 have raised a considerable number of questions, behind which has been the assumption that our task is to study problems connected with a language as it exists at one time. Such an approach is called a **synchronic** approach, and the study is referred to as synchronic linguistics. The data are the spoken and, sometimes, written utterances that we observe. The task is to find some organizing principles that allow us to make interesting claims both about language in general and about the particular language under investigation. Sometimes a language is treated as though it were thoroughly consistent and unchanging. One of the results is that "all grammars leak" because a language is not a static entity.

Anyone who has puzzled over strange spellings or come across old documents and wondered why the language they contain is both like the current language yet somehow different knows that language is not static. But is this the only evidence that languages change? What kinds of interesting observations can be made about the changes that have occurred in a particular language and about the general nature of linguistic change? Such questions are not concerned with the charac-teristics of a language at a given time; they focus instead on a language over a period of time. We discuss questions of chronological change under the general heading of **diachronic** linguistics.

INTERNAL EVIDENCE FOR CHANGE

The first kind of evidence that language changes is the existence of old inscriptions and manuscripts, that is, written evidence. Of course, the survival of such documentation is often accidental. Obviously no such relics can be found for non-literate peoples. With literate peoples the survival of evidence varies according to factors such as the attitudes that prevailed toward permanent recordkeeping, the incidence of destructive wars, and the climatic conditions affecting preservation. Writing itself is a fairly recent phenomenon. The oldest deciphered written records, those of the Sumerians, are about 6,000 years old. Alphabetic writing is an even more recent invention. Consequently, written records not only are accidental, but also provide no more than a very shallow time depth for language history, since people have been capable of language for at the very least twenty times longer than the period for which we have records.

If we assume that any surviving writing, alphabetic or not, is systematic (for otherwise it would be ineffective), and if we know the meaning of the writing, then we should be able to say something about an older stage of the language. Sometimes we do not know what a particular piece of writing is about or know only parts of the meaning, as in the case of the Mayan inscriptions in Mexico. On the other hand, the discovery of a multilingual inscription like that on the Rosetta Stone, in Greek and two varieties of Egyptian (hieroglyphic and demotic) or, more rarely, the skilled detective work of someone like Ventris in his decipherment of Linear B can provide the desired breakthrough into the past. If the writing is not in either a syllabic or an alphabetic system, we can say very little about the sounds of an older form of a language, but fortunately the majority of surviving documents do provide phonological evidence. Decipherable documents are invaluable in historical work, particularly documents whose provenance—that is, their date and place of origin—is known. In addition, good readings of such texts are mandatory; therefore some specialists (**paleographers**) choose to work on problems of determining the provenance of texts and the best readings. The quality of the data that the historical linguist finds in documentary sources can be no better than the readings provided for these sources. Paleographers and historical linguists therefore often work hand in hand, for, although there is a difference between an interest in the scribal practices of Ancient Egypt and one in historical phonology, the scribes were writing down sounds, and only some kinds of sounds were possible in Ancient Egyptian.

Much of the work on languages that are widely spoken in the world today has been done with the aid of historical documents, since numerous written records are available dating back several thousand years. With many languages of the world, however, no such documents exist to show that a language has changed or how it has changed. Consequently, other features of a language must provide the evidence for change. What these are, and how it is possible to demonstrate, in the absence of documentation, that a language such as English has changed over the centuries, are issues we shall return to later. We must first examine the uses of written evidence to see what can be inferred about previous stages of a language.

In Old English writing, scribes were careful to distinguish between *worde,* a dative and instrumental singular form meaning "to a word" or "with a word," and *worda,* a genitive plural form, meaning "of words," and between *denu,* a singular form meaning "valley," and *dena,* a plural form meaning "valleys." At a later stage, the form *worde* is used in both dative and instrumental singular and genitive plural functions. One conclusion might be that final *e* and *a* were no longer distinguished in speaking, having fallen together as one sound. Likewise, instead of *denu* or *dena* we later find *dene* meaning both "valley" and "valleys." This evidence suggests that all final vowels have fallen together and are being written *e.* At a still later stage, we find "valleys" being written as *denes,* the result apparently of the spread of the more common *s* ending for "plural" to words that did not have this ending. In certain other English documents the spelling *deleite* is found for "delight" and the spelling *niht* for "night." We can hypothesize that the second vowel in *deleite* was pronounced differently from the vowel in *niht,* having perhaps originated from a different source. However, the current spelling *delight* and the identical pronunciations of the vowels indicate that at some time in the history of English the two vowels fell together.

We can therefore draw inferences from the spellings in old texts. In much the same way we can see evidence for several current pronunciations in certain "phonetic" spellings that occur, spellings such as *procede* for *proceed* and *preceed* for *precede* providing evidence that there is no difference in the pronunciations of *-ceed* and *-cede.* Likewise, the spellings *dipthong* and *fasen* indicate actual pronunciations, and the confusion between the spellings of *complement* and *compliment* indicates that the two words are homophonous, that is, are pronounced alike.

Evidence that language changes also comes from surviving literary forms, particularly poetic forms involving rhyming conventions. The rhyme can be either front rhyme, that is, alliteration, or end rhyme. Chaucer rhymed *clean* and *mean* but not *clean* and *green.* He did not rhyme *ea* spellings with *ee* spellings. One hypothesis, the correct one, is that these vowels were different in Chaucer's time and, therefore, could not be used in rhyming. On the other hand, Shakespeare rhymed *break* and *speak, die* and *joy, grace* and *grease, far* and *war, boot* and *foot,* and *cough* and *laugh;* and still later, Pope rhymed *join* and *divine, obey* and *tea, grace* and *brass, ought* and *fault,* and *besieged* and *obliged.* The evidence from Shakespeare and Pope creates problems of a different order than does the evidence from Chaucer. It is not difficult to understand how two sounds can fall together as did the [æ] of Chaucer's *mean* with the [ē] of his *green,* but it is difficult to understand how words that rhymed for Shakespeare and Pope no longer rhyme today, particularly if we subscribe to the hypothesis that sound change is regular. Several explanations are possible for what might have happened. First of all, we could argue for the existence of more than one pronunciation for certain words in Shakespeare's and Pope's times, just as certain words today exist in more than one pronunciation. We might then postulate that in certain cases Shakespeare and Pope chose the most convenient pronunciation just to make the rhyme. A second explanation could be that subtle combinations of factors may work to produce sound change and that the modern differences in pronunciation result from combinations that effected changes only in certain environments. A final explanation could be that the sounds were once phonetically similar but phonologically different; that is, at a deep level they had different properties. We could then argue that any change in the phonological representation of one sound in each pair would account for the emergence of the phonetic differences which we observe today.

Perhaps a more basic question we might ask about any writing system concerns the kinds of conventions that are observed. English has words like *name, mete, ride, note,* and *rule* with what have been called "long vowel plus e" spellings, and the names of the letters *a, e, i, o,* and *u* are not given their "continental" values but peculiar English values. We also have spellings like *laugh, night, knee,* and *wring.* If we assume that English spelling is systematic so that the final e in the first five words and such combinations as -*gh-, kn-,* and *wr-* in the others have an explanation, then such spellings provide evidence about earlier stages of English. Likewise, when we find old documents in which the Latin words *Caesar, versus,* and *Virgilius* are spelled as *Casere, fers,* and *Firgilius* respectively, we might want to ask why such spellings occur. The spelling *Casere* indicates that the word was borrowed from Latin with an initial [k] sound and that some kind of palatalization has occurred since, so that the [k] has shifted to [s], a not unusual sound change as we shall see in Chapter 11. The spellings *fers* and *Firgilius* result from the fact that at one stage in the history of English, the period known as Old English, the sounds we associate today with *v* and *f,* that is, [v] and [f], were not phonemically distinct. They were allophonic variants of a single phoneme, [f] always being found in initial position in words, never [v]. Hence the substitution of English *f* for Latin *v.*

In many ways a still more useful source of information, but a rarer kind, is provided by the occasional writer who comments on his language or who is motivated either to preserve a certain kind of pronunciation or to reform spelling. Consequently, older grammarians provide certain kinds of evidence. About 400 B.C. the Indian grammarian Pāṇini was motivated to describe Sanskrit partly out of a desire to preserve fixed readings for sacred texts. About 800 years ago Orm was motivated to try to reform English spelling, particularly to show consistencies between short and long vowels by use of a consonant doubling convention for the former. He therefore wrote lines in his "Orrmulum" like the following:

> Annd ȝiff mann wile witenn whi icc hafe don þiss dede,
> Whi icc till Ennglissh hafe wennd goddspelles hallȝhe lare:
> Icc hafe itt don forrþi þatt all crisstene follkess berrhless
> Iss lang uppo þatt an þatt teȝȝ goddspelles hallȝhe lare
> Wiþþ fulle mahhte follȝhe rihht þurrh þohht, þurrh word, þurrh
> dede.

Such lines provide useful information about the language of late twelfth-century England in that they indicate which vowels were short and which were long at that time.

EXTERNAL EVIDENCE FOR CHANGE

So far we have discussed only the previous state of one language to illustrate that languages change. However, resemblances also occur among different languages. A simple example is that of the pronunciation of the word for "hundred" in Italian [tʃɛnto], Spanish [θjento], and French [sã]. The Italian and Spanish words are quite alike in pronunciation and the French word resembles both. The three pronunciations also have interesting similarities to the Latin word for "hundred" [kɛntum], which in turn, has a certain resemblance to English [həndrəd]. These resemblances are in such matters as the presence of a nasal or nasalized vowel, common disyllabic structure, a [d] corresponding to a [t], and so on. We can postulate a historical relationship among the different languages rather than an accidental one. An inspection of the words, cited in normal spellings, for the numbers one to ten in various languages in Figure 10-1 also leads us to conclude that a historical relationship exists among these languages; an alternative explanation of extensive borrowing among the languages is much less satisfactory.

Observations of data like these prompted Sir William Jones to make the first known statement about their importance in historical linguistics. In 1786 he addressed the Asiatic Society of Bengal as follows:

> The *Sanscrit* language, whatever be its antiquity, is of a wonderful structure; more perfect than the *Greek,* more copious than the *Latin,* and more exquisitely refined than either, yet bearing to both of them a stronger affinity, both in the roots of verbs and in the forms of grammar, than could possibly have been produced by accident; so strong indeed, that no philologer could examine them all three, without believing them to have sprung from some

English	German	Danish	Greek	Russian	Polish
one	eins	en	heis	odin	jeden
two	zwei	to	duo	dva	dwa
three	drei	tre	treis	tri	trzy
four	vier	fire	tettares	chetyre	cztery
five	fünf	fem	pente	pyat'	pięć
six	sechs	seks	hex	shest'	sześć
seven	sieben	syv	hepta	sem'	siedem
eight	acht	otte	oktō	vosem'	osiem
nine	neun	ni	ennea	devyat'	dziewięć
ten	zehn	ti	deka	desyat'	dziesięć

Latin	Italian	French	Spanish	Persian	Sanskrit
ūnus	uno	un	uno	yek	ekas
duo	due	deux	dos	do	dvā
trēs	tre	trois	tres	se	trayas
quattuor	quattro	quatre	cuatro	char	catvāras
quīnque	cinque	cinq	cinco	panj	pañca
sex	sei	six	seis	shesh	ṣaṭ
septem	sette	sept	siete	haft	sapta
octō	otto	huit	ocho	hasht	aṣṭā
novem	nove	neuf	nueve	noh	nava
decem	dieci	dix	diez	dah	daśa

FIGURE 10-1 Numbers one to ten in various languages.

common source, which, perhaps, no longer exists: there is a similar reason, though not quite so forcible, for supposing that both the *Gothick* and the *Celtick,* though blended with a very different idiom, had the same origin with the *Sanscrit;* and the old *Persian* might be added to the same family, if this were the place for discussing any question concerning the antiquities of *Persia.*

Such evidence led Jones and others to conclude that languages do change and that similarities among languages are often not accidental. We can also see that whereas certain languages do have similarities, for example English and Sanskrit, others do not, for example English and Japanese:

Sanskrit	English	Japanese
ekas	one	hitotsu
dvā	two	futatsu
trayas	three	mittsu
catvāras	four	yottsu
pañca	five	itsutsu
ṣaṭ	six	muttsu
sapta	seven	nanatsu
aṣṭā	eight	yattsu
nava	nine	kokonotsu
daśa	ten	tō

The data contained in Figure 10-1 may lead us to make hypotheses about previous states of a language, about "parent" languages, that is, languages from which other languages may have descended, and about the processes of linguistic change. Investigators need not be daunted by the absence of written records. They can use the evidence from the speech they observe and, in investigating the languages of nonliterate peoples or peoples who have left no written records themselves, can sometimes draw on observations recorded by travelers, explorers, and missionaries.

THE BASIC ASSUMPTIONS

Many interesting possibilities open up once the data are recognized, but we require basic assumptions and techniques to explore the possibilities. The most important assumption is that change is regular and systematic, not erratic nor random. Without such an assumption reputable work is impossible. Without the additional assumption that only certain kinds of changes can occur and that these changes must be "natural," we would be free to say that anything could change to anything at any time for any reason. Although it may be so that anything can change to anything else in a language, such a change must take place over a long period of time with each individual change in the total process a "natural" one.

RECONSTRUCTION

Internal Reconstruction

We can use two basic methods in reconstructing the former stages of a language: the **internal-reconstruction** method and the **comparative** method. The method of internal reconstruction is severely limited since it employs data from only one language which are often incomplete and difficult to interpret. Briefly, the method requires us to inspect a language and account for any peculiarities of phonological and grammatical distribution that might be explained by known processes of change. For example, we might find no occurrences of [k] before [ɪ], except in words obviously borrowed from other languages, but instances of all other consonants including [č] before [ɪ] in native words. There might also be no instances of [č] after vowels. The hypothesis is that such variation did not exist at some previous time in the language. We therefore postulate that at one time [k] did occur before [ɪ] but that **palatalization,** the process whereby a high front vowel affects a preceding consonant, produced a shift of [k] to [č] before [ɪ]. The English words *children* and *cold* provide examples in which palatalization occurred in the first word but not in the second when the original beginning consonants were identical [k].

The relationships between consonants and vowels and stems and affixes in pairs of words such as *sane-sanity, weep-wept, wise-wisdom, lose-lost,* and *holy-holiday* enable us to postulate the existence of a previous stage of the language in which each pair of words contained the same vowel: [æ, ē, ī, ō, ɔ̄] respectively. We can point to processes such as diphthongization, vowel shortening, and vowel raising to account for the currently observed differences. Such processes will be discussed at greater length in Chapter 11.

An obvious connection exists between the method of internal reconstruction and certain kinds of investigations into morphology (Chapter 5) and into **generative phonology** (Chapter 8). The results are often remarkably similar. The method varies in usefulness with the kind of data that are involved, for, although it is valuable in certain kinds of phonological and morphological work, it is almost useless in syntactic studies. The method is also of little use in establishing relationships among languages except for the help it provides in reconstructing earlier stages of the individual languages among which any relationships must be sought.

Comparative Method

The main method used to reconstruct an older form of a language is the comparative method in which forms in related languages are compared. The individual sounds, words, and so on that are reconstructed and for which no surviving documentary evidence exists are called **protoforms.** A reconstructed language is called a **protolanguage.** Unattested protoforms are always preceded by an asterisk when they are cited, so *oinos* would be **Proto-Indo-European** for "one." In reconstructing a protolanguage, we look for words that are **cognates,** that is, words that have similar meanings, in different languages to discover what phonological similarities exist among the words. Complete identity of meaning is not required because word meanings can change, so that the word for "beech" in one language might equate to the word for "oak" in another (as they do in English and Greek) and even the word for "cup" to the word for "head" (as does English *cup* to German *Kopf*). We must search for genuine cognates, too, not accidental ones, so that a resemblance like *mati* and *mata,* the Greek and Malay words respectively for "eye," must soon be dismissed as an accidental one on the basis of all the other evidence from the two languages which suggests that no discernible historical relationship exists between Greek and Malay.

A little more difficult to cull out are **borrowings.** French, Latin, or Greek words borrowed into English are of no use in reconstructing the English spoken long before the periods in which the words were borrowed. Instead we must use words from the native Germanic stock. Occasionally though, borrowing can be so widespread and can have occurred so far in the past that it is difficult to discover. The words for "devil" in various languages provide such a case, for example Polish *djabel,* Latin *diabolus,* French *diable,* Welsh *diafol,* German *Teufel,* English *devil,* and Danish *djœvel.* It is tempting to postulate the existence of a common ancestral form in the protolanguage from which all these languages appear to be descended, but such gaps exist in the distribution of forms and such variations occur from the expected patterns of development from Proto-Indo-European that we believe the Greeks borrowed the word for "devil" from a source now unknown and then speakers of the other languages borrowed it from the Greeks.

The comparative method can be used only with genuine cognates. Often such words refer to things like body parts, basic human relationships, articles of food and clothing, common natural objects, and the numbers one to five or ten. There is little or no necessity to borrow words for basic objects and relationships in the real world and often a great deal of resistance to any such borrowing. These words are learned early by children and are basic to social functioning; therefore, they tend to persevere.

The comparative method depends on the availability of data such as those contained in Figure 10-2. The data show numerous systematic correspondences. Our task is one of postulating some underlying historical forms from which the forms in Figure 10-2 derive. Such forms might be *[man], *[hand], *[fōt], *[hūs], *[mūs], *[lūs], *[ūt], and *[brūn]. Certain observations can be made about these postulated forms. In *[man] and *[hand] a fronting of the vowel in English [a > æ] and a devoicing of the final consonant in Dutch and German [d > t] have

	English	Dutch	German	Swedish
"man"	mæn	man	man	man
"hand"	hænd	hant	hant	hand
"foot"	fʊt	vūt	fūs	fōt
"house"	haʊs	høys	haʊs	hūs
"mouse"	maʊs	møys	maʊs	mūs
"louse"	laʊs	løys	laʊs	lūs
"out"	aʊt	øyt	aʊs	ūt
"brown"	braʊn	brøyn	braʊn	brūn

FIGURE 10-2 Selected cognates in English, Dutch, German, and Swedish.

occurred. In *[fōt] the vowel has been raised [ō > ū] in all the languages except Swedish and has undergone an additional shortening in English [ū > ʊ]; the initial fricative has also become voiced in Dutch [f > v]. In *[hūs], *[mūs], *[lūs], *[ūt], and *[brūn] one kind of diphthongization of the vowel has taken place in English and German [ū > aʊ] and another in Dutch [ū > øy]. Swedish appears to have been the least innovative of the languages as far as change is concerned, since it preserves the older forms; on the other hand, Dutch has been the most innovative in that more changes seem to have occurred in Dutch than in the other languages. Such statements as these result from an inspection of the evidence in Figure 10-2.

In the same way we might attempt to reconstruct protoforms for the numbers one to ten from such data as those given in Figure 10-1. One such reconstruction of Proto-Indo-European numbers is as follows:

Proto-Indo-European

one	*oinos
two	*dwo
three	*treies
four	*kwetwor
five	*penkwe
six	*seks
seven	*septm
eight	*okto
nine	*neun
ten	*dekm

The numbers used today in the various languages are called the **reflexes** of the numbers reconstructed for Proto-Indo-European. Each reflex is a descendant of its Proto-Indo-European ancestor, and the changes that have occurred in each descendant have resulted from various systematic processes.

	snow	*moon*	*yoke*
German	Schnee	Mond	Joch
Old English	snaw	mona	geoc
Old Norse	snær	mani	ok
Gothic	snaiws	mena	juk
Greek	nipha	men	zugon
Latin	nivis	mensis	yugum
Irish	snechte	mi	cuing
Russian	sneg	mesyats	igo
Lithuanian	sniegas	menuo	jungas
Sanskrit	snih-	mas-	yugam
Proto-Indo-European	*snigwh-	*menes-	*yugo

FIGURE 10-3 *Snow, moon,* and *yoke* in various Indo-European languages and in Proto-Indo-European.

The words cognate with English *snow, moon,* and *yoke* in Figure 10-3 provide a further illustration of the comparative method. Among the cognates cited in Figure 10-3 are some forms from Old English, Old Norse, Gothic, and Sanskrit.

Figure 10-3 shows that protoforms are quite often longer forms than their reflexes, even without their affixes, which have been omitted. Although this result may be an artifact of the comparative method, it is the only way to explain the variety of modern reflexes. Almost certainly Proto-Indo-European forms were longer than most of their modern reflexes and Proto-Indo-European was a highly inflected language.

The words cognate with English *father* in various Indo-European languages show a still more complicated problem in establishing the protoform of the word. The following cognates exist in various Germanic languages:

Gothic (fourth century)	fádar
Old English (ninth century)	fæder
Old Saxon (ninth century)	fáder
Old High German (ninth century)	fáter
Old Norse (thirteenth century)	fáðir
Old Frisian (thirteenth century)	féder

From these examples we can reconstruct a common ancestral form **fáder* in a language called Proto-Germanic. We can then compare this form with cognates found in other Indo-European languages for the purposes of reconstructing a Proto-Indo-European form:

Proto-Germanic	*fáder
Sanskrit	pitá
Greek	patér
Latin	páter
Old Irish	áðir

The reconstructed Proto-Indo-European form is **pətér.* The consonants and second vowel are fairly easy to reconstruct even from the small amount of data given above. However, the reconstruction of the first vowel is more complicated and requires access to considerable additional data, just as does the placement of stress on the second vowel in the reconstructed form.

In this way, by inspecting evidence from existing languages, we can sometimes see relationships among the languages and establish a source from which they have sprung. The comparative method relies mainly on phonological evidence, a knowledge of possible kinds of phonological change, and the principle of the systematic nature of such change. The method allows us to reconstruct a proto-system from which the systems we actually observe apparently derive. In some cases extant evidence supports the reconstructions, and this evidence may be used to check the results of the method. For example, French, Spanish, Portuguese, and Italian come from a common source called Proto-Romance, which can be reconstructed. The reconstructions can be checked against Latin. There is not a one-to-one correspondence between reconstructed Proto-Romance forms and surviving Latin forms, but the discrepancies are easily explained. Reconstruction results in a "dialect-free" system, but Latin existed in a variety of dialects and was not as homogeneous as the protolanguage. In addition, Proto-Romance forms are reconstructed forms of the spoken language, since the modern Romance languages are derived from the speech of the marketplace and of the military. In contrast, the Latin which survives does so in the form of writing so we are comparing forms from the spoken language with those from a written language. Consequently, we should not be surprised to observe differences between Proto-Romance and Latin.

LANGUAGE FAMILIES

The comparative method allows us to establish relationships among languages, common ancestors for different existing languages, and patterns of historical development. It also makes possible the groupings of languages into language "families." One such family is the Indo-European family, the ancestor of such diverse living languages as English, Russian, Persian, Hindi, Irish, and Albanian, and of languages that are no longer spoken, such as Latin, Sanskrit, Tocharian, and Gothic. The various relationships among the individual Indo-European languages together with some indication of the time each came into existence is shown in Figure 10-4.

The *centum* languages referred to in Figure 10-4 are those languages in which the word for "hundred" begins with a stop; in contrast the word for "hundred" in the *satem* languages begins with a continuant. This distinction between a stop and a continuant coincides with a distinction between the western and eastern branches of Indo-European, although the exact place of Hittite is somewhat uncertain. The territory in which the Indo-European languages are mainly spoken today also includes languages that are not Indo-European, such as Basque, Finnish, Hungarian, and Turkish. In addition, varieties of Indo-European have spread throughout the world as a result of political and economic factors.

The diagram in Figure 10-4 resembles an inverted tree. Consequently, we refer to it as the **Stammbaum,** or "family tree," model of genetic relationships among languages. While the tree does represent the relationships among the languages in a systematic way, it also creates certain difficulties. For example, it suggests that Latin is "dead" and Modern French is "alive" or that Latin is the "parent" of Modern French; however, it is more accurate to say that Latin is the French spoken in France today or that Latin has become French in France, Spanish in Spain, and so on. The tree diagram also suggests sharp separations among languages; however, languages influence each other. The notion of sharp separation is partly the result of the comparative method which treats languages as homogeneous entities and partly the result of a desire to deal with uniform systems and to make "either-or" qualitative decisions rather than "more-or-less" quantitative ones.

An alternative model is that of the **Wellentheorie** or "wave theory." This model shows a language existing in different dialects that overlap each other, as in Figure 10-5. As the dialects become separate languages, they continue to have contact with each other and to influence each other. The same kinds of linguistic changes can occur over dialect boundaries and even over language boundaries once the dialects have become separate languages. In practice, most researchers

193

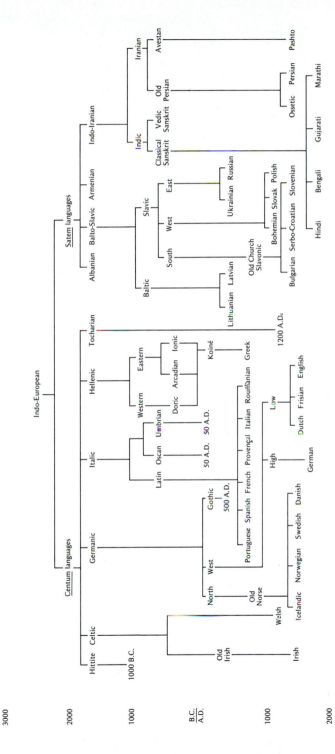

FIGURE 10-4 The Indo-European language family.

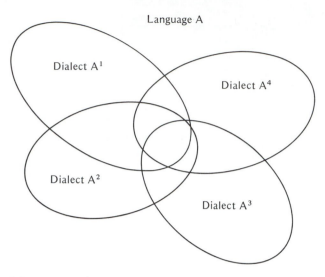

Language A

Dialect A¹

Dialect A⁴

Dialect A²

Dialect A³

FIGURE 10-5 The "wave" model of genetic relationships.

have found it harder to work with a fluid "wave" model than with a static "family tree" model, because the variables are much more difficult to control. Consequently, family relationships among language and problems of historical derivation continue to be discussed and illustrated by "trees" rather than by "waves."

We can use the methods discussed above to provide information about the previous stages of a language and ancestral forms. We might even try to say when and where the reconstructed language was spoken, that is, something about the provenance of the protolanguage. For example, when Proto-Indo-European is reconstructed, we find words for *snow, beech* (or *oak*), *goose, cow, horse, dog, sheep, pig, wolf, bear, otter, beaver, salmon, wolf, bee, yoke, wheel,* and *axle,* for terms used in weaving and sewing, for the numbers up to a hundred, for the relationships of women through marriage (for example, "daughter-in-law"), and for certain bronze tools. But no words can be reconstructed for certain other kinds of trees and animals (for example, for *palm, olive, cypress, elephant,* and *tiger*), or for corresponding relationships of men through marriage (for example, no "son-in-law"), or for iron artifacts. The time Proto-Indo-European appears to have been spoken is the Late Stone and Early Bronze Age (perhaps about 4000 B.C.) and the place appears to be in east or central Europe. Moreover, such evidence accords rather well with archeological evidence and also with the particular way in which the various Indo-European languages appear to have separated from each other as wave after wave of speakers left the original area of settlement.

Six thousand years is a very shallow time depth, but it is as far back into time as we can go in investigations of the Indo-European family with any reasonable certainty. One linguist, Morris Swadesh, did devise a controversial method called **glottochronology,** or **lexicostatistics,** with possibilities for going back even further. One version of the method employs a list of a hundred vocabulary items for common objects and concepts equivalent to the English words *cloud, eye, green, I,* *leaf, long, louse, new, star, wet,* and so on. The theory behind the method is that vocabulary items decay in languages through the process of replacement at a fixed rate over long periods of time: approximately twenty percent decay each 1,000 years. The process is somewhat analogous to the carbon-dating process used by physicists. Over a given period of time a fixed vocabulary loss is predicted to occur. Using the list, we can examine a group of languages to discover what similarities exist in the items on the list. According to the theory, the ratio between the number of correspondences and the total number of one hundred items can be used to calculate the time depth of separation from a common ancestral language. Glottochronology has intriguing possibilities but remains essentially unproven as a method for doing work in historical linguistics.

Knowing the limitations of data and available methods for use in historical work, we must be very cautious indeed in making claims about languages spoken several thousands of years ago. Still more caution is needed when questions are raised concerning the ultimate origin of language. No adequate theories exist as to the origin of language. The methods devised to date for work in historical linguistics are irrelevant to resolving the problem of the ultimate origin of language.

BIBLIOGRAPHIC NOTES

Most books on introductory linguistics contain chapters or sections on historical-comparative linguistics. However, few such treatments match Bloomfield's chapters in *Language,* which are also available under Hoijer's editorship as *Language History.* The most useful book on the subject is Anttila's *Introduction to Historical and Comparative Linguistics.* Sturtevant's *Introduction to Linguistic Science* and *Linguistic Change* are both useful books. Hoenigswald's *Language Change and Linguistic Reconstruction* is a more advanced book with an orientation toward structural linguistics. Arlotto's *Introduction to Historical Linguistics* and Lehmann's *Historical Linguistics: An Introduction* (with an accompanying workbook) are less technical treatments. King's *Historical Linguistics and Generative Grammar* attempts to deal with historical problems from the perspective of generative-transformational theory. The papers in Part One of Scott and Erickson's *Readings for the History of the English Language* are also of interest, their focus being language in general not English in particular.

The development of writing is discussed in Gelb's *Study of Writing* and the problems of decipherment in Chadwick's *Decipherment of Linear B.* Hymes provides a summary of work in glottochronology (or lexicostatistics) in his paper "Lexicostatistics So Far."

EXERCISES

10-1 Check to make sure that you understand each of the terms printed in **boldface** in Chapter 10.

10-2 Chapter 10 makes distinctions between certain terms. Explain the distinction between the following terms as clearly as you can: *synchronic linguistics* and

> *diachronic linguistics; parent language* and *daughter language; borrowing* and *change; cognate* and *reflex; family-tree model* and *wave model.*

10-3 English spelling has many peculiarities. Consequently, it is not always a safe guide to previously existing pronunciations. However, the spelling does provide a variety of data about the history of the language. Find out how the underlined letters came to be used in the words given below.

1 <u>ye</u> olde shoppe	**6** <u>k</u>iss	**11** laug<u>h</u>
2 ni<u>gh</u>t	**7** <u>qu</u>een	**12** hou<u>se</u>
3 phi<u>l</u>osophy	**8** <u>s</u>on	**13** <u>k</u>nave
4 <u>ch</u>eese	**9** dou<u>b</u>t	**14** <u>w</u>ring
5 <u>c</u>ity	**10** <u>th</u>rone	**15** <u>g</u>uest

10-4 What is the modern reflex of each of the following Old English words?

1 āscian	**11** čild	**21** hring	**31** scip
2 āþ	**12** cwic	**22** īs	**32** seolfor
3 bān	**13** cyning	**23** lēoht	**33** swēte
4 bedd	**14** cynn	**24** myrhð	**34** twelf
5 beorht	**15** dæġ	**25** norð	**35** þūsend
6 biscop	**16** eald	**26** ofer	**36** ūt
7 bisiġ	**17** fīf	**27** pāpa	**37** wæter
8 blōd	**18** fȳr	**28** rustiġ	**38** wīs
9 brād	**19** gōd	**29** sǽd	**39** wudu
10 brȳdguma	**20** hlūd	**30** sār	**40** yrre

10-5 In working with a new language, a linguist discovers that it has four vowels [i, e, a, o] and four stops and affricates [t, d, č, ǰ]. The linguist notes some peculiarities in the distribution of these sounds as follows:

[č] and [ǰ] occur only before [i] or pause
[t] and [d] do not occur before [i]

Sets like the following exist:

bib	'book'	taf	'cat'
bibi	'of a book'	tafi	'of a cat'
čit	'fish'	fač	'lamp'
tat	'rope'	faǰ	'horse'
čič	'of a fish'	fat	'small' (singular)
tač	'of a rope'	fid	'sing'
čito	'fishes'	fato	'small' (plural)
tato	'ropes'	fide	'sang'
ǰida	'foot'		

The linguist proceeds to make the following reconstructions:

*taf	'cat'	* tafi	'of a cat'
*fati	'lamp'	* titi	'of a fish'
*fadi	'horse'	* tati	'of a rope'
*tit	'fish'	* tito	'fishes'
*tat	'rope'	* dida	'foot'

Explain the reasoning.

10-6 In working with data in four languages, a linguist observes the following cognates:

	LANGUAGE A	LANGUAGE B	LANGUAGE C	LANGUAGE D
'goose'	mon	mõ	mond	mont
'nose'	bet	bet	bet	bet
'yellow'	rim	rĩ	rim	rim
'red	bon	bõ	bon	bon
'say'	dem	dẽ	dem	dem
'twig'	bed	bed	bet	bet

The linguist reconstructs the following protoforms:

'goose'	* mond	'red'	*bon
'nose'	* bet	'say'	* dem
'yellow'	* rim	'twig'	* bed

What processes does the linguist postulate as occurring between the proto-language and each of the four languages?

11

LANGUAGE CHANGE

In Chapter 10 we indicated that languages change over time. Change may be observed in the phonology, syntax, and vocabulary of a language, although only phonological changes were mentioned in Chapter 10. A second assumption is that change is regular and systematic just as language itself is systematic. A third assumption is that only certain kinds of change are possible and that these are natural. This chapter examines the kinds of change that take place in the phonology, syntax, and vocabulary of a language, says something about the different ways of describing the process of change itself, and mentions various theories that purport to explain why change occurs.

PHONETIC CHANGE

Vowels

Chapter 10 illustrated several possible kinds of sound change. For example, in Figure 10-2 the change of * [man] to [mæn] is an instance of vowel **fronting** and that of *[hūs] to [haʊs] is an instance of the **diphthongization** of a long high vowel. The falling together of the pronunciations of *clean* and *green* is an instance of vowel **raising:** [klǽn] > [klēn] > [klin] and [grēn] > [grin]. Such processes are relatively simple because vowels do tend to move to adjacent phonetic positions (forward or back, up or down) or to diphthongize.

One interesting kind of change that affects vowels is called vowel umlaut, a kind of **assimilation,** the process in which sounds come to resemble adjacent sounds in one or more features. Vowel umlaut is a change in the quality of a vowel brought about by the presence of a front vowel or a front glide in the following syllable. The vowels in *sing* and *singe* have different historical origins. In a pre-Old English stage *sing* was *[sɪngan] but *singe* was *[sɛngjan]. The presence of the *[j] in the second syllable brought about the raising of the vowel in the first syllable: *[ɛ] > [ɪ]. Some further examples of the process of umlaut can be seen in the alternations between *mouse-mice, foot-feet,* and *goose-geese:*

Germanic	Old English	Modern English	
* mūs	mūs	maʊs	"mouse"
* mūsi	mȳs	maɪs	"mice"
* fōt	fōt	fʊt	"foot"
* fōti	fēt	fit	"feet"
* gans	gōs	gus	"goose"
* gansi	gēs	gis	"geese"

The differences between the Modern English singular and plural forms result from the presence of a front vowel [i] in the second syllable of the original plural forms. Actually both umlauted and nonumlauted forms occurred for a while in certain inflections of both the singular and plural; however, the umlauted forms became identified with the plural and the nonumlauted forms with the singular.

Another kind of assimilation is in the **vowel harmony** that we find in languages such as Turkish. In vowel harmony, vowels in a word must agree in certain features such as backness and roundedness. Consequently, the allomorphs of an affix can take rather different phonemic shapes, as in the following examples from Turkish:

diš	"tooth"	dišim	"my tooth"
gul	"rose"	gulum	"my rose"

Another kind of change can be observed in the nasalization of a vowel from an original sequence of vowel plus nasal, as in French *cent* [sã] from Latin [kɛntum]. Sometimes the result is two pronunciations for a single vocabulary item depending on its grammatical distribution, so that French *bon* is pronounced [bɔn], that is, with an oral vowel and a nasal, before a vowel, but [bɔ̃], that is, with a nasalized vowel, before a pause or a consonant. Occasionally, a consonant is lost and compensatory lengthening of a preceding vowel occurs. Old English *niht* [nɪxt] "night" lost its fricative [x] and the vowel lengthened (and tensed), so that [nɪxt] became [nīt]. Eventually the [ī] diphthongized and produced the current pronunciation [naɪt]. In this case the spelling *night* still reflects the Old English pronunciation rather well, just as do the spellings of most words ending in *ght,* such as *fight, bright, knight,* and so on, as was pointed out in Chapter 10, but not *delight.* Lengthening and shortening often work to produce interesting sets of pronunciation variants when inflectional or derivational patterns are involved or when vowels occur in different syllable types, for example, in open and closed syllables or before two or more consonants. Numerous such sets exist in English, among them *wise-wisdom, keep-kept, steal-stealth, clean-cleanse, Moon-Monday,* and *holy-holiday.*

Still other changes involve the addition or loss of a vowel. The pronunciations of *film* and *athlete* as though they were spelled *filum* and *athalete* show vowel addition (**epenthesis**). Loss may occur initially, medially, or finally in a word. Initial loss (**aphesis**) leads to pronunciations such as *'fraid, 'most, 'bove (afraid, almost, above*); medial loss (**syncope**) to *secret'ry, gen'ral, reg'lar (secretary, general, regular*); and final loss (**apocope**) to *boun', fines', pas' (bound, finest, past*). We can see the process of syncope at work in the relationship between Latin *populus* and *tabula* and English *people* and *table.*

Consonants

Consonants necessarily exhibit other kinds of changes. Sometimes a stop will become a fricative, as for example in Indo-European when Proto-Indo-European *[p], *[t], and *[k] became Proto-Germanic *[f], *[θ], and *[x] respectively. Consequently, today, alongside Latin *pes, trēs,* and *centum,* we have English *foot, three,* and *hundred,* the latter showing a further change of *[x] to [h]. Often the change is a combinatorial one, that is, one that depends on the cooccurrence of some other vowel or consonant. For example, we can note the following relationships between Latin and French:

	Latin		*French*		
1	[k]	cīvitas	[s]	cité	"city"
		cinis		cendre	"ashes"
2	[k]	cēra	[s]	cire	"wax"
		centum		cent	"hundred"
3	[k]	cārus	[š]	cher	"dear"
		campus		champ	"field"
4	[k]	cor	[k]	cœur	"heart"
		cubitum		coude	"elbow"

The Latin [k] has changed in French to [s] before mid and high front vowels in 1 and 2, and to [š] before low vowels in 3. Therefore, in 1 through 3 the consonant has been fronted and the stop quality lost. It remains unchanged before mid and high back vowels in 4.

Sometimes this particular process of consonantal change is called **palatalization,** particularly when it clearly involves front vowels or glides and the change of a consonant from a stop to some kind of continuant. Some interesting examples of palatalization have occurred in English:

	Old English		*Modern English*
1 [kʸ]	ciese	[č]	cheese
	cinn		chin
	cīdan		chide
	cild		child
2 [gʸ]	gieldan	[y]	yield
	gearn		yarn
3 [kʸ]	drencean	[č]	drench
[gʸ]	sengan	[ǰ]	singe

We can compare the above words with words in which no palatalization of an original Germanic [k] or [g] occurred because [k] and [g] were not followed by a mid or high front vowel, or glide. For 1 there is a contrast with Old English *cald* (Modern English *cold*); for 2 with Old English *gōd* (Modern English *good*); and for 3 with Old English *drinkan* (Modern English *drink*) and Old English *singan* (Modern English *sing*).

Palatalization is only one instance of a sound changing in the direction of a neighboring sound. Other instances involve the devoicing of final consonants, as in the German *Bund* with a final [t] rather than [d] or *Weg* with a final [k] rather than [g], or even the loss of such consonants, as in those English dialects in which final consonants in clusters may be lost so that *old* comes to sound like *ole* and *desk* like *dess*. A voiceless consonant may become voiced in an environment in which there is considerable voicing or a particular combination of stress and voicing. For example, the medial consonant [t] in *water* and *better* is voiced to [d] or [ř] in some dialects of English in the presence of a preceding stressed vowel and a following unstressed vowel. The same consonant in *attack* remains unvoiced when the distribution of stresses is reversed. The alternation of [s] and [z] in *goose-gosling* and *house-husband* may also be explained by the same process of assimilation.

Dissimilation occurs when one of two similar sounds changes in such a way to make it less similar to the other. *Turtle* and *marble* both once had two *r*'s; the second *r* has changed to an *l*. Likewise, *pilgrim* comes from *peregrine,* another change of *r* to *l*. The pronunciation of *colonel* shows that the original first *l* has gone to *r*, a change in the opposite direction. *Chimbley* as a pronunciation of *chimney* shows the second nasal being changed to an *l* and a *b* intruded, as the *b* of *grumble* and *humble*. Intrusion of consonants is not uncommon. Intrusive *r* occurs regularly in some dialects, for example, in Boston English in *Cubar and America* and *Americar and Cuba*. The *s* in *harpsichord* is intrusive. **Spelling pronunciations** also result in **intrusive consonants,** the *t* in *often*, the *l* in *solder,* and the *h* in *herb,* for example, and sometimes even complete restructuring of pronunciations, as in *boatswain, waistcoat, forehead,* and *forecastle,* to cite but a few examples.

Clusters

Sometimes whole **consonant clusters** change. The Old English [sk] cluster found in *fisc* [fɪsk] and *scip* [skɪp] changed to [š] so that the Modern English words are *fish* [fɪš] and *ship* [šɪp]. This change has produced at least one interesting pair of English words: *shirt* and *skirt.* Both words have the same etymological source in Germanic and refer to similar garments. *Shirt,* the older English form, being present in the language before [sk] became [š], underwent this English sound change. Then, after the change took place, *skirt* was borrowed from another Germanic group, the Danes, for whom there had been no such change. It was then used with a slightly different meaning, but one which is obviously cognate.

Similar simplification results from certain other cluster changes that have occurred in English. The Old English words *wringan, hring, hlēapan, hnecca, gnagen,* and *cniht* are cognate with the Modern English words *wring, ring, leap, neck, gnaw,* and *knight.* Modern English preserves the spelling associated with the older pronunciation in many cases, but each of the Modern English forms begins with only a single consonant, the second one in the original cluster: [wr > r], [hr > r], [hl > l], [hn > n], [gn > n], and [kn > n]. An initial [h] in a cluster is preserved in certain dialects before [w] as in [hw] pronunciations of such words as *which, what, while,* and so on. However, in the other dialects of English, perhaps the majority, all such words begin with the single consonant [w], so that *which* and *witch* are homophonous.

Metathesis

Another kind of sound change is **metathesis,** the switch in position of sounds. For example, Old English *bridd* and *urnon* have become Modern English *bird* and *run.* There are also alternations in pronunciation today like *aks* and *ask, waps* and *wasp, apse* and *asp;* such alternations provide evidence of the process of metathesis in operation. So do the pronunciations *revelant* for *relevant, prehaps* for *perhaps,* and *pertty* for *pretty.* Metathesis involving *r* and *l* is apparently more frequent than other kinds.

PHONEMIC CHANGE

So far a variety of processes of sound change have been mentioned to illustrate possible changes and some ways of describing these. We should also examine the structural effects of changes. If all the vowels in a phonological system are raised and if the highest vowels diphthongize, phonetic changes have certainly occurred, but the system itself may be unaffected. The same number of phonemic contrasts may exist and the same words may contrast as minimal pairs. Only the phonetic realizations of the contrasts have changed. Of interest then are phonetic changes that result in changes in phonological systems, or stated conversely, changes in phonological systems that result in different phonemic assignments of phonetic data.

In Old English [f] was in complementary distribution with [v], and [s] was in complementary distribution with [z]. The voiced fricatives [v] and [z] occurred between vowels (intervocalically) as variants of two basically voiceless phonemes, /f/ and /s/ respectively. The weakening of final unstressed syllables and their eventual disappearance placed [f] in contrast with [v], and [s] in contrast with [z] in final position in words, that is, before pause. At the same time an influx of French vocabulary items in which both initial [v] and intervocalic [f] were prominent both hastened and consolidated the process of **phonemic split.** The eventual result was four phonemes in Modern English (/f/, /v/, /s/, and /z/) instead of the two in Old English (/f/ and /s/).

Another instance of the same phenomenon is found in the present contrast between /θ/ and /ð/ in Modern English, even though minimal pairs, such as *ether* and *either* and *thigh* and *thy* are difficult to find. Old English had a single phoneme /θ/ with two allophones [θ] and [ð] ([ð] occurring intervocalically and [θ] occurring elsewhere). In initial position the allophone was [θ]; however, there was a tendency to voice the initial [θ] to [ð] before unstressed vowels. At the same time final unstressed syllables were being weakened on their way to eventual disappearance. Consequently, [θ] and [ð] came to contrast in initial and final positions in native words although only in a very limited way. The present phonemic distinctions in English between /f/ and /v/, /s/ and /z/, and /θ/ and /ð/ are therefore developments that postdate the Old English period and that show a French influence on English. The remaining pair of contrasting English fricatives /š/ and /ž/ is still less well-established than the other pairs and also has a history of fairly recent development.

The opposite process of phonemic split is that of **phonemic coalescence,** or merger, in which a phonemic contrast is lost. This phenomenon can be illustrated with such pairs as *green* and *clean* and *meet* and *meat.* In Old English the first member of each pair had a long ē [ē] and the second member a long ǣ [ǣ]. However, during the process of vowel movement experienced by all the long English vowels the [ǣ] fell together with the [ē] on the way to both becoming [i]. The phonemic contrast that existed in Old English was therefore lost, so that the Modern English words rhyme.

CHANGE IN SYSTEMS

The Great Vowel Shift

The particular vowel movement referred to in the previous paragraph is called the **Great Vowel Shift.** The shift involves vowel raising and diphthongization, not infrequent kinds of changes; however, it does not necessarily result in any noticeable change in the total system of contrasts. For example, the Middle English long vowels may be represented as in Figure 11-1.

In the Great Vowel Shift in English, which was in progress about 500 years ago, the long vowels shown in Figure 11-1 were raised and the highest vowels diphthongized, as shown in Figure 11-2. We can note from Figures 11-1 and 11-2 that all the original contrasts are maintained following the shift except that [ǣ] and [ē] have coalesced. The phonetic values of the contrasts have changed in some cases, for example [ī] to [aɪ] and [ū] to [aʊ]. Although it produced a considerable phonetic change, the Great Vowel Shift did not produce any considerable phonemic change. We can conclude that the system of contrasts is virtually unchanged, but the rules for realizing the system have been changed.

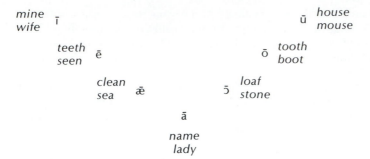

FIGURE 11-1 Vowels in certain English words before the Great Vowel Shift.

Grimm's Law

A similar kind of change producing important phonetic consequences but leaving the underlying system largely unaffected is seen in the shift between Proto-Indo-European and Germanic known as **Grimm's law.** The following correspondences can be noted among Proto-Indo-European, Latin, and English:

Proto-Indo-European	Latin	English
1 *p	p (pater)	f (father)
*t	t (trēs)	θ (three)
*k	k (cornū)	h (horn)
2 *b	b (labium)	p (lip)
*d	d (duo)	t (two)
*g	g (genus)	k (kin)
3 *bh	f (frāter)	b (brother)
*dh	f (foris)	d (door)
*gh	h (hortus)	g (garden)

ī

ē

æ

ā

ū

ō

ɔ

aɪ   aʊ

FIGURE 11-2 The Great Vowel Shift.

The above examples show that Latin apparently retains most of the original values of the Proto-Indo-European stop series, except in 3. However, a considerable change has taken place in English as a result of a general shift for Germanic languages first described by Grimm. This shift apparently occurred between 2,000 and 2,500 years ago. One way of formulating the shift is to say that a series of changes occurred, as follows:

Proto-Indo-European   *Germanic languages*

THE FIRST CHANGE

*p	became	f
*t	became	θ
*k	became	x

THEN A SECOND CHANGE

*b	became	p
*d	became	t
*g	became	k

AND THE FINAL CHANGE

*bh	became	b
*dh	became	d
*gh	became	g

Once again, the original system is unchanged so far as the actual number of contrasts is concerned, but the realizations of the contrasts have changed. Of course, still other changes took place between Proto-Indo-European and the derivative languages so that some restructuring of the consonantal systems resulted. For example, Verner observed that there were certain "exceptions" to Grimm's law that could be explained by referring to the placement of stress. **Verner's law** states the exceptions and allows us to explain such an alternation as *was* and *were* and why *forlorn* comes from *lose* and *sodden* from *seethe*. Still another sound shift differentiated High German (South, Austrian, and Swiss varieties) from Low German (North German, Dutch, and English). In High German certain voiceless stops either became affricates (compare *pound, Pfund; heart, Herz;* and *tale, Zahl*) or fricatives (compare *ape, Affe; water, Wasser; make, Machen; foot, Fuss;* and *sleep, Schlaf*).

An examination of any one of the changes noted immediately above reveals the possibility of formulating the change as one in the phonological rules of the language as these rules were described in Chapter 8. One set of rules prevails before the change and a slightly different set prevails after the change. The difference between the two sets of rules is a relatively simple one: a change in a feature, the addition or subtraction of a rule, or the reordering of two or more rules. Feature changes may result in a vowel being rounded, fronted, or raised, or a consonant losing its stop quality to become a fricative. Adding or subtracting a rule may result in a particular consonant becoming devoiced only in certain positions, for example before pause, or becoming voiced only in certain positions, for example in a particular stress environment. Reordering rules may result in apparently similar sounds differentiating or different sounds coalescing. Using the notion of rule, we can conceive of sound change as resulting from changes in the rules internalized by speakers of a language rather than from phonetic changes made by speakers because of some tendency that languages have to "drift" phonetically. More will be said on this topic later in the chapter under the heading "Accounting for Change."

Sound change goes on largely unobserved outside the consciousness of speakers. It is regular. However, sound change does produce irregularity since it tends to bring an increase in allomorphic variation as morphemes take on different pronunciations in different circumstances. Speakers sometimes try to decrease the irregularity by extending patterns which they perceive to be regular to cover the irregularities. This process is called **analogy.** Analogical creation sometimes does produce the desired effect, but it can also produce further irregularity because as different kinds of analogical relationships are postulated different effects are produced. For example, analogical creation in English has resulted in such pairs as *older–elder* and *brothers–brethren,* with the irregular form (the second one in each case) having a typically more restricted meaning and use than the regular analogical form.

GRAMMATICAL CHANGE

Change occurs in grammatical systems as well as in phonological systems, but it is more difficult to describe such change. Consequently, much more work has been done on sound change than on grammatical change, owing in part no doubt to the relative tractability of the problems. The discussion of the various kinds of grammatical change that follows is limited to observations we can make about three passages quoted from Old English, Middle English, and Chaucer. Only certain kinds of change occur in the examples, but these illustrate the kinds of phenomena that interest students of grammatical change. The passages from Middle English and Chaucer date from almost the same time; however, the former passage, being a prayer, tends to be conservative in contrast to the more innovative passage from Chaucer.

OLD ENGLISH (A.D. 1000)

Fæder ure þu þe eart on heofonum, si þin nama gehalgod; tobecume þin rice; gewurþe þin willa on eorðan swa swa on heofonum; urne gedæghwamlican hlaf syle us to dæg; and forgyf us ure gyltas, swa swa we forgyfað urum gyltendum; and ne gelæd þu us on costnunge, ac alys us of yfele, soþlice.

MIDDLE ENGLISH (A.D. 1400)

Oure fadir þat art in heuenes, halwid be þi name; þi reume or kyngdom come to þe. Be þi wille done in herþe as it is doun in heuene. Ʒeue to vs to-day oure eche dayes bred. And forʒeue to vs oure dettis, þat is oure synnys, as we forʒeuen tu oure dettouris, þat is to men þat han synned in vs. And lede vs not in-to temptacion, but delyuere vs from euyl. Amen, so be it.

CHAUCER (A.D. 1400)

Ther was also a Nonne, a Prioresse,
That of hir smylyng was ful symple and coy;

Hire gretteste ooth was but by Seinte Loy;
And she was cleped madame Eglentyne.
Ful weel she soong the service dyvyne,
Entuned in hir nose ful semely,
And Frenssh she spak full faire and fetisly,
After the scole of Stratford atte Bowe,
For Frenssh of Parys was to hire unknowe.

Morphology

One of the first differences is that the Old English passage contains a greater variety of word endings than does either of the other passages. For example, there are three forms corresponding to *our: ure, urne,* and *urum* and there are nouns ending in *-um, -a, -e, -an,* and *-as.* The number of such endings appears to have been reduced considerably between Old English and the English spoken today, Modern English. This evidence accords with other evidence, so we may conclude that the number of inflectional endings in English has decreased over the last thousand years. We can observe the loss of another affix in words that begin in the Old English passage with *ge-,* as in *gehalgod, gewurþe, gedæghwamlican,* and *gelæd,* for this prefix is completely absent from Modern English. Some further instances of changes in morphology are revealed in the composition of the word *gedæghwamlican* ("daily") and of the phrase *swa swa* ("just as"); neither is found in Modern English.

Syntax

There are noticeable differences in word order among the three passages. For example, the Old English excerpt begins *Fæder ure* in comparison with the *Oure fadir* beginning of the Middle English version of the Lord's Prayer. Furthermore, the word order of the Middle English version more closely resembles the word order of Modern English than does the word order of the Old English version: *urne gedæghwamlican hlaf syle us to dæg* ("our daily loaf give us today") and *ʒeue to vs to-day oure eche dayes bred* ("Give to us today our each day's bread"). The syntax of the lines from Chaucer appears to be even more modern than that of the Middle English version of the Lord's Prayer, even though an instance of an adjective postposed to a noun occurs in *service dyvyne,* undoubtedly because of the influence of French on English at the time.

In the cases of negation and inserting relative clauses into sentences, a very noticeable development is apparent within the three passages. The negation in the Old English passage is achieved through the use of a particle *ne* preposed to the verb *gelæd.* In the Middle English passage there is the more familiar *lede vs not,* and in the passage from Chaucer the participle *unknowe.* The embedding of a subordinate relative-type clause is achieved with considerable difficulty in the Old English passage in *Fæder ure* [þu þe eart on heofonum]. The embedding is much easier in Middle English in *Oure fadir* [þat art in heuenes] and in Chaucer in *Ther was also a Nonne, a Prioresse,* [*That of hir smylyng was ful symple and coy*]. We see a similar kind of apparent awkwardness in Old English in the final phrase in *gewurþe þin willa on eorðan* [*swa swa on heofonum*] with which we can compare the Middle English *Be þi wille don in herþe* [*as it is doun in heuene*]. The Chaucer passage sounds much more modern than the Middle English passage in the way the clauses are related to each other.

Another possible approach to syntax is to focus on the development of a particular verb to see how it changes and sometimes develops. The verb *be,* for example, could be singled out for attention in the above passages. *Be* is found with the forms *eart* and *si* in the Old English passage, *art, be,* and *is* in the Middle English passage, and *was* in the Chaucerian passage. Furthermore, the phrases *Ther was* and *she was cleped* show interesting developments of the verb *be* that the other two passages do not and, in the case of the Old English passage at least, could not show, developments with *there* and with the passive voice.

Both versions of the Lord's Prayer communicated to their readers in their day. The Middle English version is easier to understand today because language changes. When we observe that between Old English and Middle English the use of inflections declined and that certain syntactic devices having to do with negation, relative clause embedding, and the forms of the verb *be* developed, we do not mean that Middle English and, in its turn, Modern English are better than Old English on some absolute scale: they are different not better, for we have no such scale by which to judge "good" and "bad" in language.

A final observation should be made about the three passages. The Old English passage employs vocabulary and devices typical of Germanic languages: *rice* (compare the Modern German *Reich*), *gewurþe,* and *soþlice* to cite a few instances. The Middle English passage contains two interesting doublets: *reume or kyngdom* and *dettis, þat is oure synnys;* and a paraphrase: *oure dettouris, þat is to men þat han synned in vs.* In each case a non-Germanic word is explained with a Germanic one or with a paraphrase. The Middle English passage contains the word *temptacion* instead of the *costnunge* of the Old English passage. The different vocabulary selections support a claim that can be advanced to explain some of the changes that occurred in English between the Old English and Middle English periods, namely that many changes were either brought about by or hastened by the influence of French on English after the Norman Conquest of 1066. The passage from Chaucer shows a similar French influence, and even part of the subject matter of the passage is the particular French spoken by the nun.

VOCABULARY CHANGE

The mention of some vocabulary differences in the passages from Old English, Middle English, and Chaucer serves as an introduction to the final area of change to be discussed, vocabulary change. Such change occurs in a variety of ways: by developing the inner resources of the language, by borrowing, and by semantic change.

Inner Resources

The inner resources of a language are used in such a process as compounding when two or more existing words are brought together to form a compound, as in *strongman, bellhop, highball, bloodcount, cakewalk, sit-in,* and *downgrade.*

Sometimes a complex rather than a compound word results when a derivational affix is used on a stem on which it has not been previously used, as in *disaffiliate, emplane, inflationary, stardom, sexy, hospitalize,* and *officialese.* **Back formation** occurs when a word is formed by removing part of it which looks like an affix, but which is not: *burgle* from *burglar, donate* from *donation, edit* from *editor, audit* from *auditor,* and even *pea* from *pease.* The technical term for a new creation is a **neologism.**

Other processes for creating new vocabulary items from the inner resources of the language exist. Words can be deliberately created, like *Kodak, Yahoo, chortle, altruism,* and *gas.* Two or more words can be blended together, as in *brunch, slanguage,* and *blurb,* although the sources of the latter are rather obscure. Various **acronyms** can take on a life of their own, like *WASP, Gestapo, NATO,* and *radar.* Perhaps the best-known of these acronyms is *OK,* or *okay,* the exact origin of which is still in some doubt. Still another process involves generalizing a proper name to certain kinds of persons and objects, as with *quisling, boycott, sandwich, curie,* and *volt.*

Morphemic split occurs when a word splits (sometimes with a deliberate spelling change) to take on two different meanings, though not often very different meanings: *effect, affect; capital, capitol; principle, principal; flour, flower; past, passed;* and *of, off.* **Morphemic merger** is the opposite process: two different meanings coalesce into one morpheme. This is a much rarer process. A good example is *queen,* which contains the old meanings of both *queen* and *quean,* the one a royal personage and the other a harlot. The second meaning is still found to some extent in *a dancehall queen* and slang uses of the word.

Borrowing

Borrowing is another way of adding new vocabulary items to a language. Speakers of a language often have contact with speakers of other languages. If a speaker of one of these languages does not have a readily available word for something in the world and a speaker of the other language does, the first speaker often borrows the word from the second speaker. The first settlers in North America had contact with the Indians who had already developed names for places and things peculiar to the North American continent. Consequently, the settlers borrowed such words as *Massachusetts, Wisconsin, Michigan, Illinois, Chicago, Oshkosh,* and *Mississippi* to mention a few place-names only.

Another large group of words came into English as a result of contact through invasion, in this case the Norman Conquest of England in 1066. Various kinds of words were borrowed into English: for matters of government like *crown, country, duke, court,* and *prince;* for matters of law like *judge, jury, crime, accuse, marry,* and *prove;* for matters of war like *battle, arms, soldier, siege, danger,* and *march;* and for matters of religion like *angel, saint, pray, save, blame, virtue,* and *vice.* Then, too, today we find interesting pairs of words such as *cow* and *beef, sheep* and *mutton, calf* and *veal,* and *pig* and *pork* in which the first item, the name of the animal, is Germanic in origin and the second item, the meat of the animal, is a borrowing from French. Perhaps the occurrence of such pairs reflects a society in which the conquered Englishman raised the animals for the table of the conquering Norman.

Several points can be made about the Norman Conquest. First, the borrowings from French do not show much, if any, cultural superiority in the invaders. French borrowings into English having to do with high fashion and culture, in the sense of refinement, considerably postdate the French invasion of the eleventh century. Secondly, although the Normans were conquerors, they eventually gave up their French to become speakers of English, just as their ancestors had eventually given up their Germanic language when they invaded France. Thirdly, the borrowings do not show the same intimate relationships between conquered and conqueror as the borrowings that resulted from the earlier Danish invasions of the ninth and tenth centuries, when "everyday" words such as *egg, sky, gate, skin, skirt, skill, skull, scrape, scatter, sister, law, weak, give, take, call,* and *hit,* and particularly the pronouns *they, them,* and *their,* and the verb *are* were borrowed from the Danish invaders.

The kinds of contact speakers have with each other may often be assessed from the particular items that are borrowed. For example, English has borrowed numerous words from French having to do with clothing, cosmetics, and luxury goods, like *negligee, crochet, chemise, ensemble, lingerie, suede, perfume, rouge, champagne,* and *deluxe.* From German have come words associated with food like *sauerkraut, delicatessen, wiener, hamburger,* and *lager,* and also the "untranslatable" German words *Weltanschauung, Gestalt, Gesundheit,* and *Gemütlichkeit.* From Italian have come musical words like *piano, opera, solo, sonata, soprano, trombone,* and *serenade.* From various Indian languages have come words for once exotic dress items like *bandana, sari, bangle,* and *pajamas.* And from Arabic have come some interesting words beginning with *al-* (the Arabic determiner): *alcohol, alchemy, almanac,* and *algebra.*

Of course, Latin and Greek have provided English with the richest resource for borrowing more formal learned items. Large numbers of words have been borrowed into English from both languages, particularly learned polysyllabic words. Numerous **doublets** also exist in English, that is, words that have been borrowed twice, once directly from Latin, and the second time through another language, most often French:

Latin	*English*	*French*	*English*
camera	camera	chambre	chamber
computare	compute	compter	count
magister	magistrate	maître	master
sēcūrus	secure	sûr	sure

Sometimes a word is not borrowed, but is translated. Such an English word as *superman* is a loan translation of the German *Übermensch* just as *marriage of convenience* is a loan translation of the French *mariage de convenance* and *it goes without saying* of the French *ça va sans dire.*

North American English shows a wide contact with other languages in its borrowings: French (*levee, prairie*); Spanish (*mesa, patio*); German (*fatcakes, smearcase*); Dutch (*coleslaw, cooky, stoop*); American Indian (*squash, moccasin, squaw, wigwam, tomahawk*); and various African languages (*banjo, gumbo, voodoo*).

At different times speakers of certain languages have shown noticeable resistance to borrowing words, and they have preferred either to exploit native resources or to resort to loan translations instead. The German language provides a particularly good example of this phenomenon especially during periods of extreme German nationalism. Two good examples from German are the words *Wasserstoff* and *Sauerstoff* for the more widespread *hydrogen* and *oxygen* respectively. However, in recent years there has been a noticeable introduction of English words directly into German, examples such as *aftershave, barbecue, blue jeans, cartoon, jazz, jet, pilot, protest, teach-in,* and *weekend* all having been noted.

Borrowings are also assimilated to different degrees. Sometimes a borrowing is pronounced in a decidedly foreign way for a while, but it is usually soon treated according to native sound patterns if it occurs frequently. The Japanese have borrowed the word *baseball* from English, but its pronunciation is almost unrecognizable to a speaker of English now that the word is treated within the Japanese sound system. Likewise, in English, words such as *pueblo, garage, Nkrumah, salon, masseur, ghoul,* and *hickory,* borrowed from a variety of foreign languages, are pronounced according to the sound system of English and not according to the phonological rules of the source languages.

SEMANTIC CHANGE

Once words come into the language, no matter what their origin, they are subject not only to the rules of pronunciation of that language but also to **semantic change,** that is, change in meaning. There are various processes of semantic change and various ways of classifying changes. We will illustrate only a few kinds.

Narrowing and Widening

One process involves **narrowing** the meaning of a word so that the word achieves a more restricted meaning over the course of time. *Meat* now means a particular kind of food, not food in general, as it does in the following quotation from the King James version of Genesis: *And God said, Behold, I have given you every herb bearing seed, which is upon the face of the earth, and every tree, in which is the fruit of a tree yielding seed; to you it shall be for meat.* Likewise, *deer* now refers to a particular kind of animal, not animal in general, as it did in Shakespeare's words *But mice and rats and such small deer have been Tom's food for seven long year. Worm* now refers to a particular kind of crawling creature, not any crawling creature, although some of the original more general meaning is contained still in *slowworm, blindworm,* and *glowworm. Fowl* and *hound* refer to particular kinds of bird and dog and *wife,* to a particular kind of woman. However, in the case of the last word we can note a more general meaning in *midwife, wife of Bath,* and perhaps *housewife.* Finally, North Americans use the word *corn* in a narrow meaning to refer to maize, whereas the British use it to refer to grain in general. Keats' Ruth standing *amid the alien corn* is not standing in a field of maize.

The opposite process is **widening** of meaning. In this process a word achieves a more general meaning. The words *bird* and *dog* once referred to specific types of birds and dogs, not to the species in general. The word *virtue* described a characteristic associated with men, but not with women, just as only women could be said to be *hysterical,* since men were not possessed of wombs (*hystera* being the Greek word for "uterus"). The word *sensible* once meant "sensitive," as it still does in French, and *alibi* referred to the fact that a person was elsewhere when something happened, not that he had some kind of excuse for something.

Elevation and Degradation

The meanings of words may also be elevated or degraded. The words *knight, squire,* and *earl* were once used for people who were not very important, nor were the activities subsumed under *chivalry* particularly refined. But times and meanings changed and each word assumed the elevated meaning it has today. The opposite process to that of **elevation** is that of **degradation** and it is perhaps much more common. The words *villain, churl, wench,* and *knave* have all taken on pejorative connotations they did not once have, as have *lust, lewd,* and *silly* in their way. Still others are words having to do with smell, such as *stench* and *odor,* and even *smell* itself, and with certain kinds of skill, such as *sly, cunning,* and *crafty.* The word *homely* has been degraded in North America where it is now synonymous with *plain;* however, the meaning in England remains synonymous with *homey.*

Folk Etymology

The two phenomena of borrowing and semantic change often cooccur in a particularly interesting process known as **folk etymology.** In this process a word or phrase is borrowed from a foreign language and its sound and meaning are reshaped during the process of borrowing because of certain similarities it has with words already in the language. In this way *crawfish* has taken on an association with *fish, female* with *male, muskrat* with both *musk* and *rat, penthouse* with *house, gooseberry* with *goose,* and *woodchuck* with both *wood* and *chuck.* The same process of folk etymology occurs with words of native stock as a result of sound change within the language, borrowing between dialects, and unfamiliarity with actual referents of the words. Consequently, we have folk etymologies in English for *belfry, bridegroom, helpmate, pickax, shamefaced, titmouse,* and *wormwood.*

Euphemism

Euphemisms result when roundabout, elegant, or modified expressions are deliberately used to avoid harsh or explicit meanings. People *pass on* or *pass away* rather than *die* and are attended to by a *mortician* rather than by an *undertaker. Bad breath* becomes *halitosis, inability to read* becomes *dyslexia,* and *old people* become *senior citizens.* Girls *glow,* men *perspire,* and only horses *sweat. Gee whiz, Jimminy Cricket,* and *Jeepers Creepers* substitute for *Jesus Christ,* and *darn* and *tarnation* replace *damn* and *damnation.* And so on, and so on, for euphemism is a very fertile field for the insecure and pretentious in society.

ACCOUNTING FOR CHANGE

Languages change in all kinds of ways, but the ways themselves are to some extent predictable. Only certain kinds of change take place. In phonology, a feature changes, or rules are switched, or some other kind of restructuring takes place. In syntax, a certain syntactic device develops, or case endings weaken, or word order patterns change. In meaning, changes result from language contact, from cultural developments requiring new vocabulary, and from reshaping existing meanings. But in no case does a radical change occur overnight. The processes are predictable in that only certain kinds of things happen and they happen slowly. The exact changes are not predictable, for example that a certain set of stops will lose their stop quality and become fricatives, or a particular inflection will disappear, or a particular item will stay in the language after it has been borrowed or undergone a change in meaning. Nor is the process of change itself well understood.

Many reasons for change have been advanced, but mainly by nonlinguists and persons only peripherally interested in language. The subject has been almost as fascinating as those of the creation of language and of the possibilities of intraspecies and interspecies communication. Consequently, theories of change have been advanced to fit many systems of esthetics, politics, economics, and so on. Linguists have tended to keep clear from all three subjects, believing that most questions are premature in that they too soon seek definitive answers to problems that cannot clearly be formulated with current knowledge. They have tended to focus on describing the changes that have taken place, as far as they can discover these changes, on establishing systems for discussing such changes, and on creating protosystems, rather than on speculating on reasons for change itself. However, we should mention some of the theories proposed to account for language change, particularly one that is gaining currency today.

Some Explanations

One theory of change, associated with the names of Curtius, Whitney, and Zipf, involves the principle of least effort whereby speakers tend to make things easy to pronounce in order to economize time and effort in the work of expression. This explanation appears plausible in that we all feel that the English spoken today is easier for us than the English of King Alfred, Chaucer, or Shakespeare would be. There is also the evidence of assimilations, of contractions, and of shortenings through the use of either acronyms or words like *cab, mob, fan, pants, bike,* and *bus.* Yet, since each language must preserve a large amount of redundancy if it is to function efficiently, least effort in one direction will be offset by more effort in some other direction. For example, English verb inflection has decreased over the centuries, but a complex phrasal verb system has replaced the inflections.

A second hypothesis, proposed by the French linguist Martinet, is that there is an inherent tendency in languages toward economy. All languages have unsymmetrical features, and this lack of symmetry produces a certain imbalance that speakers try to correct. The hypothesis is that attempts at correction do not always result in symmetry, but do result in change.

A third hypothesis, which again tries to account seriously for linguistic evidence, is the substratum hypothesis associated with Ascoli. According to this hypothesis, languages are often learned by speakers who have already learned another language as their native language. The result is a kind of imperfect learning of the second language or some disruption in the first language, either of which produces conditions necessary for change. Proponents of this theory have argued that Celtic produced a substratum effect for the Anglo-Saxons and that still later the Norman Conquest produced a further substratum effect for English. The changes in Indo-European described as Grimm's law are also sometimes attributed to the substratum effect of non-Indo-Europeans learning Indo-European.

Other theories are less convincing. One, associated with Croce and Vossler, attempts to account for change by postulating some inner esthetic drive in speakers and in the languages they speak. Another, associated with Grimm and Humboldt, tries to relate change to the racial characteristics of speakers, even to their psychology. Still another claims that geographic influences may affect the articulatory base of language, for example, changing its characteristic rhythms and intonations. Historical events have been proposed by such an important linguist as Jespersen as influencing linguistic change, and wars, invasions, famine, and pestilence have all been related to certain kinds of changes. Social changes and social unrest have figured heavily in the writings of the Frenchman Meillet and the Russian Marr as the causes of change, and cultural changes have been proposed by Wundt. Certainly industrialization, colonization, urbanization, migration, the development of mass communication, and technological diffusion must have had some role to play in language change. But to argue that any one of these factors or even all acting together cause the linguistic changes that *sometimes* cooccur is almost certainly to confuse correlation with causation.

A Current View

Most linguists who have considered the subject of change find little of value in the above theories. Few of the theories really attempt to deal with linguistic issues, and those that do, for example those of least effort, economy, and substratum, are too inexact to be of much value. Linguists acknowledge that languages are not neat systems. For example, they are usually spoken in a variety of dialects (the subject of the following chapter), and each person usually has contact with several dialects. Language is only completely systematic in the grammars we write, and even these grammars are fragmentary works. People too continue to learn more about the language they speak as they get older, and changes in age bring about changes in usage, as certain usages become appropriate to certain ages, a phenomenon known as **age-grading.** Languages also have to be learned anew by every generation, and even though we might want to claim that certain kinds of principles do not have to be learned, because they are innate, enough must be learned so that variation between generations is likely to occur.

Perhaps the clue to language change resides in that last observation. Children must learn the language of the community into which they are born. Nevertheless, that language is not a completely static, fixed entity. It has many variations according to dialect, age, sex, and usage. Of course, a specific child is not alone in this learning task. Other children, some older and some younger, are engaged in the same task. The learners share a common characteristic, however, and that is a tendency to internalize the maximally efficient set of rules to account for the kind of language that meets with the approval of immediate peers and acquaintances, and to a lesser extent, of the general community of speakers. This maximally efficient set of rules will vary between succeeding generations. The consequence of this variation is linguistic change over a period of time; however, this change will be almost imperceptible between successive generations.

BIBLIOGRAPHIC NOTES

The main concern of this chapter is with certain aspects of the history of the English language. Topics in other languages are discussed in various places in the literature cited for Chapter 11. Numerous single-volume histories of the English language are available. Baugh's *History of the English Language,* Bryant's *Modern English and Its Heritage,* Pyles' *Origins and Development of the English Language* (with an accompanying workbook by Algeo and Pyles), Robertson and Cassidy's *Development of Modern English,* and Schlauch's *English Language in Modern Times (since 1400)* focus less on modern linguistic issues than do Bloomfield and Newmark's *Linguistic Introduction to the History of English,* Marckwardt's *Introduction to the English Language,* Peters' *Linguistic History of English* (with an accompanying workbook), Pyles and Algeo's *English: An Introduction to Language,* and Stevick's *English and Its History.* Parts 2 through 4 of Scott and Erickson's *Readings for the History of the English Language* contain a good selection of papers on linguistic topics in the history of English. Traugott's *History of English Syntax* deals with a number of syntactic developments from a generative-transformational prospective. Linguistic change in general (with special reference to English) is discussed in Samuels' *Linguistic Evolution.*

   Read's "First Stage in the History of 'O.K.'" provides a good introduction to the kind of careful work necessary in one variety of historical work. Jespersen's *Language: Its Nature, Development and Origin* contains a long discussion of possible causes of linguistic change and of "progress" and "decay" in language. Pages 192 to 197 of Langacker's *Language and Its Structure* present certain current views of how language change occurs.

EXERCISES

11-1 Check to make sure that you understand each of the terms printed in **boldface** in Chapter 11.

11-2 Chapter 11 makes distinctions between certain terms. Explain the distinction between the following terms as clearly as you can: *open syllable* and *closed syllable; phonetic change* and *phonemic change; phonemic split* and *phonemic coalescence; elevation* and *degradation.*

11-3 Here are some Old English words and their Modern English reflexes. What sound changes have occurred in each case?

1 brȳd	[brȳd]	bride	7 hlūd	[xlūd]	loud
2 crabba	[krabba]	crab	8 hnutu	[xnʊtʊ]	nut
3 fisc	[fɪsk]	fish	9 læfan	[lævan]	leave
4 fūl	[fūl]	foul	10 scip	[skɪp]	ship
5 gāt	[gāt]	goat	11 sōna	[sōna]	soon
6 henn	[hɛnn]	hen	12 tēþ	[tēθ]	teeth

11-4 Determine with the aid of a good dictionary the source language of each of the following words:

1 blouse	6 cruise	11 halo	16 shibboleth
2 book	7 deaf	12 language	17 skill
3 bungalow	8 equal	13 meek	18 supper
4 cheese	9 geisha	14 penguin	19 tea
5 cousin	10 gold	15 robot	20 whiskey

11-5 Trace the ultimate origin of the following doublets and account for the variation found today:

1 camera, chamber	6 guest, host
2 dike, ditch	7 pauper, poor
3 fragile, frail	8 regal, royal
4 glamour, grammar	9 secure, sure
5 guardian, warden	10 shirt, skirt

11-6 Each of the following words has an interesting etymology. Try to explain what is of interest in each case.

1 apron	7 derring-do	13 newt	19 sherry
2 bridegroom	8 garlic	14 nickname	20 sirloin
3 bylaw	9 gooseberry	15 nostril	21 teetotal
4 cherry	10 gospel	16 orange	22 walnut
5 daisy	11 helpmate	17 pea	23 walrus
6 dandelion	12 mushroom	18 sheriff	24 woman

11-7 What is the meaning of each of the following acronyms?

1 AWOL	4 FBI	7 Nabisco	10 SEATO
2 CARE	5 Gestapo	8 NATO	11 snafu
3 CIA	6 GI	9 radar	12 UNESCO

11-8 From what sources is each of the following blends derived?

1 bash	4 clash	7 motel	10 splatter
2 blurt	5 flare	8 prissy	11 slanguage
3 brunch	6 medicare	9 smog	12 transistor

11-9 Each of the following words has a folk etymology in addition to its regular etymology. What is the folk etymology and the regular etymology of each?

1 belfry	3 female	5 hiccough	7 shamefaced
2 crayfish	4 greyhound	6 penthouse	8 sirloin

11-10 Each of the following words has changed its meaning to some extent as a result of elevation or degradation. Give the original more degraded or more elevated meaning in each case.

1 crafty	**5** idiot	**9** lust	**13** steward
2 dame	**6** impertinent	**10** mischievous	**14** villain
3 dizzy	**7** lady	**11** silly	**15** vulgar
4 hussy	**8** lord	**12** smirk	**16** wench

11-11 Each of the following words has changed its meaning to some extent as a result of narrowing or widening. State the original wider or narrower meaning in each case.

1 assassin	**4** disease	**7** flesh	**10** injury
2 cattle	**5** doctor	**8** fowl	**11** liquor
3 dean	**6** fee	**9** frock	**12** ordeal

11-12 Each of the following words is based on a proper name. Who or what was the original?

1 ascot	**5** euphemism	**9** quisling	**13** stoic
2 braille	**6** guillotine	**10** sandwich	**14** syphilis
3 diesel	**7** leotard	**11** saxophone	**15** tawdry
4 donnybrook	**8** macadam	**12** silhouette	**16** watt

11-13 What are the simple everyday equivalents of each of the following euphemisms?

1 attendance officer	**11** liquidate
2 building superintendent	**12** mentally unsound
3 comfort station	**13** pass away
4 domestic help	**14** perspiration
5 ecdysiast	**15** powder room
6 extermination engineer	**16** prevaricate
7 financial resources	**17** protective custody
8 gosh darn	**18** senior citizens
9 inebriated	**19** studio apartment
10 intestinal fortitude	**20** urban renewal

12

LANGUAGE VARIATION

From time to time in previous chapters mention was made of language variation. Linguists have tended to disregard such variation in favor of linguistic models that stress unvarying systems and regularity. For example, some have concerned themselves with describing the speech of only one speaker, concentrating on his speech, or **idiolect,** and disregarding certain stylistic variations that occur even in such a sample. Others, particularly Trager and Smith, have attempted to describe an overall system for a language from which individuals select a system. An overall system does allow for variation in language, but only within a supersystem. Still others, notably Chomsky, stressing a distinction between linguistic competence and linguistic performance, have taken for their goal the description of an "ideal" linguistic competence and considered many kinds of variation to be instances of linguistic performance and, therefore, of only peripheral concern. Even in historical work, the comparative method of reconstruction and the family-tree model of genetic relationships work best when we disregard most kinds of variation.

Although we have tended to ignore linguistic variation because of the need to develop models to account for what is general and universal in language rather than for what is individual and idiosyncratic, a commonsense view of the "facts" tells us that considerable variation does occur within language. Speakers of a language speak it differently. There are good speakers and bad speakers of a language such as English. There are intelligible speakers and almost unintelligible speakers. And *good, bad, intelligible,* and *unintelligible* seem to vary in many different ways. If we have not said much about this commonsense view, it is because we have been more vitally concerned with trying to clarify the nature of language itself than with making what could easily become unsystematic observations about surrounding phenomena. Linguists have not completely ignored variation, however, and it is the purpose of this chapter to indicate some ways in which linguistic variation has been examined in a spirit motivated by the kind of scientific inquiry described in this book. The particular focus of most of the chapter will be upon dialect variation.

SOME VARIETIES OF LANGUAGE

By Age

Of course, other kinds of variation than dialect variation occur, and linguists have shown an interest in some of these varieties. For example, language varies according to the age of the person using it. It varies in this way because language must be learned, and there appear to be stages through which individuals progress in the process of language acquisition. However, six-year-old children seem to have gone through most of these stages. Changes do still continue to occur, but these changes are more typical of the age-grading phenomenon, alluded to at the end of Chapter 11, than of the kinds of changes that occur during the acquisition process. We all recognize that old people speak differently from young people and that linguistic generation gaps exist. Likewise, accepted patterns exist for communicating between and within the generations: old people to young, young to old, fathers to young children, young children to fathers, adolescents to their peers, and so on. Consequently, variation by age is one kind of linguistic phenomenon we can study and about which we can ask a variety of linguistic, psychological, and sociological questions.

By Sex and Occupation

Language also varies according to sex and occupation. The language of men differs subtly from that of women. Men do not usually use expressions such as *It's darling,* and women tend not to use profanity as extensively as men. Likewise, the language used in addressing men and women varies subtly: we can compliment a man on a new necktie with the words *What a pretty tie that is!* but not with *How pretty you look today!,* an expression reserved for complimenting a woman. The occupation of a person causes his language to vary, particularly in the use he makes of technical terms, that is, in the use he makes of the **jargon** of his vocation. Soldiers, dentists, hairdressers, mechanics, yachtsmen, and skiers all have their particular special vocabularies. Sometimes the consequence is that such persons experience difficulty in communicating with people outside the vocation on professional matters because the technical vocabulary is not shared by all. Although we can relate certain kinds of jargon to levels of education and professional training, we must also note that all occupations employ some jargon, even those of the criminal underworld. There may well be a more highly developed use of jargon in occupations that require considerable education, in which words, and the concepts they express, are manipulated rather than objects, for example in the legal and teaching professions and in the world of finance.

By Function

Still another kind of variation is related to function. There are both formal and informal styles of speaking and writing. Writing also tends to be more formal than speaking in the sense that more conscious manipulation of vocabulary and syntax takes place. The most informal styles of speaking are often unjustly condemned, for very few words used to describe **slang** are anything other than pejorative. Slang, with its clipped and shortened forms, its novel uses and combinations of words, and its exotic quicksilver display of language, is a universal linguistic phenomenon. Slang is easier to criticize than to study, because its very transience does not leave behind in the language the kind of evidence linguists prefer to study. Discussions of slang tend to bring out expressions of dismay and condemnation from those who misunderstand its natural function as the exuberant wordplay of a group often used to achieve some kind of group identity. Slang in particular and linguistic **usage** in general have been studied in terms of cultural associations and functional uses. Yet the educated public has shown little acceptance of the few objective statements that can be made about the varieties of usage that occur in a language like English. Good evidence of this attitude can be seen in the predominantly hostile criticism that greeted the publication of *Webster's Third New International Dictionary* in 1961, which had the "audacity" to describe the language as it is rather than to prescribe it as it should be. Dictionaries published after that dictionary were less stridently objective and consequently more palatable to the critics, a result that is more a commentary on the state of the art of criticism than of the art of dictionary-making.

REGIONAL VARIATION

The kind of variation that has most interested linguists is dialect variation. Such an interest results in part from the connection between modern linguistics and older philological studies in which languages were seen as continually fragmenting through dialect variation. This process led to the evolution of new languages, for example the evolution of Proto-Indo-European into Greek, Latin, Sanskrit, and so on, and then, in turn, Latin into French, Spanish, and Italian. Consequently, linguists have studied dialects in relation to their geographic distribution since they recognize that people in one location often speak a language differently from speakers somewhere else, and that speakers in a third place speak it differently again. In recent years a new dimension has been added to dialect studies partly as a result of the growth of sociology and the development of refined techniques for sampling large populations of speakers. This new dimension is that of the social variation of language in social dialects. The concern of the rest of this chapter than is with these two aspects of language variation: regional dialect and social dialect.

A **dialect** itself is a variety of a language associated with a particular group of speakers and mutually intelligible with other varieties. According to this definition, Cantonese and Mandarin, both of which are often called Chinese, are different languages rather than different dialects of one language because they are not mutually intelligible in their spoken forms. However, Danish and Norwegian, sometimes called two different languages, are really dialects of one language in that they have a high degree of mutual intelligibility.

Types of Variation

We will now consider each of phonology, grammar, and vocabulary in turn to see how dialects can be established and how the regional speech of one area may be said to differ from that of other areas. We will use examples drawn from North American English. The differences referred to are all well known, having been pointed out in a number of studies. Only a few differences are mentioned in each category.

In phonology, linguists have investigated such matters as the inventory of vowels and consonants of a particular region and the phonetic values of the phonemic contrasts that exist. For example, the vowels of New York City English differ from those of Austin, Texas, and each dialect has its own set of contrasts and its own phonetic realizations of these contrasts. In examining regional dialects, we try to determine the phonetic values of the vowels in such words as *house, tide,* and *noise,* that is, those vowels that are usually pronounced as diphthongs in most varieties of English but which may have very different phonetic realizations of the diphthongs. In some dialects too these words may contain monophthongs rather than diphthongs. The tense vowels of words such as *beat, bait,* and *boat* also show interesting variations from dialect to dialect. Certain contrasts may be present or lacking, particularly in combination with certain phonemes, for example, before /r/ or a nasal phoneme. *Mary, merry,* and *marry* may show no distinction, one distinction, or two distinctions in pronunciation. *Horse* and *hoarse* may be pronounced alike or they may be contrasted in pronunciation, as may *pin* and *pen.* A dialect may also lack a distinction that most other dialects have, as when *cot* and *caught* become homophonous in some areas. The choice of vowel phoneme often varies from region to region, for example in words such as *hot, hog, orange, creek,* and *roof.* In some areas the vowel of *house* has a very noticeably different phonetic value from that of the first vowel in *houses,* and a similar difference may exist between the vowels of *wife* and *wives.*

Consonantal differences are generally much less useful in establishing dialect boundaries than vowel differences. The presence or absence of postvocalic /r/ is important, however, for *caught* and *court* can easily become homophonous. Likewise, the pronunciations of the initial consonants in *whip* (/w/ or /hw/) and *tune* (/t/ or /ty/) and the mid consonant in *greasy* (/s/ or /z/) correlate with important dialect areas. Certain other differences can be important, as for example the choice of the initial consonant in *then* (/d/ or /ð/), or of the final consonant or consonants in *cold* (/l/ or /ld/) and *singing* (/ŋ/ or /n/), but such differences are often less regional in distribution than they are social, a matter to which we will return later in the chapter.

Grammatical differences among dialects are largely morphological in nature. For example, the "past tense" forms and "past participle" forms of certain verbs often have interesting variants, as in such verbs as *dive* (*dived, dove, div*), *wake* (*waked, waked up,* and so on), and *climb* (*climbed, clum*). The plurals of *wasp* and *post* sometimes occur as *waspes* and *postes*.

Certain phrasal forms reveal different usages that can be related to regional characteristics: *quarter* (*of, till, to*) *ten: named the boy* (*after, at, for, from*) *his father; she was sick* (*at, in, of, on, to*) *her stomach;* and *he stood* (*behind, back of, in back of*) *the door* are representative examples. In still larger syntactic units other variations appear: *he* (*didn't ought, hadn't ought, ought not*) *to do it; he* (*doesn't have any, ain't got none, hasn't any*); and *that's* (*yours, yourn*). Some of these last differences are possibly related more closely to level of education than they are to particular regions. Syntactic differences are apparently less tolerated than are phonological differences among educated speakers of a language; therefore, such speakers tend to eliminate them. These stigmatized differences are regarded as nonstandard by linguists, **nonstandard** being the nonpejorative equivalent of the more usual designation, **substandard.**

Differences in vocabulary may also be observed among dialects. Such differences often relate to the commonplace activities of life rather than to what are usually regarded as scientific, cultural, and business activities, for which the vocabulary tends to be quite uniform throughout the language. The "folk" vocabulary often contains the clearest differences. There are different names for a window covering that can be rolled up: *blinds, shades, window blinds, window shades, roller shades;* for a web made by a spider: *web, cobweb, spider's web, dust web;* for the grass strip between the sidewalk and the street: *boulevard, lawn extension, tree lawn, city strip;* for relatives: *folks, kin, kinfolks, relations, family;* for a worm used in fishing: *angleworm, fish bait, earthworm, fishworm;* for a carbonated soft drink: *pop, soda, tonic, soft drink;* for a certain kind of nut: *peanuts, goobers, ground nuts;* and for a piece of playground equipment: *teeter-totter, teeter-horse, seesaw, riding horse.*

Dialect Atlases

During the last hundred years linguists have developed more and more refined ways of investigating the regional variations of a language. The earliest comprehensive survey, that of Georg Wenker for a dialect atlas of Germany, began in 1876. Wenker eventually developed a questionnaire which he distributed to village schoolmasters who were asked to write out certain sentences in the local dialect forms. In this way he attempted to discover how much phonological, grammatical, and vocabulary variation existed in German. He then followed up some of the more interesting variations with specific investigations. At the turn of the century Jules Gilliéron employed a single fieldworker, Edmond Edmont, for his dialect work in France. Edmont interviewed what he considered to be representative informants in 600 communities in France and adjoining areas of Belgium, Italy, and Switzerland for their responses to a very long questionnaire containing some 2,000 items. After World War I, the work of Jaberg and Jud in Italy and Switzerland further refined techniques for eliciting data from informants, particularly those living in towns and cities. More recent work in the British Isles, Japan, and North America has profited greatly from the experiences of these forerunners in collecting data.

In North America the most interesting project completed to date is that of the *Linguistic Atlas of New England.* This project, conducted under the direction of Hans Kurath during the 1920s and 1930s, employed a questionnaire containing 814 items that nine highly skilled investigators administered in 213 carefully selected communities to 416 informants. The questionnaire items were decided on after a preliminary investigation; the communities were picked out following demographic work on population distributions and movements; the informants were chosen to represent two and sometimes three levels of age and education in each community; and the investigators were selected because they were trained phoneticians and linguists whose work could be coordinated and whose transcriptions could be carefully compared for individual variations and accuracy. However, little attempt was made in the survey of New England to investigate language variation within large urban communities.

The results of such investigations are often published in the form of a **dialect atlas;** that is, the geographical distribution of linguistic variables is shown on elaborate maps. One map might show the distribution of the different pronunciations of a vowel in a certain word, another the distribution of the "past tense" variants of a certain verb, and still another the distribution of the different names that people use for a certain object. Often clear geographical divisions are apparent between areas so that one variant is found in one area and a second variant in another. In such cases dialect geographers draw a line between the two areas and call that line an **isogloss.** Sometimes several such lines, or isoglosses, will run together for long distances as two areas show a number of clear differences. This bundle of isoglosses is generally taken to mark the boundary between two dialect areas, and is referred to as a **dialect boundary.** One of the best known dialect boundaries is that between Low German (north) and High German (south) in Germany. Low German has the following pronunciations for words equivalent to English *make, village,* and *that:* [maken], [dorp], and [dat], whereas High German has [maxen], [dorf], and [das]. The isoglosses run together in the east but fan out in the west of Germany in a phenomenon known as the **Rhenish fan.**

Sometimes the isoglosses appear to be concentric or to fan out from a particular location, as in Figure 12-1. A point such as A in Figure 12-1 is called a **focal**

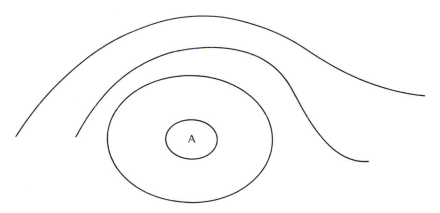

FIGURE 12-1 A dialect focal area.

area. Boston is a well-known focal area in North America, as evidenced by the spread into outlying areas of the word *tonic* for a carbonated soft drink. The Hudson Valley is another focal area.

Occasionally the opposite effect is observed. Isoglosses appear to be moving toward a particular location from various other locations, as in Figure 12-2. A point such as B in Figure 12-2 is called a **relic area.** Martha's Vineyard, with its *smurring up,* meaning "becoming foggy," and Cape Cod are two well-known relic areas in North America. Still a third kind of area, one in which the isoglosses crisscross in an apparently unsystematic way, is called a **transition area.** Northwest Virginia and Oklahoma are examples of transition areas in North America.

Once focal, relic, and transitional areas have been located and dialect boundaries established from an analysis of the data collected by field workers, some attempt is usually made to relate such areas to one or more of a variety of factors. For example, the settlement history of a region is often closely related to language variation. Older settled areas often seem to be less innovative than newly settled areas and also to display comparatively more variation over comparably sized territories. We need do no more than compare the great amount of linguistic variation found in New England with the degree of linguistic uniformity of much of California to appreciate the importance of settlement history. Likewise, the place of origin of the settlers makes a difference. Different parts of New England were settled from different parts of the British Isles; the Midwest was settled by people from various parts of Europe in addition to the British Isles, and also from the East; and California has been settled from all over the United States but contains in addition a large indigenous Spanish-speaking population. When a particular group in an area speaks a different language from the standard or national language, that language is likely to produce some dialect differences, as for example did the speaking of German in parts of Pennsylvania, particularly in the Pennsylvania Dutch region.

Dialect boundaries are often related to migratory routes, such as water, road,

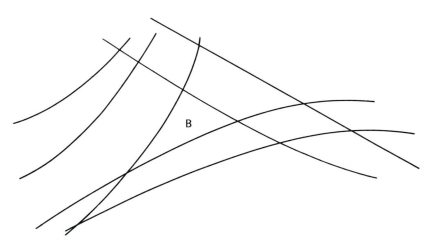

FIGURE 12-2 A dialect relic area.

or rail routes. For example, the Great Lakes area shows linguistic distributions related to water routes, as do the Mississippi and Ohio Valleys. More recently, northward migration in the United States, particularly of whites from Appalachia and blacks from the southern states, has produced linguistic effects in and around large northern cities such as New York, Detroit, Cleveland, and Chicago. In this case the population movement has been on a very large scale, and it is still too early to assess the full results. We also experience much more difficulty in surveying linguistic variation in a complex, fluid, urban setting than in a simple, static, rural one.

Recent developments in transportation have reduced the extent to which geographic barriers and the availability of easy routes of communication are important in determining population settlement. For example, the Blue Ridge Mountains in Virginia were an early obstacle to western expansion and mark a dialect boundary. Now they are no longer such an obstacle, so the dialect boundary may be expected to diminish in importance in time. Geographic mobility tends to reduce dialect differences.

Finally, certain forms may be associated with centers of prestige and culture. London and Oxford in England, Paris in France, and Boston, Charleston, Richmond, and Philadelphia in the United States are examples of cities which have acquired prestige as national capitals, or as educational, commercial, or cultural centers. Consequently, certain linguistic forms appear to radiate from these centers as features of prestige dialects are adopted by speakers in other places. Occasionally the results of such adoptions are strange: certain migrants to New York City find it very desirable to learn the distinctive characteristics of New York City speech whereas second- and third-generation residents—that is, native New Yorkers themselves—often condemn the same characteristics. New York City speech, therefore, is regarded as prestigious by one group, but as lacking in prestige by the other. Other kinds of ambivalent attitudes exist too, as witnessed by the very different feelings people have about the speech of Boston.

AMERICAN AND BRITISH ENGLISH

Regional differences within the United States are not as apparent to most speakers of English as are regional differences within the British Isles, where many of the same factors account for the differences. Then, of course, American English and British English differ from each other. There are differences between the two in the phonetic values of certain vowels, particularly conspicuous in the tense vowels and diphthongs of the variety of British English known as **Received Pronunciation,** the variety taught to Eliza Doolittle by Professor Higgins in Bernard Shaw's play *Pygmalion,* and sometimes caricatured in the expression *How now, brown cow.* Different phonemic choices are also apparent, as for example in *bath, either, clerk, fertile,* and in the pronunciation of *z* (as *zee* in America and as *zed* in Britain). Stress patterns differ, as do the numbers of syllables in words such as *medicine, necessary, laboratory,* and *missionary,* and the intonation contours for sentences.

Vocabulary differs between American and British English as a result of certain cultural differences, divergent developments in word meanings, and the parallel development of certain inventions, for example, the automobile and the railroad.

Vocabulary differences are seen in the following American words, the British equivalent, if any, being bracketed: *bayou, moccasin, peanuts (monkey nuts), suspenders (braces), clerk (shop assistant), homely (plain), letter carrier* or *mailman (postman), railroad (railway), tie (sleeper), hood (bonnet), trunk (boot), TV (telly), billboard (hording), taxes (rates), subway (underground),* and *checkers (draughts).*

The most subtle differences of all are the syntactic ones. British English has a preference for the use of *have* as a full verb in *Haven't you any?* as opposed to an American preference for *Don't you have any?* Likewise, the use of *those* and *ones* together in *Give me those ones* is a British usage, just as the tendency to add prepositions to verbs as in *visit with* and *call up* is an American usage. The claim has been made that American speech is more exuberant and vital than British speech, but, though we can show certain areas where this is apparently so, as in the use of slang, names, honorifics, and profanity, such a thesis is probably unprovable and really little more than the statement of a personal preference for one variety of English over the other.

HISTORICAL DIALECTOLOGY

We can use some of the techniques developed for describing contemporary existing dialects for studies in historical dialectology. One group of investigators gathered together a number of fourteenth-century English documents of known provenance, that is, documents whose dates and geographic origins were well established. Then, using their knowledge of the history of the language and of modern British English dialects, they examined these documents for linguistic features that appeared to be characteristic of the region in which each document was written. They found certain very interesting dialect differentiations reflected in the writings. *Stane* was a northern variant for *stone; vrom* was a southwestern variant for *from; them* was a northern variant for *hem; mon* was a west midland variant for *man; sun* or *syn* were west midland and southern variants for *sin;* and so on. The same vowel and consonant alternations showed up in other words too, as in *hame* (northern) for *home,* and *vather* (southwestern) for *father* in a quite systematic way.

On the basis of such evidence, the investigators established isoglosses and dialect areas for Middle English, noting at the same time certain less obvious characteristics of each area such as the northern preference for *ui* rather than *oo,* as in *buik* and *bluid* (*book* and *blood*), and for spelling words beginning with [hw] as *qu-.* They proceeded to use this information to locate possible places of origin for documents the provenance of which was uncertain. A document with *hem* (for *them*), *zuyn* (for *sin*), and *velaʒe* (for *fellow*) is very southern in its characteristics, whereas one with *allane* (for *alone*), *quhar* (for *where*), *mon* (for *man*), and *them* (for *hem*) is northern. It is likely that each document originated in the region whose characteristics it bears.

SOCIAL VARIATION

Almost all the dialect differences discussed so far have been regional differences, although we made brief mention of differences associated with social and educational level. The questionnaire surveys of the dialect geographer do not allow us to say very much about social dialects because the sampling techniques, for both data and informants, are not designed for this purpose. This coverage of data works out quite well for purposes of making geographically based observations, since it is nearly always possible to compare equivalent responses from old people, generally of limited education and mobility, by region. Nevertheless, the surveys cannot be used to say very much about the social distribution of dialects, nor to make many observations about the speech of densely populated areas and the varieties of speech within such areas. Different sampling techniques are required for such work together with a different approach to language variation, one which recognizes that the speech of any individual may show a variety of characteristics, each dependent on a particular set of circumstances, rather than a uniform set of characteristics appropriate to all circumstances.

Recent work in large cities such as Washington, Detroit, Chicago, New York, and Philadelphia, particularly work by William Labov, has employed sampling procedures derived from sociological surveys. Consequently, the speech of a sample which is representative of the total community is subject to linguistic analysis. In one approach the speech of each speaker within a sample is recorded in a variety of circumstances: reading a passage from a book; answering a set of questions; and participating in unguarded conversation, particularly with peers. The investigator also collects information about the mobility characteristics, social groupings, and such matters as educational level, income level, color, sex, age, and regional origin of each informant. Such investigations collect large amounts of data concerning the speech of certain cities and provide opportunities for relating the data to a variety of social and regional factors.

Analyses of the data show that the incidence of certain variations is often more important than a decision that a particular variation does or does not occur. For example, many speakers are not completely r-less or completely r-pronouncing in words like car and cart, but show variation in the incidence of r's according to circumstances. If speakers consider r's to be prestigious and they are in a setting in which r's are generally pronounced, they will probably pronounce r's to an extent greater than they would in circumstances in which prestige is of no concern. They will also probably be quite unaware of what they are doing. In like manner, this may be pronounced with either a beginning /d/ or /ð/, singing may end in /ŋ/ or /n/, unstressed vowels may or may not be eliminated (because or 'cause), stresses may be shifted (pólice or políce; Détroit or Detróit), and negatives may be used singly or multiply, all depending on the particular social context of an utterance.

Each item that is investigated is called a **linguistic variable.** For example, r-pronouncing, the alternation between /d/ and /ð/ in then, or between /iŋ/ and /in/ as "progressive" verb endings are linguistic variables. The occurrences of the variants of each variable must be related to the circumstances of their occurrence. The evidence gathered in such circumstances is therefore quantitative rather than qualitative, that is, evidence which must be treated statistically (in terms of more or less) rather than absolutely (in terms of the presence or the absence of a particular feature). Linguists try to interpret their data in relation to social class by relating observed linguistic variations to socio-economic status, patterns of language contact, social mobility, and group norms. What has emerged is a very complex portrait of each of the communities that has been investigated in contrast to the kinds of sketches produced by those who worked in the atlas-making tradition. In fact, new insights from demography, sociology, statistics, and linguistics have completely revolutionized the study of dialects.

Some of the most interesting recent work on the language of cities in the United States has focused on the varieties of English spoken by many black citizens. Such speakers appear to share certain linguistic features as a result of the early settlement history of the United States and recent migratory patterns. For example, they often show a considerable amount of vowel **neutralization.** This neutralization combined with the lack of pronunciation of postvocalic r can lead to **homophonous** pronunciations of *guide, god,* and *guard.* Final stop consonants are often lost in totally voiceless or totally voiced clusters so that *pass* and *past* become homophonous, as do *Ben* and *bend.* This last reduction is particularly important because it conceals certain past tense and past participle forms, making *they bake* homophonous with *they baked* and *they beg* with *they begged,* and since the g in this last case is sometimes realized phonetically as [k], all four forms may be pronounced the same. Certain other consonantal distinctions vary in frequency of occurrence, sometimes being made but more generally not, for example the distinctions between *taught* and *thought, three* and *free,* and *Ruth* and *roof.* The result is a considerable amount of homophony in parts of the system in which other dialects have contrasting forms. Together with phonetic realizations for the resulting vowels that differ from the realizations in other dialects, the homophony produces a dialect of English that is noticeably distinct.

The distinctness of this variety of English is reinforced by certain characteristics of intonation, vocabulary, syntax, and styles of use. The most noticeable syntactic characteristics occur in expressions in which other varieties require a particular form of the verb *be* (*He sick, He be sick*), a single negative (*It ain't no help*), a certain kind of construction for indirect questions (*He asked could he go, I want to know did he go*), or an expletive *there* (*It's a man outside*). The characteristic forms of this dialect that are given in parentheses are perfectly well formed and consistently used within the dialect; they are therefore grammatical for the speakers in question. Nevertheless, the rules are different from those of speakers of more standard varieties of English. It is not unusual for speakers of such a dialect to learn a standard dialect, and it is quite usual for such institutions as the public schools to attempt deliberate teaching of a standard dialect to these speakers.

INTERDIALECT COMMUNICATION

A particularly interesting question to ask about dialects is how it is that speakers of different dialects of a language understand each other when numerous differences exist. One answer is that they sometimes do not, for many people have had the experience of being hardly able to communicate with someone who was obviously speaking English, but who was speaking a very different dialect from their own. On the whole, however, easy communication is possible because all speakers use very much the same system of rules. The system varies little from dialect to dialect; indeed a dialect may be defined as one of the systems of slightly varying rules the whole set of which comprises a language. A particular dialect may have a neutralization rule for a pair of vowels in a certain environment (/i/ and /e/ before nasals), another rule for dropping certain syllables (initial unstressed syllables) or certain consonants (final stops in totally voiced or totally voiceless clusters, or postvocalic *r*'s), and still another rule for negation (negate every word that can be negated: *He ain't never done nobody no harm*), rules that are not found in other dialects. In each case, however, the dialect is produced by the systematic application of rules and shares the vast majority of its rules with the other dialects of the language.

This systematic operation of rules in dialects can be illustrated by reference to three well-known examples of dialect variation. In one dialect the work *desk* is pronounced like *dess*, phonetically [dɛs] and its plural is *desses* [dɛsəz]. The pronunciations of these words can be predicted from knowing that in this dialect final voiceless stops are not pronounced in voiceless clusters, and that this rule applies before plurals are added. Consequently, [dɛsk] becomes [dɛs] by a rule peculiar to this dialect, and then pluralizes to [dɛsəz] by a general English rule that adds [əz] after coronal stridents, as described in Chapter 5. In still another dialect the vowel in *wife* differs in quality from that in *wives*, beginning in a more central position: phonetically [wəɪf] and [waɪvz]. This characteristic results from a rule that centralizes such a diphthong before voiceless consonants, [f] in this case, but not before voiced consonants, [v] in this case. An identical centralization is sometimes found in the pair *house* and *houses* ([həʊs] and [haʊzəz]), which involves a different diphthong.

The third example is perhaps the most interesting of all. It involves the pronunciation of the words *writer* and *rider*, in which there are two potential differences, the quality of the diphthong and of the medial consonant. Often medial *t*'s are voiced in English so that medial underlying phonemic /t/ is pronounced phonetically as [d] (or [ɾ]). In dialect A this rule operates before the rule to centralize the diphthong before voiceless consonants. Consequently, *writer* is pronounced as follows:

writer = /raɪtər/ → [raɪdər]

In this case the centralization rule cannot apply because there is no voiceless consonant following the diphthong. However, in dialect B the order of rules is reversed so that the rule to centralize the diphthong before voiceless consonants applies first and then the voicing rule for /t/ applies. The result is the following pronunciation:

writer = /raɪtər/ → [rəɪtər] →]rəɪdər]

Consequently, in dialect A *writer* is phonetically [raɪdər] and in dialect B it is [rəɪdər]. However, in both dialects *rider* is pronounced [raɪdər] by still a third rule which lengthens the diphthong before the /d/ in the underlying phonemic representation of *rider* (/raɪdər/). Consequently, *writer* and *rider* are kept apart in both dialects: by vowel length in dialect A and by a combination of vowel quality and vowel length in dialect B.

The last dialect examples using rules and rule-ordering bring us back to the problems of what language is and how languages change. To speak a language is to have mastered a set of rules for producing sentences in that language. However, a language is not an unvarying system. All kinds of people speak it in a variety of ways and circumstances. Children learning a language must construct the most economical system they can from the varieties that are present in the environment. They must compose their own rules and devise their own grammars. In large measure the grammar each child constructs will be the same as everyone else's, but it will have idiosyncracies, particularly if the child is in an environment in which many different varieties of the language are spoken. It appears inevitable that in such circumstances linguistic change will occur over the generations as learners add, delete, and rearrange rules in their attempt to construct optimal grammars to suit the variations to which they are exposed.

BIBLIOGRAPHIC NOTES

Two useful sources of information on slang are Partridge's *Dictionary of Slang and Unconventional English* and Wentworth and Flexner's *Dictionary of American Slang.* Joos' *Five Clocks* is an intriguing study of levels of usage and Sledd and Ebbitt's *Dictionaries and* THAT *Dictionary* is an informative account of the critical reception given to *Webster's Third New International Dictionary.*

The three European dialect atlases referred to in Chapter 12 are Wenker's work edited by Wrede in the *Deutscher Sprachatlas,* Gilliéron and Edmont's *Atlas Linguistique de la France,* and Jaberg and Jud's *Sprach- und Sachatlas Italiens und der Südschweiz.*

The North American atlas is Kurath's *Linguistic Atlas of New England,* from which several interesting works have derived: Kurath's *Word Geography of the Eastern United States,* Kurath and McDavid's *Pronunciation of English in the Atlantic States,* and Atwood's *Survey of Verb Forms in the Eastern United States.* Good introductory materials for a study of American dialects can be found in McDavid's chapter in Francis' *Structure of American English,* and Shuy's *Discovering American Dialects.* Brook's *English Dialects* provides an introduction to British dialects.

American English is the concern of Marckwardt's *American English,* Mencken's *American Language,* and Krapp's *English Language in America.* Historical dialectology using documents of known provenance is described in Moore, Meech, and Whitehall's "Middle English Dialect Characteristics and Dialect Boundaries" and in Chapter Five of Bloomfield and Newmark's *Linguistic Introduction to the History of English.* Part Five of Scott and Erickson's *Readings for the History of the English Language* contains papers on a variety of topics.

In social dialectology Labov's *Social Stratification of English in New York City, Study of Nonstandard English, Language in the Inner City,* and *Sociolinguistic Patterns* are key works. Trudgill's *Sociolinguistics: An Introduction* is a useful brief introduction to the general topic and Wolfram and Fasold's *Study of Social Dialects in American English* is a sound introduction to social dialectology. "Black English" is the subject of Dillard's *Black English* and Burling's *English in Black and White.*

EXERCISES

12-1 Check to make sure that you understand each of the terms printed in **boldface** in Chapter 12.

12-2 Chapter 12 makes distinctions between certain terms. Explain the distinction between the following terms as clearly as you can: *language* and *dialect; social dialect* and *regional dialect; focal area* and *relic area; nonstandard* and *substandard.*

12-3 Select a short piece of technical writing. Pick out some words which are instances of jargon peculiar to the topic. Pick out other words which are being used in a special sense.

12-4 Find a dozen slang expressions which you think are not well known to the majority of people. Provide glosses.

12-5 The following sentences contain examples of different usages. For each sentence find out which usage is recommended by prescriptivists. Indicate the places where you disagree with the prescription or where you consider more than one usage acceptable.

   1 This room is *awfully/extremely* cold.
   2 *Whom/Who* do you want?
   3 Is that you? Yes, it's *I/me.*
   4 He's completely *uninterested/disinterested* in school these days.
   5 I don't like *those/that* kind of people.
   6 He *dove/dived* into the pool after her.
   7 I'm right, *ain't I/aren't I/am I not?*
   8 The broom is (*in*) *back of/behind* the door.
   9 I don't have anyone *to talk to/to whom I can talk* anymore.
   10 Stand up *like/as* a man.
   11 This one is different *than/from* that one.
   12 We *will/shall* sing, "We *Will/Shall* overcome."
   13 If it *was/were* to happen, what would you do?
   14 He took it *off of/off/from/from off* the table.
   15 She *graduated/was graduated* from Vassar.
   16 I wonder *if/whether* he'll come.
   17 *Lay/Lie* down, Fido.
   18 There are *fewer/less* reasons for doing that now.
   19 It looks *as though it will/like* rain.
   20 *This/These* data *is/are* correct.
   21 The reason he did it was *that/because* he was tired.
   22 Please write to John and *I/me* when you get back.
   23 I don't approve of *him/his* doing that.
   24 Try *and/to* finish it soon.
   25 *Can/May* I open the window, please?
   26 He *surely/sure/certainly* knows about it now.
   27 You should be able to judge *a book's contents/the contents of a book* by now.
   28 I don't doubt *but what/that* they will agree.
   29 *Because of/Due to* a power failure the show was canceled.
   30 The members of the faculty supported *each other/one another.*

12-6 Record your pronunciation of the following words. Record the pronunciations of two other people of very different backgrounds from each other and from you.

1 creek	sick	seek		
2 Mary	marry	merry		
3 ask	aunt	bath	bat	
4 water	Washington			
5 fog	log	hog	dog	
6 time	fine	house	houses	
7 horse	hoarse	poor	pour	
8 apricot	tomato			
9 height	humor			
10 balm	bomb			
11 the grease	to grease	greasy		
12 on	off	cot	caught	
13 roof	broom	food	good	
14 many	Minnie	pin	pen	
15 which	witch	what	Watt	
16 calm	alms	arms		
17 saw	sore	bawd	bored	board
18 cot	court	caught	coat	
19 since	cents	scents	sense	
20 Ben	bent	bend	bends	Ben's
21 Tess	test	tests	Tess's	
22 thin	thing	singing		

12-7 What word (or words) do you use for each of the following? Write down any other words you know for each. By whom are they used? What conclusions, if any, can you draw from your data?

1 a meal eaten in the middle of the day
2 a grass strip between the sidewalk and the street
3 a severe but short rainstorm
4 a limited-access road
5 a rainstorm accompanied by thunder and lightning
6 a large truck with a trailer attached
7 a large covered porch
8 a vehicle for pushing a baby
9 an iron utensil used for frying
10 a building in which fire engines are kept
11 a paper container used to carry groceries
12 a place where trains stop
13 a cover for a bed when the latter is not in use
14 the fuel for a lamp
15 an insect that glows in the dark
16 a road with an asphalt surface
17 a nonpedigreed, nondescript dog
18 a call made to get a horse moving
19 a call made to bring in cattle
20 to be illegally absent from school
21 bread made from cornmeal
22 flat cakes made from flour often eaten for breakfast
23 a call by children to interrupt a game for a moment
24 thick sour milk
25 a window covering on rollers
26 a black and white animal capable of emitting a strong odor

27 to become ill
28 a worm used for bait
29 a large sandwich which is a meal in itself
30 a web made by a spider
31 a phrase used to refer to one's immediate family
32 a children's cry at Hallowe'en
33 a familiar word for *father*
34 a familiar word for *mother*
35 a derogatory phrase for a person from the country
36 a bad dive, resulting in a large splash
37 a carbonated drink
38 a garment worn by men for swimming

12-8 Give the equivalent North American word or phrase for the following British word or phrase:

1 clothes-peg	**8** sweets	**15** engine driver	**22** high street
2 trousers	**9** petrol	**16** public school	**23** queue
3 braces	**10** windscreen	**17** shop assistant	**24** spanner
4 waistcoat	**11** boot (of a car)	**18** reel (of thread)	**25** electric torch
5 turnups	**12** railway engine	**19** drawing pin	**26** the underground
6 biscuits	**13** return ticket	**20** to pay rates	**27** cinema
7 crisps	**14** guard's van	**21** zebra crossing	**28** interval

12-9 Give the equivalent British word or phrase for the following North American word or phrase:

1 janitor	**7** fender	**16** billboard	**24** wrench
2 deck	**8** railroad	**17** cop	(tool)
(of cards)	**9** freight train	**18** pharmacist	**25** principal
3 frosting	**10** tracks	**19** elevator	(of school)
(on cake)	**11** checkers	**20** second floor	**26** attorney
4 vacation	**12** homely	**21** billion	**27** co-ed
5 can	**13** traffic circle	**22** a raise	**28** faucet
("container")	**14** sidewalk	**23** grade	
6 hood	**15** truck	(in school)	

12-10 Try to describe the major differences between your most careful style of speaking (as in giving a formal lecture) and your most relaxed style (as in casual conversation with your peers).

12-11 Choose a linguistic variable such as the pronunciation of the *-ing* endings of verbs. Try to discover the incidence of the variants (of the /ɪŋ/ and /ɪn/ pronunciations) and relate the occurrences to the circumstances of their production.

GLOSSARY

This glossary lists all the linguistic terms that are printed in boldface in the text together with a number of other terms that beginning students of linguistics are likely to meet in their reading. The list is by no means exhaustive, nor will the definitions always be exactly appropriate, since individual linguists tend to coin special terms or give accepted terms special meanings. The illustrative examples are drawn almost exclusively from English.

abstract The semantic feature of being without discernible physical attributes. *Hope* and *love* are abstract nouns so are marked with the semantic feature [−concrete]. Compare **concrete.**

acronym A word formed from the initial letters or syllables of a set phrase, for example, *NATO* from *North Atlantic Treaty Organization* and *Benelux.*

active Designating the form of a verb in which the subject performs the action; for example, *chased* in *John chased the cat* and *paid* in *John paid for the tickets.* Compare **passive.**

adjective A form class often marked in English by the ability to take the comparative and superlative suffixes; for example, *long, longer, longest* and *good, better, best* are adjectives.

adverb   A form class sometimes marked in English by the ability to take the *-ly* suffix; for example, *wisely, usually,* and *heavily* are adverbs.

affix   A bound morpheme attached to a stem; for example, *pre-* in *prehistory, -ic* in *historic,* and *-s* in *cats.*

affricate   A stop with a fricative release; for example, the initial sounds in *cheese* and *jump.*

age-grading   The characteristic language of a particular age group.

agent   The animate performer of the action of a verb; for example, *John* in *John ate the candy* and *the cat* in *The cat chased the mouse.*

agreement   A dependency between two or more words involving inflection for one or more of such characteristics as case, gender, number, and person.

allomorph   A positional variant of a-morpheme. The endings of *cats, dogs,* and *churches* all have the meaning "plural" but differ phonemically (/s/ ~ /z/ ~ /əz/) and are therefore allomorphs of the "plural" morpheme.

allophone   A positional variant of a phoneme. The initial sound in *pin* [pʰ] and the second sound in *spin* [p] are phonetically different, but this difference is quite predictable in English and never results in a difference in meaning; it is therefore an allophonic difference, not a phonemic one.

alphabet   A system of writing in which letters are used to represent individual sounds.

alveolar   Referring to the hard ridge behind the top teeth. The sounds at the beginning of *Ted, dead,* and *Ned* are alveolar consonants.

alveopalatal   Indicating the positioning of the front part of the tongue on, or in the region of, the alveolar ridge and hard palate. The sounds at the beginning of *choose, Jack,* and *show* and in the middle of *measure* are alveopalatal consonants.

ambiguity   The property of having at least two distinct meanings; for example, *seal, criminal lawyer,* and *He likes entertaining guests* are all ambiguous.

amelioration   See **elevation.**

analogy   The extension of a pattern or a rule to data not previously covered by the pattern or rule. The plural of *criterion* is sometimes *criterions* instead of *criteria* by analogy to words such as *champion* and *scorpion.*

anaphora   Reference to something that has already been mentioned through a process of substitution. For example, *did too* in *I said it and he did too* avoids the repetition of *said it.*

anaphoric pronoun   A pronoun which makes reference back to a noun phrase in a sentence or series of sentences; for example, *he* in *I spoke to the man and expected he would answer.*

animate   Having life and movement; however, plants are usually excluded. *Boy, dog,* and *caterpillar* are animate nouns and are assigned the semantic feature [+animate] as opposed to *tree* and *rock* which are [−animate] (or **inanimate**).

antecedent   The word or group of words to which a pronoun refers. In *He gave it to the people who came, the people* is the antecedent of *who* and in *The foolish hunter wounded himself, the foolish hunter* is the antecedent of *himself.*

antonym   A word with a meaning opposite to that of another word, as in the pairs *black* and *white, young* and *old,* and *wise* and *foolish.* Compare **synonym.**

aphesis   The loss of an unstressed vowel at the beginning of a word, as in *'bout* for *about.*

apical Involving the tip of the tongue; for example, the sounds at the beginnings of *Ted, dead, Ned,* and *red* (the last being apical as well as retroflex).

apicoalveolar Made by touching the tip of the tongue to the ridge behind the upper teeth.

apocope The loss of a sound or sounds at the end of a word, as in *tes'* for *test.*

arbitrariness The lack of a logical connection between the form of something and its expression in sounds.

archiphoneme A class of phonemes lacking contrast in a particular environment. In German /t/ and /d/ do not contrast in final position, so certain linguists claim that the archiphoneme /T/ occurs finally. In English /p/ and /b/ do not contrast after /s/, so *spin* is sometimes said to contain the archiphoneme /P/ and is written as /sPin/. In English /i/ and /iy/ do not contrast before /r/, so *hear* is sometimes said to contain the archiphoneme /I/ and is written as /hIr/. See **neutralization.**

argot The specialized language and vocabulary of a particular group of people, especially of a criminal or underworld group.

article A word such as *the* or *a,* the former the definite article, the latter the indefinite article.

articulation The alterations of the various cavities and passages of the vocal tract to produce the sounds of speech.

articulator A movable organ of speech such as the various parts of the tongue and the lower lip.

aspect The marking of a verb to indicate whether an action is beginning, completed, in progress, repeated, and so on; for example, *Shirley is knitting a sweater* is marked for progressive aspect.

aspiration A puff of air accompanying the release of a stop, as with the initial stops of *pan, tan,* and *can.*

assimilation The process by which a sound changes to become phonetically more like an adjacent sound, so that the first /n/ of *incongruous* sometimes becomes /ŋ/ and the final /n/ of *ribbon* sometimes becomes /m/.

autonomous phonemes See **taxonomic phonemes.**

auxiliary verb A verb that combines with another verb to form a verb phrase; for example, *have* in *have gone* or *will* in *will go.*

back Produced in the back of the mouth or with the back of the tongue. The vowels in *boot, good, boat,* and *bought* are back vowels, whereas those in *bit, bet,* and *bat* are front vowels.

backed Produced in a position further back in the mouth than what may be regarded as the basic position of the sound. The initial consonant of *cool* is backed in comparison with the initial consonant of *calm.*

back formation The creation of a new word from an already existing word in the belief that the existing word is a derivative of a word that actually exists. *Burgle* is a back formation from *burglar.*

base A morpheme to which affixes can be added; for example, *wise* in *wisely* and *-vise* in *revise.* See also **phrase-structure component.**

bilabial Produced by both lips. *Pin* and *bin* begin with bilabial stops.

bimorphemic Composed of two morphemes, as are *cats, men, produce, took,* and *player.*

binary Made up of two parts.

biuniqueness Being able to go from either phonemic to phonetic or phonetic to phonemic notations leaving nothing unaccounted for in the rules that are employed.

blend A word coined from parts of existing words; for example, *slanguage* and *motorcade.*

borrowing Adding new items to a language or dialect by taking them from another language or dialect.

bound morpheme A morpheme that must occur with at least one other morpheme; for example, the *-s* in *cats,* the *-ing* in *singing,* and the *-duce* in *reduce.*

braces { } In generative-transformational grammar a convention for showing that one, and only one, of the linear choices enclosed in the braces must be made in the rewriting of a particular constituent.

bundle of isoglosses The cooccurrence of several isoglosses that marks a dialect boundary.

cardinal-vowel system A system devised by Daniel Jones for describing vowels by making use of certain vowels as reference points for all possible discriminable vowels.

case An inflected form of a word which indicates the syntactic relationship of that word to another word in a grammatical construction. For example, *him* is in the objective case in *I like him* and *his* is in the genitive (or possessive) case in *He ate his dinner.* In the last sentence *he* is not marked for case, although it is sometimes said to be in the nominative case.

case grammar A theory of syntax and semantics in which nouns in deep structure are said to be related to verbs in cases such as agent, object, dative, instrumental, and so on.

causative verb A verb which can be paraphrased as "cause to ____" or "cause something to ____"; for example, *fell* can be paraphrased as "cause to fall" and *kill* as "cause to die." *Broke* is used causatively in *He broke the window,* that is, "caused the window to break."

central Produced in the center of the mouth. The vowel in *but* is a central vowel.

checked vowel The vowel in a closed syllable, as in *at, get, ape,* and *bite.* The English vowels in *at* and *get* can occur only in closed syllables, so these vowels are always checked; the vowels in *ape* and *bite* may also occur unchecked in open syllables. Compare **free vowel.**

citation form A linguistic form pronounced in isolation; for example, *have* rather than the *'ve* of *I could've gone* or *them* rather than the *'em* of *I saw 'em.*

class A set of linguistic forms sharing a common characteristic; for example, nouns can be pluralized, relative pronouns require antecedents, and questions seek a response.

class dialect The dialect of a particular social class.

clause A construction containing a subject and a finite verb.

closed syllable A syllable ending in one or more consonants; for example, *cat, bump, apt,* and *strength.* Compare **open syllable.**

closed system A system that allows for only a finite set of possibilities.

cluster A sequence of two or more consonants made without an intervening vowel; for example, the beginning of *scream* (/skr-/) and the end of *glimpsed* (/-mpst/).

coarticulation The concurrent articulation of two sounds; for example, in certain languages labial and velar stops are produced together: [k͡p] and [g͡b].

cognate A morpheme or word related to another morpheme or word by reason of descent from a common linguistic source; for example, English *foot,* German *Fuss,* and Latin *pes* are cognates.

collocation The likelihood that several words will occur in the same environment; for example, *car, road, drive,* and *wheel.*

comparative method A method for doing historical-comparative work which employs cognates in different languages in order to postulate ancestral forms of which the cognates may be said to be the historical reflexes.

competence The ability of native speakers to create and understand grammatical sentences, to detect deviant and ungrammatical sentences, and to make other linguistic judgments about utterances in their language. Compare **performance.**

complement A word or group of words that follows a verb or verb phrase so as to complete a predicate; for example, *happy* in both *John is happy* and *I made him happy* and *John's father* in *It was John's father.*

complementary distribution The occurrence of variants of a linguistic unit in different environments. Two or more linguistic variants are in complementary distribution when they have no common environment; for example, the allomorphic variants /s/ of *cats* and /z/ of *dogs,* both meaning "plural," and the allophonic variants [pʰ] of *pin* [pʰɪn] and [p] of *spin* [spɪn], belonging to the phoneme /p/.

complementation A grammatical construction consisting of a verb or verb phrase and a complement; for example, the relationship between *made him* and *happy* in *I made him happy* and *was* and *John's father* in *It was John's father.*

complementizer A grammatical form which introduces a complement of some kind; for example, *to* in *I want to go.*

complex nucleus A diphthong in a syllable. Each of the syllables *bough, buy,* and *boy* contains a complex nucleus.

complex sentence A sentence containing one independent clause and one or more dependent clauses or embedded verbals.

componential analysis The analysis of sets of related words into their minimal components of meaning so that *uncle* is analyzed into such components as "male," "one generation removed," and "related to father or mother as either sibling or sibling's spouse."

compound A new form made by joining together two or more freely occurring forms; for example, *houseboat* is a compound formed from *house* and *boat,* and *I sing and dance* is a compound formed from *I sing* and *I dance.*

compounding Joining together two linguistic forms which can function independently; for example, noun-compounding in *paperweight,* phrase-compounding in *The old men and young children left;* and clause-compounding in *Jack sings and Jill dances.*

compound sentence A sentence containing two or more independent clauses and no dependent clauses.

concord See **agreement.**

concrete Having discernible physical attributes. *Man, rock,* and *plant* are concrete nouns and are marked with the semantic feature [+concrete]. Compare **abstract.**

conjugation See **paradigm.**

conjunction A word usually used to join one clause to another; for example, *and, but,* and *or* are coordinating conjunctions which conjoin phrases or clauses with similar grammatical functions, and *although, since,* and *until* are subordinating conjunctions which join dependent clauses to independent ones.

consonant   A contrastive unit in the sound system of a language characterized in pronunciation by constriction of the airstream in the vocal tract; also a letter to symbolize such a sound.   Compare **vowel.**

consonant cluster   A sequence of consonants; for example, /skr/ is a permissible English initial cluster (*scream*) but */sgr/ is not.

constituent   One of the parts of a construction.

constituent structure   A mapping of a sentence or part of a sentence into its constituents.

construction   A relationship between constituents; for example, the relationship between *old* and *man* in *old man, John* and *slept* in *John slept,* and *come* and *when I signal* in *Come when I signal.*

content words   Words such as *man, go, slow,* and *red,* which are often inflected and have considerable semantic content.   Compare **structure words.**

contoid   A sound involving some kind of constriction in its production.   Compare **vocoid.**

coordination   A grammatical construction consisting of two constituents joined by *and, but,* or *or,* as in *bread and butter, very tired but extremely happy,* and *We'll sink or swim.*

copula   Any part of the verb *be* used as the main verb in the predicate of a clause.

count   Being countable.   *Sheep, boy, mile,* and *deed* are count nouns and so are assigned the semantic feature [+count].   Compare **mass.**

cultural transmission   The handing down of certain patterns of behavior from generation to generation by nongenetic means.

dative   A grammatical inflection which is not found in English but which in other languages is sometimes used in nouns to indicate the recipient of something.   In case grammar, dative refers to the animate undergoer of the action of the verb; for example, *John* in both *Fred killed John* and *John died* is said to be in the dative case.

declarative   A statement; for example, *He likes pizzas* and *Joe was happy.*

declension   See **paradigm.**

deep structure   The abstract structure postulated as underlying a sentence, containing all the information necessary for both the syntactic and semantic interpretation of the sentence.   Compare **surface structure.**

deep subject   The noun phrase which is the subject of a deep structure but which may or may not become the surface subject.   In *Jim kicked Tom* and *Tom was kicked by Jim, Jim* is the deep subject of both sentences but the surface subject of only the first sentence.

degradation   A change of meaning which results in a word describing something less worthy, desirable, or pleasant than it previously did; for example, *wench, knave,* and *odor.*   Also called **pejoration.**   Compare **elevation.**

deictic   Pointing out or demonstrating something; for example, *this, that, here,* and *there.*

dental   Referring to the use of the top teeth in the process of articulating a sound.

dependent clause   A clause that cannot function as an utterance of sentence without being joined in some way to an independent clause.

derivation The process by which noninflectional affixes are added to bases to form words, as is *en-* in *enjoin*, *-ful* in *hopeful*, and both *dis-* and *-ful* in *distrustful*.

determiner A word such as *the, a, my, his, this,* and *that* usually followed, though not always immediately, by a noun.

deviant sentence A sentence that appears strange or unusual to a native speaker for semantic reasons; for example, *Colorless green ideas sleep furiously* and *The fishes spoke square apples.*

diachronic Historical, involving change. Compare **synchronic.**

diacritic A phonetic symbol indicating a phonetic characteristic of secondary importance and written either as a subscript or superscript; for example, voice-lessness [͜] in [m̥], labialization [ʷ] in [tʷ], and aspiration [ʰ] in [pʰ].

dialect The variety of a language spoken in a particular area (regional dialect) or by a particular social group (social dialect).

dialect atlas A set of maps showing the distributions of dialect features.

dialect boundary A border resulting from the cooccurrence of several isoglosses.

differential meaning The meaning difference that exists when two utterances are not repetitions. *He killed a cat* and *He killed a rat* show minimal differential meaning.

diphthong A vowel sound involving noticeable tongue movement during its production but which functions as the nucleus of a single syllable. *Shout, bite,* and *coil* all contain diphthongs.

diphthongization The process by which a vowel develops a noticeable off-glide and changes its quality; for example, [ī] becoming [aɪ] and [ū] becoming [aʊ] in the Great Vowel Shift in English.

direct object The noun phrase that follows a transitive verb in a verb phrase; for example, *Mary* in *John hugged Mary* and *a book* in both *I gave a book to the boy* and *I gave the boy a book.*

discontinuous constituent A constituent which is in two parts because of the presence of another constituent between the parts; for example, *are ready* in *Are you ready?*

discourse A group of sentences related in some sequential manner.

discovery procedure A procedure which, if applied to linguistic data, reveals the facts about a language.

discreteness The property that language has of making use of qualitative distinctions rather than quantitative ones. For example, a sound is voiced or voiceless ([b] or [p]) in English, not more or less voiced.

displacement The property that language has of allowing speakers to talk about past and future events as well as present ones.

dissimilation The process by which a sound changes to become phonetically less like an adjacent sound; for example, English *marble* from French *marbre* containing two *r*'s.

distinctive feature A member of one of the basic oppositions, such as front-back, high-low, vocalic-consonantal, voiced-voiceless, nasal-oral, tense-lax, and so on, out of which phonemic systems are formed.

distribution The set of environments in which a particular linguistic form appears.

disyllabic Having two syllables.

dorsovelar Made by touching the back of the tongue to the soft palate.

doublet A pair of words in a language ultimately from a single source but with different derivational histories, as are *compute* and *count* and *skirt* and *shirt*.

duality The characteristic of having a system of sounds and a system of meanings.

economy The principle that states that given two explanations that account for a given body of data, the briefer one is to be preferred.

egressive Made during exhalation.

elevation A change of meaning which results in a word describing something more worthy, desirable, or pleasant than it previously did; for example, *squire, earl,* and *chivalry.* Compare **degradation.**

ellipsis A deleted part of a construction which can be recovered from knowledge of the part that remains.

embedded sentence A sentence that is included in another sentence; for example, (*when*) *I arrived* is embedded in *He left when I arrived.*

emic Functional. Any functional unit in a language is an emic unit. Compare **etic.**

emphatic pronoun A pronoun such as *himself* in *He himself did it* which emphasizes an adjacent noun phrase.

endocentric construction A construction containing a head with the same distributional characteristics as the whole construction; for example, the construction *old man* is endocentric because *man* has the same distributional characteristics as the phrase as a whole. Compare **exocentric construction.**

epenthesis The insertion of a sound in pronunciation; for example, the insertion of [t] in *fence.*

etic Any discriminable linguistic datum without regard to possible function. Compare **emic.**

etymology The history and derivation of a word.

euphemism The substitution of one or more words in order to "soften" the force of an expression; for example, *pass away* for *die* and *underprivileged* for *poor.*

exocentric construction A construction of which no part has the same distributional characteristics as the whole; for example, *John died.* Compare **endocentric construction.**

eye dialect The practice of using spellings such as *wuz* for *was* and *could of* for *could've* to suggest dialect differences.

false cognates Two words in different languages apparently descended from a common source but in actuality not.

final pitch contour The movement of the pitch of the voice (up, level, down) at the end of an utterance. Compare *He left yesterday.* (↓) with *He left yesterday?* (↑) and *He left yesterday* (→), *I said* (↓).

final position Before a pause or boundary of some kind, as are *t* in *cat,* [t] in [kʰæt], *man* in *postman,* and *outside* in *He's outside.*

finite verb A verb that indicates time; for example, *went* in *I went* and *goes* in *He goes there regularly.*

flap A sound made with a very rapid movement of the tongue to the top of the mouth; for example, the medial consonant in the American English pronunciation of *butter.*

focal area An area from which a linguistic feature seems to be spreading to outlying areas.

folk etymology A popular etymology for a word leading to some restructuring of the phonology and morphology of the word according to its supposed derivation; for example, *bridegroom* from *brȳdguma* (instead of *bridegoom*).

form class A set of words that often take certain affixes or distribute similarly.

Nouns often take a plural suffix (*cats*) and a possessive suffix (*cat's*), verbs often take tense and participle suffixes (*baked, baking*), and adjectives often take a comparative suffix (*wiser*) and a superlative suffix (*wisest*).

free form A linguistic form that can occur as an independent word, like *cat, judge,* and *happy,* but not the *-s* of *cats,* the *-ment* of *judgment,* or the *un-* of *unhappy.*

free variation Nonsignificant linguistic variation between two or more linguistic forms; for example, final stops may be released or unreleased and the *-ing* verbal ending (/iŋ/) may vary with *-in'* (/in/).

free vowel A vowel that may appear in an open syllable (a syllable that does not end in a consonant) such as the vowels in *may, see,* and *sue.* (Note that these same vowels frequently occur in English in closed syllables, as in *made, seed,* and *suit.*) Compare **checked vowel.**

fricative A speech sound in which the airstream is forced through a narrow opening with resulting friction; for example, the initial sounds of *fat, vat, sin, zoo, thin, this,* and *shin* are fricatives.

front Produced in the front of the mouth or with the front of the tongue. The vowels in *beat, bit, bait, bet,* and *bat* are front vowels, whereas those in *boot* and *bought* are back vowels.

fronted or **fronting** Produced in a position further forward in the mouth than what may be regarded as the basic position of the sound. The initial consonant of *cat* is fronted in comparison with the initial consonant of *calm.*

functional shift A change in the syntactic function of a word from its normal function; for example, *black* from adjective to noun in *in the black* and *brother* from noun to verb in *Don't brother me!*

function words See **structure words.**

gender A classification of words usually related in some way to the sex of the referents in Indo-European languages.

generalization A change of meaning which results in a word covering a wider range of meaning than it once did; for example, *virtue* and *alibi.*

generate Produce by rule.

generative grammar A grammar that generates sentences and assigns a structural description to each sentence that is generated.

generative phonology A phonology that employs a set of rules to generate phonetic representations from underlying phonological units.

generative semantics A grammar that generates the underlying meanings of sentences and then transforms their meaning into actually produced sentences.

generative-transformational grammar A grammar that generates sentences, assigns structural descriptions to these sentences, and relates their deep structures and meanings to the surface structures and sounds.

genetic relationship The relationship that exists between two or more languages descended from a common source.

genitive case A grammatical inflection often indicating possession; for example, *John's* in *John's hat* is marked for the genitive case.

glide The change of a vowel that occurs in a complex nucleus when the tongue moves to another position. The vowels in *high, now,* and *boy* all contain noticeable glides.

gloss The meaning associated with a particular form.

glottal stop A sound produced in the larynx by closing off the airstream in the glottis.

glottis The opening between the vocal cords in the larynx.

glottalization A partial or whole closure of the glottis during the articulation of a sound.

glottochronology See **lexicostatistics.**

grammar A description of the possible arrangements of words in a language, and sometimes also of the possible arrangements of sounds.

grammatical Accepted by native speakers as a possible arrangement of words in a language. Conforming to the rules of the grammar of a language.

grammatical marking The inflecting of words for certain characteristics. For example, one set of English words may be called nouns because they all can be marked for "plural": *cat, cats; dog, dogs; church, churches; man, men.*

grammatical subject See **surface subject.**

grapheme A significant unit in the writing system of a language.

Great Vowel Shift A noticeable change in the quality of English tense vowels that occurred between Middle English and Modern English.

Grimm's law A series of correspondences between certain Germanic consonants and consonants in cognates in other Indo-European languages.

head One of the constituents in a structure of modification; for example, *man* in *old man* and *speaks* in *speaks clearly.*

high Produced with the tongue placed relatively high in the mouth. The vowels in *beat, bit, boot,* and *good* are high vowels.

homograph A word spelled like another word but having a different meaning and often a different pronunciation; for example, *wind* meaning both "to coil" and "a current of air."

homonym A word pronounced like another word but often having a different spelling and always having a different meaning; for example, *bore* and *boar* and *scene* and *seen.* Also used as a cover term for **homograph** and as a synonym for **homophone.**

homophone See **homonym.**

idiolect The language or dialect of an individual speaker.

idiom Morphemes or words which have a particular meaning by virtue of their occurrence in a certain construction; for example, *put up with* and *kick the bucket.*

immediate constituents (IC's) The parts, usually two, of a construction, as *house* and *wife* are the immediate constituents of *housewife, birds* and *sing* the IC's of *Birds sing,* and *un-* and *happy* the IC's of *unhappy.*

imperative A command; for example, *Stand up!, Be gone!,* and *Don't do that!*

inanimate Not having life and movement. *Tree* and *rock* are inanimate nouns and so are assigned the semantic feature [−animate]. Compare **animate.**

independent clause A clause that can function alone as a complete utterance or sentence.

indirect object One of the noun phrases that follows certain verbs that take two noun phrases as part of the verb phrase; for example, *Mary* in *I gave Mary the book.*

Indo-European The language family of which English is a member.

infinitive The completely unmarked form of a verb often preceded by *to;* for example, *to go* in *I want to go* and *dance* in *She can dance.*

infix An affix placed within a morpheme.

inflection An affix (in English, usually a suffix) that changes the form of a word without changing its form class or basic meaning: *cat* and *man* may be inflected for "plural" (*cats, men*) or "possessive" (*cat's, man's*) or both (*cats', men's*).

informant A person who contributes linguistic data.

ingressive Made during inhalation.

initial position Occurring after a pause of some kind or at the beginning of a linguistic unit such as a syllable, word, or utterance.

instrumental In case grammar, designating the case for objects with which actions are performed; for example, *hammer* in both *I struck the nail with the hammer* and *The hammer struck the nail* is said to be in the instrumental case.

interchangeability The property that a language has of being freely usable in all ways by everyone who has mastered its forms and meanings.

interdental A sound made by placing the tip of the tongue between the teeth; for example, the initial sounds of *thin* and *this* are interdental fricatives.

internal reconstruction A method for doing historical work in linguistics employing data from a single language in order to postulate older forms that no longer survive.

International Phonetic Alphabet (IPA) A widely accepted system of phonetic notation.

interrogative A question; for example, *Are you going?* and *Where are you going?*

intervocalic Occurring between vowels.

intonation contour The pattern of rising or falling pitches with which a sentence is pronounced.

intransitive verb A verb that does not take an object; for example, *died* in *He died* and *ran* in *She ran away.* Compare **transitive verb.**

intrusive consonant A consonant which occurs only as a linking phenomenon; for example, the *r* in *Cuba(r) and China.*

inversion A change in what may be considered as the normal word order, as in *Are you happy?* (*You are happy*) and *Never have I seen such foolishness* (*I have never seen such foolishness*). In the first case the inversion is required by the grammatical rules of English; in the second it is a stylistic or rhetorical device.

irregular Not conforming to the general rule for the language. *Men* is an irregular English noun plural and *sang* an irregular past tense. Regular forms would be **mans* and **singed* (compare *pans* and *winged*). Compare **regular.**

isogloss A line on a dialect map marking a boundary between linguistic features.

jargon The technical vocabulary of a particular occupation.

juncture The transition from one phonological segment to the next, either open or close. Also, the pause at the end of a phrase or utterance.

kernel sentences A term used in certain versions of generative-transformational grammar to describe active, positive, and declarative sentences from which passive, negative, imperative, and interrogative sentences could be derived.

kinesics The study of the body and facial movements used in communication.

labial Referring to the use of the lips in the process of articulating a sound. *Pat, bat, fat,* and *vat* begin with labial consonants.

labialization Any noticeable rounding of the lips occurring during the production of a consonant.

labiodental A sound articulated with the bottom lip and top teeth; for example, the initial sounds in *fat* and *vat.*

language A set of sentences generated by a grammar.

language universals   Characteristics which all languages share.

larynx   The "voice box" in which the basic sound stream on which speech depends is brought into existence.

lateral   An *l*-like sound.

lax   Referring to a distinctive sound feature characterized by very little muscular tension in the articulators; for example, [z] is lax whereas [s] is tense, and the vowel in *bet* is lax whereas the vowel in *bait* is tense.

lexeme   A word or phrase that is a meaningful unit.

lexical   Meaningful.

lexicon   The vocabulary of a language.

lexicostatistics   The application of statistical techniques to problems in historical linguistics in an attempt to estimate when languages separated.

linguistic geography   The study of the distributions of languages and dialects.

linguistics   The scientific study of language.

linguistic variable   A unit in the language system which varies from speaker to speaker or occasion to occasion; for example, the forms which negation takes can vary as can the pronunciations of the initial consonant in *then* and the final consonant in *singing.*

liquid   An *r*- or *l*-like sound, that is, a frictionless, vowel-like consonant.

loan translation   A phrase borrowed from another language after being translated; for example, *marriage of convenience* from French *mariage de convenance.*

loan word   A word borrowed from another language and then partly or fully "naturalized"; for example, *masseur* from French and *lager* from German.

long vowel   A tense vowel, such as the vowels in *beat, bait,* and *boot.*   Compare **short vowel.**

low   Produced with the tongue placed low in the mouth.   The vowels in *bat* and *father* are low vowels.

main clause   See **independent clause.**

marked   Having a characteristic or feature not possessed by a closely related unit; for example, *baked* is marked for "past tense" but *bake* is unmarked, and the phoneme /b/ is marked for voicing but /p/ is unmarked.

mass   Not being countable.   *Milk, butter,* and *water* are mass nouns and so are assigned the semantic feature [−count].   Compare **count.**

medial   Occurring in middle position; for example, the *st* in *mistake* is a medial consonant cluster.

metalanguage   A language for describing language.

metalinguistics   The study of the relationship between linguistic and nonlinguistic factors in society.

metathesis   The transposition of letters, sounds, and sometimes even syllables within a word; for example, *revelant* for *relevant.*

mid   Produced with the tongue placed neither high nor low in the mouth.   The vowels in *bait, bet, but,* and *boat* are mid vowels.

minimal pair   Two utterances distinguished by a single contrast, as are *pat* and *bat, It's a battle* and *It's a bottle,* and *He's ready* and *He's ready?*

modality   The possibility, probability, necessity, reality, or obligation expressed in a clause.

modal verb   A verb such as *can, will, shall, may, must,* or *ought.*

modification A grammatical construction consisting of a head and a modifier; for example, *walks slowly* and *new girl.*

monophthong A vowel sound without any noticeable tongue movement. *Bit, bet,* and *bat* all contain monophthongs.

mood See **modality.**

morph Any phoneme or sequence of phonemes that can be associated with an identifiable meaning; for example, the /s/ in /kæts/ and the /z/ in /dɔgz/ are separate morphs.

morpheme The minimal unit of meaning. *Cats* contains two such units and *unwisely* contains three.

morphemic merger The situation which exists when two morphemes merge into one; for example, *queen* and *quean* into *queen.*

morphemic split The situation which exists when one morpheme splits into two; for example, the splits of *of* and *off* and *flour* and *flower.*

morphological conditioning Specification of the distribution of an allomorph by reference to a morphemic environment rather than to a phonemic one; for example, English "plural" has the allomorph /ø/ in /dir/ (*deer*) and /(æ) → e/ in /men/ (*men*). Compare **phonological conditioning.**

morphology The study of morphemes and their combination in words.

morphophoneme A phonological unit corresponding to a set of phonemes that occur within the allomorphs of a particular morpheme: the distribution of the set of phonemes in the morphophoneme is explicable in terms of phonological environments. For example, the //s// morphophoneme of the English plural is predictably realized in three ways (/s ~ z ~ əz/) according to the final phoneme of the noun to which it is attached (*cat, dog, church*).

morphophonemics The morphophonemic variations of a particular language or the study of these variations.

morphotactics The possible sequences of morphemes in a language.

narrowing A change of meaning which results in a word describing a narrower range of meaning than it once did; for example, *meat* and *deer.* Compare **widening.**

nasal Produced by the release of air through the nose. The *m, n,* and *ng* (/ŋ/) of *Pam, pan,* and *pang* are nasal consonants.

nasality A distinctive sound feature characterized by use of the nasal cavity in the articulation of speech sounds.

nasalization The release of air through the nasal cavity during the production of a sound.

natural class A class of sounds sharing one or more distinctive features; for example, [s, z, š, ž] are all coronal stridents.

natural language A language spoken naturally by human beings, in contrast to the artificial languages of computers, mathematics, and symbolic logic, or languages like Esperanto, or the communication systems of other species.

naturalness The principle that linguistic rules and changes should conform to natural parameters and be known to occur or to have occurred.

neologism A new word or phrase.

neutralization The absence of a contrast between two phonemes in a particular phonological environment: /i/ and /iy/ contrast before most consonants, for example in *bit* and *beat,* but not before /r/, so *here* may be written as either /hir/ or /hiyr/, or even with a special symbol (an **archiphoneme**) as /hɪr/.

neutral vowel   See **schwa.**

nonsignificant   Not resulting in a difference in sound or a difference in meaning.

nonstandard dialect   A dialect diverging noticeably from a standard dialect in pronunciation, lexicon, or grammar.

noun   A form class often marked in English by the ability to take plural and possessive suffixes; for example, *dog, dogs, dog's* and *man, men, man's, men's* are nouns.

noun phrase   A grammatical construction that usually contains a noun as its central constituent.

object   The noun phrase or phrases that follow the verb in a verb phrase or the preposition in a prepositional phrase; for example, *Fred, two dollars,* and *his work* in *I gave Fred two dollars for his work.*

obligatory transformation   A transformation that must be applied if required by a certain structure.   Compare **optional transformation.**

obstruent   A voiced stop or nonresonant sound; for example, the initial sound in *bail, dale,* and *gale.*

off-glide   The final part of a complex nucleus.   The vowels in *high, now,* and *boy* have off-glides.

open juncture   A type of transition between neighboring sounds symbolized as /+/.

open syllable   A syllable ending in a vowel sound; for example, *be, they,* and *sigh.* Compare **closed syllable.**

open system   A system that allows for an infinite set of possibilities; natural languages are open systems.

optional transformation   A transformation that may be applied to a structure that satisfies its requirements.   The result of the application is a stylistic variation between two or more sentences.   Compare **obligatory transformation.**

oral   Designating a speech sound in which all the air passes through the mouth.

orthography   A system of spelling.

palatal   Designating a sound involving placing the front of the tongue near or against the hard palate; for example, the sound at the beginning of *yet* is a palatal.

palatalization   A change in the quality of a sound produced by the presence of a high front vowel.

paleography   The description and decipherment of ancient writings.

paradigm   A list of all the forms of a form class, as in a noun declension (*man, man's, men, men's*) or verb conjugation (*sing, sings, singing, sang, sung*).

paralanguage   A system of phonetic characteristics overlaid on the phonological system and conveying certain meanings.

paraphrase   A restatement of the meaning of a word, phrase, or sentence in other words.

parentheses   ( ) In generative-transformational grammar a convention for showing that the item or items enclosed in the parentheses may optionally be chosen in the rewriting of a particular phrase-structure constituent.

parse   To assign words, phrases, and clauses to grammatical forms and functions.

part of speech   A form class, such as noun and verb, or a particular kind of function word, such as determiner or preposition.

passive   Designating the form of a verb in which the subject receives or undergoes the action; for example, *was chased* in *The cat was chased by John.* Compare **active.**

pejoration See **degradation.**

performance The actual utterances produced by speakers of a language. Compare **competence.**

performatives Verbs such as *name, beg,* and *sentence* in *I name this ship Explorer, I beg you to leave,* and *I sentence you to thirty days.* These verbs "perform" the acts of naming, begging, and sentencing.

philology An earlier term for linguistics as linguistics was practiced in the nineteenth century.

phone A discriminable speech sound.

phoneme A minimal significant contrastive unit in the phonological system of a language.

phoneme-grapheme correspondence The relationship between a contrastive sound unit (phoneme) and a contrastive alphabetic unit (grapheme or letter), as for example, between an English phoneme /æ/ and its usual grapheme correspondent *a,* or between /č/ and *ch* or *tch.*

phonemic coalescence The loss of a phonemic contrast over a period of time.

phonemic notation A system for recording the phonemes of a language. Such notation is written within diagonal bars: *cat* is written as /kæt/ and *high* as /hay/ in the Trager-Smith system of phonemic notation.

phonemics The procedures for establishing the phonemes of a language; also, the system that results. Compare **phonetics.**

phonemic split The development of a phonemic contrast over a period of time.

phonetic feature A minimal phonetic characteristic, such as the use of the lips, or of the top teeth, or of low tongue position, or of the nasal cavity.

phonetic notation A system for recording all discriminable phonetic features. Such notation is written within square brackets: *cat* is written [kʰæt].

phonetics The study of the production, transmission, and reception of speech sounds. Compare **phonemics.**

phonetic similarity The sharing of at least one phonetic feature by two or more sounds, as [m] and [p] share the feature "bilabial" and [g] and [t] the feature "stop."

phonetic variant See **allophone.**

phonics A way of teaching reading in which children are taught the relationships of written symbols to sounds.

phonological component The part of a generative-transformational grammar that deals with the pronunciation of sentences.

phonological conditioning Specification of the distribution of an allomorph by reference to a phonemic environment; for example, English "plural" has the allomorph /s/ after certain voiceless phonemes. Compare **morphological conditioning.**

phonological process Any change that a sound undergoes either over a period of time (diachronically) or in the generation of an utterance (synchronically).

phonology A cover term for both phonetics and phonemics.

phonotactics The possible sequences of phonemes in a language.

phrase Any construction except one containing a subject and a predicate.

phrase-structure component The part of a generative-transformational grammar that generates deep structures. Sometimes called the **base.**

phrase-structure grammar A grammar that describes the grammatical structures of sentences without the use of transformations.

phrase-structure rule A rule in the phrase-structure component.

pitch The frequencies used in the production of speech.

pitch contour See **intonation contour.**

place (or point) of articulation The place (or point) to which an articulator moves in the production of a sound.

plosive See **stop.**

possessive See **genitive case.**

postvocalic Occurring after a vowel.

predicate The verb phrase of a clause.

predication A grammatical construction consisting of a subject noun phrase and a verb phrase; for example, *The boy left* and *John sings.*

prefix An affix attached to the beginning of a base or stem; for example, *re-* in *rewrite* and *im-* in *import.*

preposition A word that introduces a prepositional phrase; for example, *at* in *at the back* and *under* in *under the floor.*

prescriptivism The doctrine that part of the grammarian's task is to prescribe good linguistic usage in order to improve general use of the language.

presupposition The real world conditions that must be met if a sentence is to be interpreted in the way intended.

prevarication The property that language has of allowing speakers to communicate falsehoods (that is, tell lies).

prevocalic Occurring before a vowel.

PRO constituent A constituent not fully specified in all features and therefore to be deleted or modified in some way by rule.

productivity The property that language has of being endlessly creative.

progressive Indication that an action is in progress through use of *be + ing.*

projection rules A set of rules for combining the meanings of the individual words of a sentence into a possible meaning for the whole sentence according to their syntactic relationships.

pronoun (or pronominal) A word that can replace a noun phrase, as *he* can replace *the old man* in *The old man left* (*He left*).

proposition In case grammar the verb and related nouns in a sentence.

protoform A hypothesized form from which cognates in various languages appear to have descended. Protoforms are usually starred (preceded by an asterisk) in the writings of linguists.

Proto-Indo-European The hypothesized language from which the present Indo-European languages appear to have descended.

protolanguage A hypothesized language from which various languages appear to have descended.

proxemics The study of how people use the space around them in communicating.

psycholinguistics The study of the interrelationships of psychological and linguistic behavior.

raising Pronounced in a higher position. Moved to a higher clause.

Received Pronunciation (RP) The pronunciation of a prestigious variety of British English.

reciprocal pronouns Pronouns such as *each other.*

recursiveness The property of being infinitely expandable; for example, *This is the dog that worried the cat that killed the rat that ate the malt that lay in the house that Jack built. . . .*

reduplication A process in which a word or part of a word is repeated; for example, *wishy-washy, mish-mash.*

referent That to which a noun or noun phrase refers.

reflex An observable datum for which a historical or underlying abstract or "deep" explanation may be provided. The spelling *night* is a reflex of a much different pronunciation of this word in Middle English. The *you* of *Wash yourself* is a reflex of a deep structure containing *you* (Imp *you* pres *will wash you*).

reflexiveness The property that language has of being its own metalanguage.

reflexive pronoun A pronoun such as *himself* in *John hurt himself.*

regional dialect The dialect spoken in a particular region.

register The kind of language used in a particular set of circumstances or context.

regular Conforming to the general rule for the language. *Cats* is a regular English noun plural and *baked* is a regular English past tense (compare *men* and *sang*). Compare **irregular.**

relative clause A clause that is part of a noun phrase and modifies the head noun of that phrase; for example, (*that*) *I want* in *Give me the book* (*that*) *I want.*

relative pronoun (or relativizer) The pronoun which introduces a relative clause and which substitutes for a noun phrase in that clause; for example, *that* in *The story that I told* and *where* in *the place where I live.*

relic area An area into which linguistic features are spreading from neighboring areas.

replacive allomorph A change such as that of *man* to *men* to form the "plural" is sometimes attributed to the presence in *men* of a replacive allomorph: /e/ replacing /æ/.

resonant A voiced continuant.

retroflex A speech sound made by curling the tip of the tongue upward and back in the mouth; for example, *red* begins with a retroflex.

Rhenish fan The effect produced by the isoglosses which differentiate High German from Low German.

role In case grammar the relationship between a noun and the verb in a proposition.

root See **base.**

rounded A noticeable rounding of the lips during the production of a vowel; for example, *boot* contains a rounded vowel and *beat,* an unrounded one.

rule A statement of a linguistic relationship.

rune A grapheme from the ancient Germanic writing system, the futhark.

schwa The lax mid central vowel symbolized as [ə].

segmental phoneme One of the vowels or consonants in a phonemic notation.

semantic change A change of meaning of a word over a period of time; for example, *squire, deer,* and *villain* have all undergone semantic changes.

semantic component The part of a generative-transformational grammar that deals with meaning.

semantic feature A distinguishable element of meaning in a lexical item; such as animate, human, or male.

semanticity The property that language has of being concerned with the communication of a wide variety of meanings.

semantic projection rules The rules in a grammar which combine the meanings of the lexical items to make "sense" of sentences.

semantics The study of meaning.

semivowel A vowel-like sound functioning as a consonant; for example, /y w/ and, according to Trager and Smith, /h/.

sentence A basic or primitive unit in language: the initial S of a generative-transformational grammar.

sentence pattern A pattern such as Noun + Verb + Noun that may be used to characterize the structures of sentences. *Birds sing* is Noun + Verb and *The man gave his friend a dollar* is Noun^1 + Verb + Noun^2 + Noun^3. (The superscripts 1, 2, 3, refer to the fact that the nouns have different referents.)

short vowel A simple lax vowel, such as the vowels in *bit, bet,* and *bat.* Compare **long vowel.**

sibilant An *s*-like sound; for example, the middle sound in *kissing, freezing, wishing,* and *pleasure.*

significant Resulting in a difference in meaning in certain circumstances.

simple sentence A sentence containing a single clause.

slang Very informal language employing vigorous and generally evanescent words and expressions.

social dialect The dialect spoken by a particular social group.

sociolinguistics The study of the interrelationships of social and linguistic behavior.

specialization The property that language has of not involving the whole human organism in the production of utterances. See also **narrowing.**

spectrogram The visual record produced by a spectrograph.

spectrograph A piece of apparatus used to record and analyze the sounds of speech using such parameters as frequency and intensity.

spelling pronunciation A pronunciation which reflects the spelling of a word rather than the pronunciation which results from changes which have occurred in the language.

spirant See **fricative.**

Stammbaum The "family-tree" model of language relationships.

standard language The particular dialect of a language accepted for use in education, government, commerce, and the media of mass communication.

stative Having some permanent or enduring quality.

stem A morpheme or morphemes to which an affix can be added.

stop A consonantal sound made by completely blocking the airstream; *pole, toll, coal, bowl, dole,* and *goal* all begin with stop consonants.

stress The intensity with which a sound is pronounced relative to that of other sounds.

stridency A distinctive sound feature characteristic of fricatives.

string A sequence of morphemes or grammatical constituents.

structure See **construction.**

structure words Words such as *the, not, in, to, quite,* and *very* which do not take inflections and often have little lexical meaning, but which perform important syntactic functions. Compare **content words.**

subject The noun phrase that usually precedes the verb in English; for example, *John* in *John kissed Mary* and *John left.*

subject raising The subject of an embedded sentence becomes a constituent of a higher sentence; for example, the *he* of *He was expected to go* comes from *He goes* embedded in *Someone expected something.*

subordinate clause See **dependent clause.**

subordination A grammatical construction consisting of a subordinator and either a phrase or clause which is subordinated; for example, *at the back* and *after the war ended.*

subordinator A preposition or conjunction used in a structure of subordination.

substandard A pejorative variant of **nonstandard.**

substitute A word such as a pronoun that replaces some other word or phrase.

substratum The hypothesized residue of a previously spoken language in a successor language.

suffix An affix attached to the end of a base or stem; for example, *-s* in *cats* and *-ize* in *winterize.*

suppletive allomorphs Allomorphs having no phonemic resemblance; for example, parts of *go* and *went, am, be* and *is,* and *good* and *best.*

suprasegmental phoneme One of the phonemes of stress, pitch, or pause.

surface structure The grammatical relationships among the words of an actually observed sentence. Compare **deep structure.**

surface subject The subject in the surface structure of a sentence. Compare **deep subject.**

syllabary A writing system, the basic units of which represent syllables.

syllabic consonant A consonant such as the final one in *ridden* ([rɪdn̩]) which functions as a syllable.

syllabification The process of dividing words into syllables; for example, *re-peat* and *a-loud.*

syllable A unit in the phonological system of a language with a vowel as its nucleus.

symmetry The principle that languages tend to have symmetrical systems. Thus, if a language has four voiceless stops and affricates contrasting with each other (/p t č k/) and also a set of voiced stops and affricates contrasting with these voiceless ones, this voiced set is also likely to number four (/b d ǰ g/).

synchronic Descriptive of a particular time or stage of development. Compare **diachronic.**

syncope The loss of one or more sounds in the middle of a word; for example, *secret'ry* for *secretary.*

synonym Two words having very similar meanings; for example, *stench* and *stink.* Compare **antonym.**

syntactic component The part of a generative-transformational grammar that deals with syntax.

syntax The arrangements and interrelationships of words, phrases, clauses, and sentences.

systematic phonemes The phonemes of a language as postulated by a generative-transformational linguist. Compare **taxonomic phonemes.**

tactics The possible sequences of phonological and grammatical units in a language.

tautology A meaningless repetition; for example, *My brother is an unmarried bachelor.*

taxonomic phonemes The phonemes of a language as analyzed by a structural linguist. They are established by using either minimal pairs or the principles of phonetic similarity and complementary distribution. Compare **systematic phonemes.**

tense A distinctive sound feature characterized by noticeable muscular tension in the articulators; for example, [s] is tense, whereas [z] is lax, and [e] is tense whereas [ɛ] is lax. Also the time indicated by a verb; for example, past or present.

terminal contour See **final pitch contour.**

tone See **pitch.**

transformation A rule for changing one grammatical structure into another by adding, deleting, or rearranging constituents.

transformational grammar See **generative-transformational grammar.**

transition area An area lacking linguistic features of its own and sharing features of various neighboring areas.

transitive verb A verb that takes an object; for example, *sells* in *Mary sells oranges.* Compare **intransitive verb.**

tree diagram A visual representation of parsing.

trill A speech sound produced by the rapid vibration of an articulator.

triphthong A syllable nucleus consisting of a sequence of three vowels.

ultimate constituent The lowest level unit in the system that is being analyzed.

umlaut The process by which the frontness feature of a vowel in one syllable is added to the vowel of the preceding syllable.

unaspirated Having no accompanying puff of air, like the *t* of *stop,* in contrast to the aspirated *t* of *top.*

ungrammatical Not generated by the grammar or not accepted as normal by native speakers. Ungrammatical forms are usually starred (preceded by an asterisk) in the writings of linguists: **He no come. *Come you the garden into.*

universal A linguistic feature common to all languages.

unmarked The neutral member of a marked-unmarked contrastive pair. Compare **marked.**

unreleased Without audible release.

unrounded Characterized by the absence of lip rounding.

usage The language actually used by a particular group of people.

utterance A spoken sentence or part of a sentence.

variant The form a linguistic unit takes in a particular context; for example, an allophone of a phoneme or an allomorph of a morpheme.

velic The opening from the mouth into the nasal cavity.

velum The back of the roof of the mouth, the rear of the soft palate. The sounds at the beginnings of *coal* and *goal* are velar consonants; the sound at the end of *bring* is a velar nasal.

verb A form class often marked in English by the ability to take the third person, past, and progressive suffixes; for example, *bake, bakes, baked,* and *baking* is a verb.

Verner's law A sound change which describes certain exceptions to Grimm's law.

vocal Realized in the sounds of speech.

vocoid A sound lacking constriction in its production. Compare **contoid.**

voice The quality produced by vibrating the vocal cords.

voiced Produced with vibration of the vocal cords, as are the initial sounds in *van, bin, then, nose,* and *be.*

voiceless Produced with no vibration of the vocal cords, as are the initial sounds in *fan, pin,* and *thin.*

vowel A contrastive unit in the sound system of a language characterized in pronunciation by lack of constriction in the vocal tract; also a letter to symbolize such a sound.   Compare **consonant.**

vowel harmony The process by which the vowel or vowels in one morpheme are made to conform in some feature to the vowel or vowels in another morpheme to which it is affixed.

vowel reduction A change in vowel quality in certain environments, as, for example, under weak stress.   Compare the vowels in *man* and *postman;* in *men* and *postmen;* and in *Canadian* and *Canada.*

Wellentheorie The "wave-theory" model of language relationships.

well-formed Conforming to the rules of a grammar.

widening A change of meaning which results in a word describing a wider range of events or activities than it once did; for example, *alibi* and *virtue.*   Compare **narrowing.**

word A morpheme or combination of morphemes which native speakers regard as a minimal pronounceable meaningful unit.

zero allomorph An allomorph without phonemic content; for example, the zero "plural" in *deer* and *sheep.*

BIBLIOGRAPHY

Abercrombie, David, *Elements of General Phonetics*. Chicago: Aldine, 1967.

Algeo, John, and Thomas Pyles, *Problems in the Origins and Development of the English Language*. New York: Harcourt, Brace & World, 1966.

Allen, Harold B., *Linguistics and English Linguistics*. New York: Appleton-Century-Crofts, 1966.

Alyeshmerni, Mansoor, and Paul Taubr, *Working with Aspects of Language*. New York: Harcourt, Brace & World, 1970.

Anttila, Raimo, *An Introduction to Historical and Comparative Linguistics*. New York: Macmillan, 1972.

Arlotto, Anthony, *Introduction to Historical Linguistics*. Boston: Houghton Mifflin, 1972.

Atwood, E. Bagby, *A Survey of Verb Forms in the Eastern United States*. Ann Arbor: University of Michigan Press, 1953.

Austin, J.L., *How to Do Things with Words*. Cambridge: Harvard, 1962.

Bach, Emmon, *Syntactic Theory*. New York: Holt, 1974.

Bach, Emmon, and Robert T. Harms, eds., *Universals in Linguistic Theory*. New York: Holt, 1968.

Baugh, Albert C., *A History of the English Language.* New York: Appleton-Century-Crofts, 1957.

Birdwhistell, Ray L., *Kinesics and Context.* Philadelphia: University of Pennsylvania Press, 1970.

Bloomfield, Leonard, *Language.* New York: Holt, 1933.

Bloomfield, Morton W., and Leonard Newmark, *A Linguistic Introduction to the History of English.* New York: Knopf, 1963.

Bolinger, Dwight, *Aspects of Language,* 2d ed. New York: Harcourt Brace Jovanovich, 1975.

Bolinger, Dwight, "The Atomization of Meaning," *Language,* 41 (1965), 555–573.

Bolinger, Dwight, "On Defining the Morpheme," *Word,* 4 (1948), 18–23.

Brook, G. L., *English Dialects.* London: Andre Deutsch, 1963.

Brown, Roger, *Words and Things.* Glencoe, Ill.: Free Press, 1958.

Bryant, Margaret M., *Modern English and Its Heritage,* 2d ed. New York: Macmillan, 1962.

Burling, Robbins, *English in Black and White.* New York: Holt, 1973.

Burling, Robbins, *Man's Many Voices.* New York: Holt, 1970.

Burt, Marina K., *From Deep to Surface Structure.* New York: Harper & Row, 1971.

Carroll, John B., *Language and Thought.* Englewood Cliffs, N.J.: Prentice-Hall, 1964.

Carroll, John B., ed., *Language, Thought, and Reality: Selected Writings of Benjamin Lee Whorf.* Cambridge: M.I.T., 1956.

Chadwick, John, *The Decipherment of Linear B.* New York: Random House-Knopf, 1958.

Chafe, Wallace L., *Meaning and the Structure of Language.* Chicago: University of Chicago Press, 1970.

Cherry, Colin, *On Human Communication.* Cambridge: M.I.T., 1957.

Chomsky, Noam, *Aspects of the Theory of Syntax.* Cambridge: M.I.T., 1965.

Chomsky, Noam, *Language and Mind.* New York: Harcourt, Brace & World, 1968.

Chomsky, Noam, *Syntactic Structures.* The Hague: Mouton, 1957.

Chomsky, Noam, and Morris Halle, *The Sound Pattern of English.* New York: Harper & Row, 1968.

Deese, James, *Psycholinguistics.* Boston: Allyn and Bacon, 1970.

Denes, Peter B., and Elliot N. Pinson, *The Speech Chain: The Physics and Biology of Spoken Language.* New York: Bell Telephone Laboratories, 1963.

Dillard, J. L., *Black English.* New York: Random House, 1972.

Dinneen, Francis P., *An Introduction to General Linguistics.* New York: Holt, 1967.

Falk, Julia S., *Linguistics and Language.* Lexington, Mass.: Xerox, 1973.

Farb, Peter, *Word Play.* New York: Knopf, 1974.

Fast, Julius, *Body Language.* New York: M. Evans, 1970.

Fillmore, C. J., and D. T. Langendoen, eds., *Studies in Linguistic Semantics.* New York: Holt, 1971.

Fodor, Jerry A., and Jerrold J. Katz, eds., *The Structure of Language: Readings in the Philosophy of Language.* Englewood Cliffs, N.J.: Prentice-Hall, 1964.

Fowler, Roger, *Understanding Language.* London: Routledge, 1974.

Francis, W. Nelson, *The Structure of American English.* New York: Ronald, 1958.

Fries, Charles C., *The Structure of English.* New York: Harcourt, Brace & World, 1952.

Fromkin, Victoria, and Robert Rodman, *An Introduction to Language.* New York: Holt, 1974.

Gardner, R. A., and Beatrice T. Gardner, "Teaching Sign Language to a Chimpanzee," *Science,* 165 (1969), 664–672.

Gardner, R. A., and Beatrice T. Gardner, "Two-Way Communication with an Infant Chimpanzee," in A. Schrier and F. Stollnitz, eds., *Behavior of Nonhuman Primates.* New York: Academic, 1971.

Gelb, Ignace J., *A Study of Writing,* rev. ed. Chicago: University of Chicago Press, 1963.

Gilliéron, Jules L., and Edmond Edmont, *Atlas Linguistique de la France.* Paris: H. Champion, 1902–1920.

Gimson, A. C., *An Introduction to the Pronunciation of English.* London: Edward Arnold, 1962.

Gleason, Henry A., *An Introduction to Descriptive Linguistics,* rev. ed. New York: Holt, 1961.

Gleason, Henry A., *Workbook in Descriptive Linguistics.* New York: Holt, 1955.

Goodenough, Ward, "Componential Analysis and the Study of Meaning," *Language,* 32 (1956), 195–216.

Greenberg, Joseph H., *Anthropological Linguistics: An Introduction.* New York: Random House, 1968.

Greene, Judith, *Psycholinguistics.* Baltimore: Penguin, 1972.

Grinder, John T., and Suzette H. Elgin, *Guide to Transformational Grammar.* New York: Holt, 1973.

Gudschinsky, Sarah C., *How to Learn an Unwritten Language.* New York: Holt, 1967.

Hall, Edward T., *The Hidden Dimension.* New York: Doubleday, 1966.

Hall, Edward T., *The Silent Language.* New York: Doubleday, 1959.

Halle, Morris, "On the Bases of Phonology," in Jerry A. Fodor and Jerrold J. Katz, eds., *The Structure of Language.* Englewood Cliffs, N.J.: Prentice-Hall, 1964.

Halle, Morris, "Phonology in Generative Grammar," *Word,* 18 (1962), 54–72. Also in Fodor and Katz.

Harms, Robert T., *Introduction to Phonological Theory.* Englewood Cliffs, N.J.: Prentice-Hall, 1968.

Harris, Zellig S., *Structural Linguistics.* Chicago: University of Chicago Press, 1951.

Haugen, Einar, and Morton Bloomfield, eds., *Language as a Human Problem.* New York: Norton, 1974.

Hayakawa, S. I., *Language in Thought and Action,* 2d ed. New York: Harcourt, Brace & World, 1964.

Hayes, C., *The Ape in Our House.* New York: Harper & Row, 1951.

Heffner, Roe-Merrill S., *General Phonetics.* Madison: University of Wisconsin Press, 1952.

Hill, Archibald A., *Introduction to Linguistic Structures.* New York: Harcourt, Brace & World, 1958.

Hockett, Charles F., *A Course in Modern Linguistics.* New York: Macmillan, 1958.

Hockett, Charles F., *A Manual of Phonology.* Baltimore: Waverley, 1955.

Hockett, Charles F., and Robert Ascher, "The Human Revolution," *Current Anthropology,* 5 (1964), 135–168.

Hoenigswald, Henry M., *Language Change and Linguistic Reconstruction.* Chicago: University of Chicago Press, 1960.

Hoijer, Harry, ed., *Language History* from *Language* by Leonard Bloomfield. New York: Holt, 1965.

Hyman, Larry M., *Phonology: Theory and Analysis.* New York: Holt, 1975.

Hymes, Dell, "Lexicostatistics so Far," *Current Anthropology,* 1 (1960) 3–44.

International Phonetic Association, *The Principles of the International Phonetic Association.* London: International Phonetic Association, 1949.

Jaberg, Karl, and Jakob Jud, *Sprach- und Sachatlas Italiens und der Südschweiz.* Zofingen: Ringier, 1928–1940.

Jacobs, Roderick A., and Peter S. Rosenbaum, *English Transformational Grammar.* Waltham, Mass.: Blaisdell, 1968.

Jacobs, Roderick A., and Peter S. Rosenbaum, eds., *Readings in English Transformational Grammar.* Waltham, Mass.: Ginn, 1970.

Jakobson, Roman, C. Gunnar, M. Fant, and Morris Halle, *Preliminaries to Speech Analysis.* Cambridge: M.I.T., 1965.

Jakobson, Roman, and Morris Halle, *Fundamentals of Language.* The Hague: Mouton, 1956.

Jespersen, Otto, *Language: Its Nature, Development and Origin.* New York: Norton, 1964.

Jones, Daniel, *An Outline of English Phonetics,* 9th ed. Cambridge: Heffer, 1960.

Joos, Martin, *The Five Clocks.* Bloomington: Publications of the Research Center in Anthropology, Folklore, and Linguistics, No. 22, 1962.

Joos, Martin, ed., *Readings in Linguistics,* 2d ed. New York: American Council of Learned Societies, 1958.

Katz, Jerrold J., *The Philosophy of Language.* New York: Harper & Row, 1966.

Katz, Jerrold J., *Semantic Theory.* New York: Harper & Row, 1972.

Katz, Jerrold J., and Jerry A. Fodor, "The Structure of a Semantic Theory," *Language,* 39 (1963), 170–210. Also in Fodor and Katz.

Kenyon, John S., *American Pronunciation,* 10th ed. Ann Arbor: Wahr, 1950.

King, Robert D., *Historical Linguistics and Generative Grammar.* Englewood Cliffs, N.J.: Prentice-Hall, 1969.

Koutsoudas, Andreas, "The Morpheme Reconsidered," *International Journal of American Linguistics,* 29 (1963), 160–170.

Krapp, George P., *The English Language in America,* 2d ed. New York: Ungar, 1960.

Kuhn, Thomas S., *The Structure of Scientific Revolutions.* Chicago: University of Chicago Press, 1962.

Kurath, Hans, *Word Geography of the Eastern United States.* Ann Arbor: University of Michigan Press, 1969.

Kurath, Hans, et al., *Linguistic Atlas of New England.* Providence, R.I.: Brown, 1939–1943.

Kurath, Hans, and Raven I. McDavid, *The Pronunciation of English in the Atlantic States.* Ann Arbor: University of Michigan Press, 1961.

Labov, William, *Language in the Inner City.* Philadelphia: University of Pennsylvania Press, 1973.

Labov, William, *The Social Stratification of English in New York City.* Washington, D.C.: Center for Applied Linguistics, 1966.

Labov, William, *Sociolinguistic Patterns*. Philadelphia: University of Pennsylvania Press, 1973.

Labov, William, *The Study of Nonstandard English*. Champaign, Ill.: National Council of Teachers of English, 1970.

Ladefoged, Peter, *A Course in Phonetics*. New York: Harcourt Brace Jovanovich, 1975.

Ladefoged, Peter, *Elements of Acoustic Phonetics*. Chicago: University of Chicago Press, 1962.

Lakoff, George, *Irregularity in Syntax*. New York: Holt, 1970.

Landar, Herbert, *Language and Culture*. New York: Oxford, 1966.

Langacker, Ronald W., *Language and Its Structure*, 2d ed. New York: Harcourt Brace Jovanovich, 1973.

Langendoen, D. Terence, *Essentials of English Grammar*. New York: Holt, 1970.

Langendoen, D. Terence, *The Study of Syntax*. New York: Holt, 1969.

Leech, Geoffrey, *Semantics*. Baltimore, Md.: Penguin, 1974.

Lehmann, Winfred P., *Exercises to Accompany Historical Linguistics: An Introduction*. New York: Holt, 1962.

Lehmann, Winfred P., *Historical Linguistics: An Introduction*. New York: Holt, 1962.

Lenneberg, Eric H., *Biological Foundations of Language*. New York: Wiley, 1967.

Liles, Bruce L., *An Introduction to Linguistics*. Englewood Cliffs, N.J.: Prentice-Hall, 1975.

Liles, Bruce L., *An Introductory Transformational Grammar*. Englewood Cliffs, N.J.: Prentice-Hall, 1971.

Linden, Eugene, *Apes, Men, and Language*. New York: Saturday Review Press, 1974.

Longacre, Robert E., "String Constituent Analysis," *Language*, 36 (1960), 63–88.

Lorenz, Konrad, *King Solomon's Ring*. New York: Crowell Collier & Macmillan, 1952.

Lounsbury, Floyd, "Semantic Analysis of the Pawnee Kinship Usage," *Language*, 32 (1956), 158–194.

Lyons, John, *Introduction to Theoretical Linguistics*. New York: Cambridge, 1968.

Lyons, John, *Noam Chomsky*. New York: Viking, 1970.

Malinowski, Bronislaw, "The Problem of Meaning in Primitive Languages," in Charles K. Ogden and I. A. Richards, *The Meaning of Meaning*, 3d ed. New York: Harcourt, Brace & World, 1930.

Malmberg, Bertil, *Phonetics*. New York: Dover, 1963.

Marchand, Hans, *The Categories and Types of Present-Day English Word-Formation*, 2d ed. München: C. H. Beck, 1969.

Marckwardt, Albert H., *American English*. New York: Oxford, 1958.

Marckwardt, Albert H., *Introduction to the English Language*. New York: Oxford, 1942.

Matthews, P. H., *Morphology*. London: Cambridge University Press, 1974.

McDavid, Raven I., and Donald C. Green, *Workbook: The Structure of American English*. New York: Ronald, 1966.

Mencken, Henry L., *The American Language: The Fourth Edition and The Two Supplements*, abridged. Raven I. McDavid, ed. New York: Knopf, 1963.

Miller, George A., *Language and Communication*. New York: McGraw-Hill, 1963.

Minnis, Noel, ed., *Linguistics at Large.* New York: Viking, 1971.

Moore, Samuel, Sanford B. Meech, and Harold Whitehall, "Middle English Dialect Characteristics and Dialect Boundaries," in *Essays and Studies in English and Comparative Literature,* University of Michigan Publication, Language and Literature XIII. Ann Arbor: University of Michigan Press, 1935.

Nida, Eugene A., "The Identification of Morphemes," *Language,* 24 (1948), 414–441.

Nida, Eugene A., *Morphology: The Descriptive Analysis of Words,* 2d ed. Ann Arbor: University of Michigan Press, 1949.

Ogden, Charles K., and I. A. Richards, *The Meaning of Meaning,* 3d ed. New York: Harcourt, Brace & World, 1930.

Osgood, Charles E., and Thomas A. Seboek, eds., *Psycholinguistics: A Survey of Theory and Research Problems.* Bloomington: Indiana University Press, 1965.

Osgood, Charles E., George J. Suci, and Percy H. Tannenbaum, *The Measurement of Meaning.* Urbana: University of Illinois Press, 1957.

Partridge, Eric, *A Dictionary of Slang and Unconventional English,* 7th ed. New York: Macmillan, 1970.

Pedersen, Holger, *The Discovery of Language.* Bloomington: Indiana University Press, 1962.

Peters, Robert A., *A Linguistic History of English.* Boston: Houghton Mifflin, 1968.

Peters, Robert A., *Student Workbook to Accompany A Linguistic History of English.* Boston: Houghton Mifflin, 1968.

Pike, Kenneth L., "Grammatical Prerequisites to Phonemic Analysis," *Word,* 3 (1947), 155–172.

Pike, Kenneth L., "On the Phonemic Status of English Diphthongs," *Language,* 23 (1947), 151–159.

Pike, Kenneth L., *Phonemics.* Ann Arbor: University of Michigan Press, 1947.

Pike, Kenneth L., *Phonetics.* Ann Arbor: University of Michigan Press, 1943.

Pittenger, Robert E., and Henry L. Smith, "A Basis for Some Contributions of Linguistics to Psychiatry," *Psychiatry,* 20 (1957), 61–78.

Postal, Paul M., *Aspects of Phonological Theory.* New York: Harper & Row, 1968.

Premack, David, "The Education of S*A*R*A*H," *Psychology Today,* 4:4 (1970), 54–58.

Premack, David, "Language in the Chimpanzee?," *Science,* 172 (1971), 808–822.

Pyles, Thomas, *The Origins and Development of the English Language.* New York: Harcourt, Brace & World, 1964.

Pyles, Thomas, and John Algeo, *English: An Introduction to Language.* New York: Harcourt, Brace & World, 1970.

Quine, Willard V., *Word and Object.* Cambridge: M.I.T., 1960.

Read, Allen W., "The First Stage in the History of 'O.K.'," *American Speech,* 38 (1963), 5–27.

Reed, Carroll E., *Dialects of American English.* Cleveland: World Publishing, 1967.

Reibel, David A., and Sanford A. Schane, eds., *Modern Studies in English.* Englewood Cliffs, N.J.: Prentice-Hall, 1969.

Roberts, Paul, *Patterns of English.* New York: Harcourt, Brace & World, 1956.

Robertson, Stuart, and Frederic G. Cassidy, *The Development of Modern English,* 2d ed. Englewood Cliffs, N.J.: Prentice-Hall, 1954.

Robins, R. H., *A Short History of Linguistics.* Bloomington: Indiana University Press, 1968.

Samarin, William J., *Field Linguistics*. New York: Holt, 1967.

Samuels, M. L., *Linguistic Evolution*. London: Cambridge University Press, 1972.

Sapir, Edward, *Language*. New York: Harcourt, Brace & World, 1921.

de Saussure, Ferdinand, *A Course in General Linguistics*. New York: Philosophical Library, 1959.

Schane, Sanford A., *Generative Phonology*. Englewood Cliffs, N.J.: Prentice-Hall, 1973.

Schlauch, Margaret, *The English Language in Modern Times* (*since 1400*). London: Oxford, 1964.

Scott, Charles T., and Jon L. Erickson, eds., *Readings for the History of the English Language*. Boston: Allyn and Bacon, 1968.

Sebeok, Thomas A., ed., *Animal Communication*. Bloomington: Indiana University Press, 1960.

Shannon, Claude E., and Warren Weaver, *The Mathematical Theory of Communication*. Urbana: University of Illinois Press, 1959.

Shuy, Roger W., *Discovering American Dialects*. Champaign, Ill.: National Council of Teachers of English, 1967.

Sledd, James, "Review of George L. Trager and Henry L. Smith, *An Outline of English Structure* and Charles C. Fries, *The Structure of English*," *Language*, 31 (1955), 312–345.

Sledd, James, and Wilma R. Ebbitt, *Dictionaries and That Dictionary*. Chicago: Scott, Foresman, 1962.

Slobin, Dan I., *Psycholinguistics*. Glenview, Ill.: Scott, Foresman, 1971.

Steinberg, Danny D., and Leon A. Jakobovits, eds., *Semantics*. London: Cambridge University Press, 1971.

Stevick, Robert D., *English and Its History*. Boston: Allyn and Bacon, 1968.

Sturtevant, Edgar H., *An Introduction to Linguistic Science*. New Haven: Yale, 1947.

Sturtevant, Edgar H., *Linguistic Change*. Chicago: University of Chicago Press, 1917.

Thomas, Charles K., *An Introduction to the Phonetics of American English*, 2d ed. New York: Ronald, 1958.

Trager, George L., and Henry Lee Smith, *An Outline of English Structure*. Norman: Studies in Linguistics, Occasional Papers, 3, 1951.

Traugott, Elizabeth Closs, *A History of English Syntax*. New York: Holt, 1972.

Trudgill, Peter, *Sociolinguistics: An Introduction*. Baltimore: Penguin, 1974.

Von Frisch, Karl, *Bees, Their Vision, Chemical Senses, and Language*. Ithaca: Cornell University Press, 1950.

Wardhaugh, Ronald, *The Contexts of Language*. Rowley, Mass.: Newbury House, 1976.

Waterman, John T., *Perspectives in Linguistics*, 2d ed. Chicago: University of Chicago Press, 1970.

Weinreich, Uriel, "Explorations in Semantic Theory," in Thomas A. Sebeok, ed., *Current Trends in Linguistics, Volume III, Theoretical Foundations*. The Hague: Mouton, 1966.

Wells, Rulon S., "Immediate Constituents," *Language*, 23 (1947), 81–117.

Wentworth, Harold, and Stuart B. Flexner, eds., *Dictionary of American Slang*. New York: Crowell-Collier, 1944.

Wolfram, Walt, and Ralph W. Fasold, *The Study of Social Dialects in American English*. Englewood Cliffs, N.J.: Prentice-Hall, 1974.

Wrede, Ferdinand, *Deutscher Sprachatlas*. Marburg: N. G. Elwert, 1926–1956.

Ziff, Paul, *Semantic Analysis*. Ithaca: Cornell University Press, 1960.

INDEX